THE **STRANGE** TALENT OF

LUTHER STRODE

IMAGE COMICS INC.

Robert Kirkman — Chief Operating Officer
Erik Larsen — Chief Financial Officer
Todd McFarlane — President
Marc Silvestri — Chief Executive Officer
Jim Valentino — Vice-President
Eric Stephenson — Publisher
Corey Murphy — Director of Sales
Jeff Boison — Director of Publishing Planning & Book Trade Sales
Jeremy Sullivan — Director of Digital Sales
Kat Salazar — Director of PR & Marketing
Emily Miller — Director of Operations
Branwyn Bigglestone — Senior Accounts Manager
Sarah Mello — Accounts Manager
Drew Gill — Art Director
Jonathan Chan — Production Manager
Meredith Wallace — Print Manager
Briah Skelly — Publicist
Sasha Head — Sales & Marketing Production Designer
Randy Okamura — Digital Production Designer
David Brothers — Branding Manager
Addison Duke — Production Artist
Vincent Kukua — Production Artist
Tricia Ramos — Production Artist
Jeff Stang — Direct Market Sales Representative
Emilo Bautista — Digital Sales Associate
Leanna Caunter —Accounting Assistant
Chloe Ramos-Peterson — Administrative Assistant

www.imagecomics.com

THE STRANGE TALENT OF LUTHER STRODE
Third printing. July 2016. ISBN: 978-1-60706-531-9

WRITTEN BY **JUSTIN JORDAN**

ART BY **TRADD MOORE**

COLORS BY **FELIPE SOBREIRO**

LETTERING BY **FONOGRAFIKS**

BOOK DESIGN BY **DREW GILL**

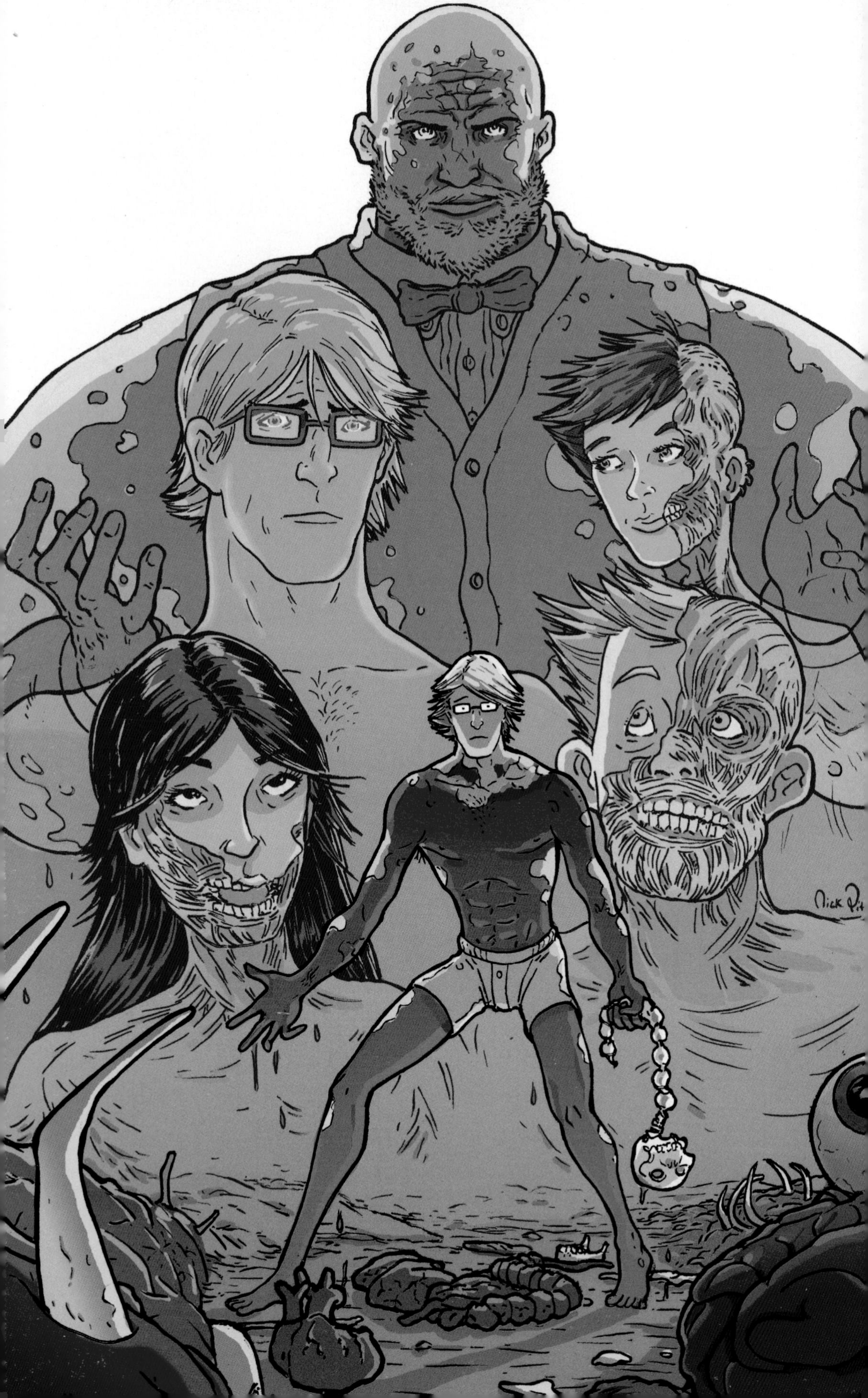

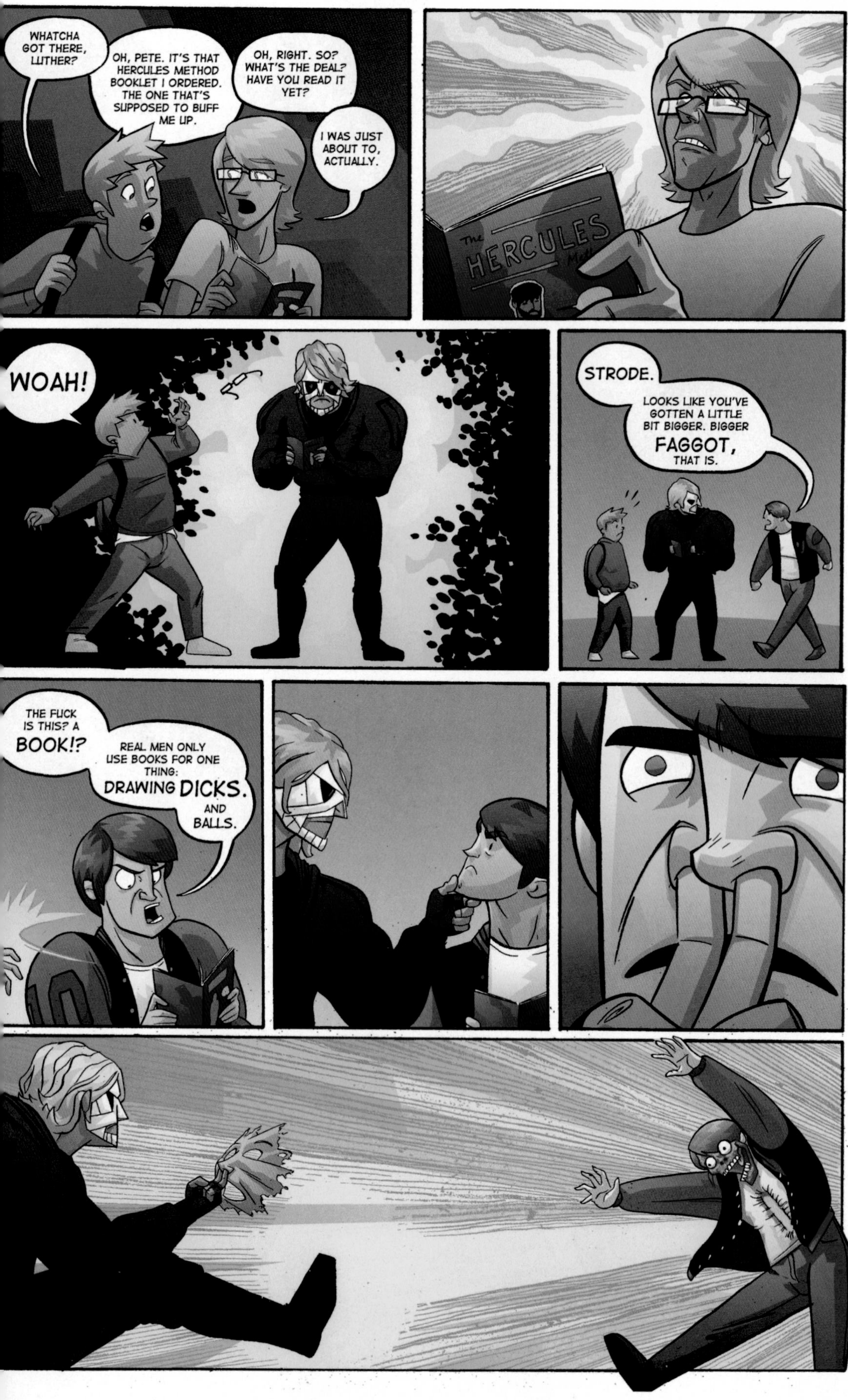
WHATCHA GOT THERE, LUTHER?
OH, PETE. IT'S THAT HERCULES METHOD BOOKLET I ORDERED. THE ONE THAT'S SUPPOSED TO BUFF ME UP.
OH, RIGHT. SO? WHAT'S THE DEAL? HAVE YOU READ IT YET?
I WAS JUST ABOUT TO, ACTUALLY.
The HERCULES
WOAH!
STRODE.
LOOKS LIKE YOU'VE GOTTEN A LITTLE BIT BIGGER. BIGGER FAGGOT, THAT IS.
THE FUCK IS THIS? A BOOK!?
REAL MEN ONLY USE BOOKS FOR ONE THING: DRAWING DICKS.
AND BALLS.

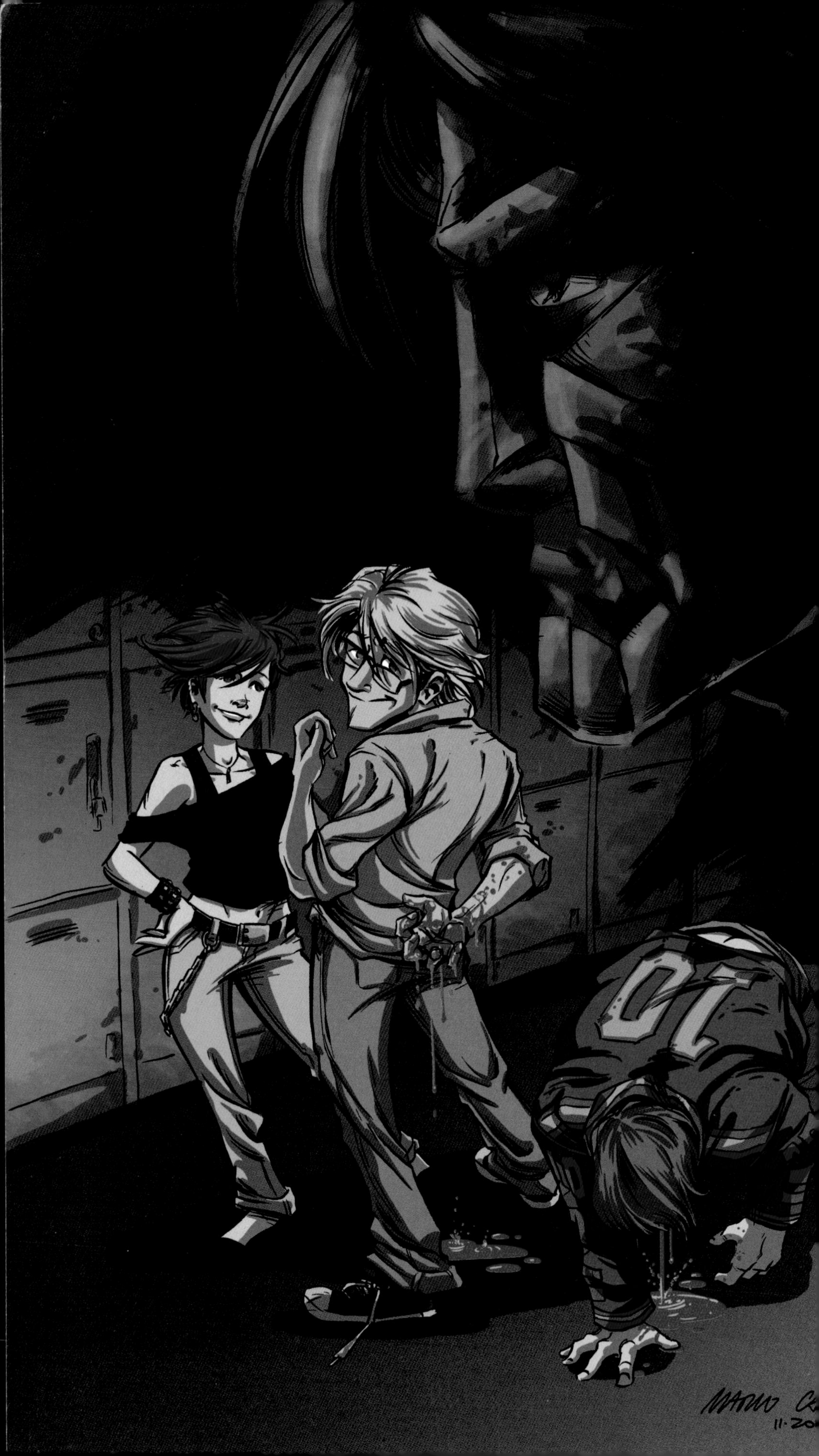

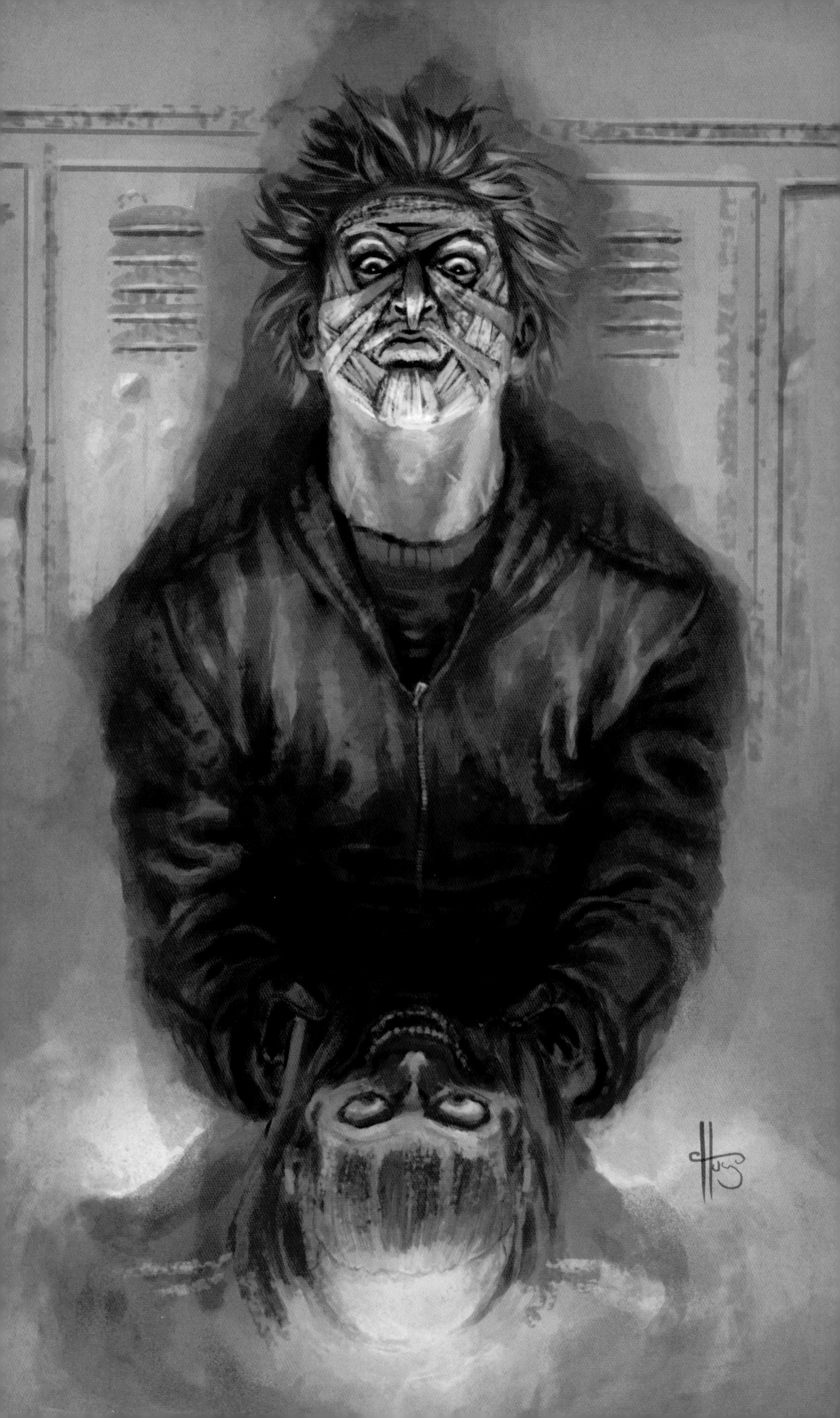

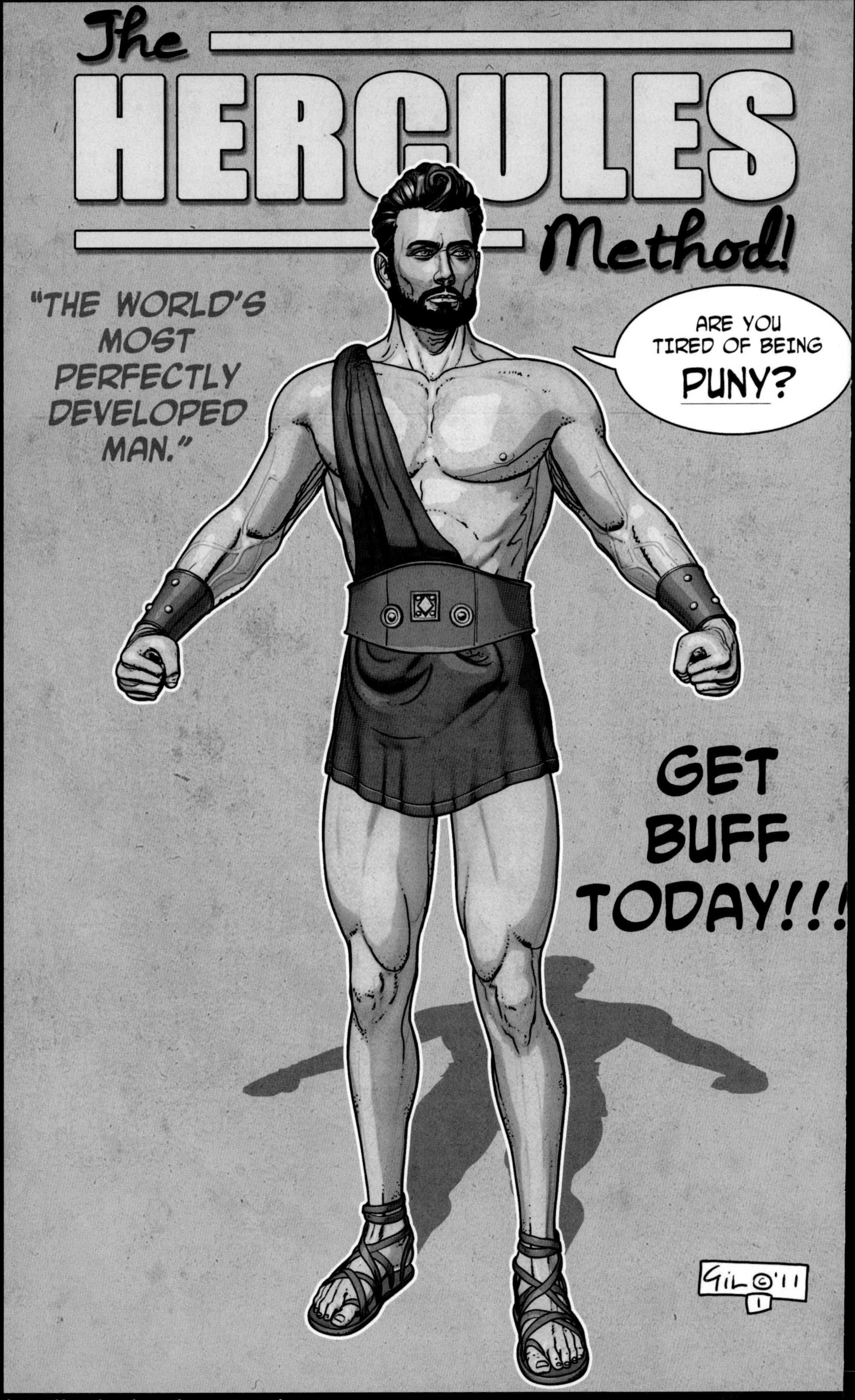
The HERCULES Method!
"THE WORLD'S MOST PERFECTLY DEVELOPED MAN."
ARE YOU TIRED OF BEING PUNY?
GET BUFF TODAY!!!
GIL ©'11

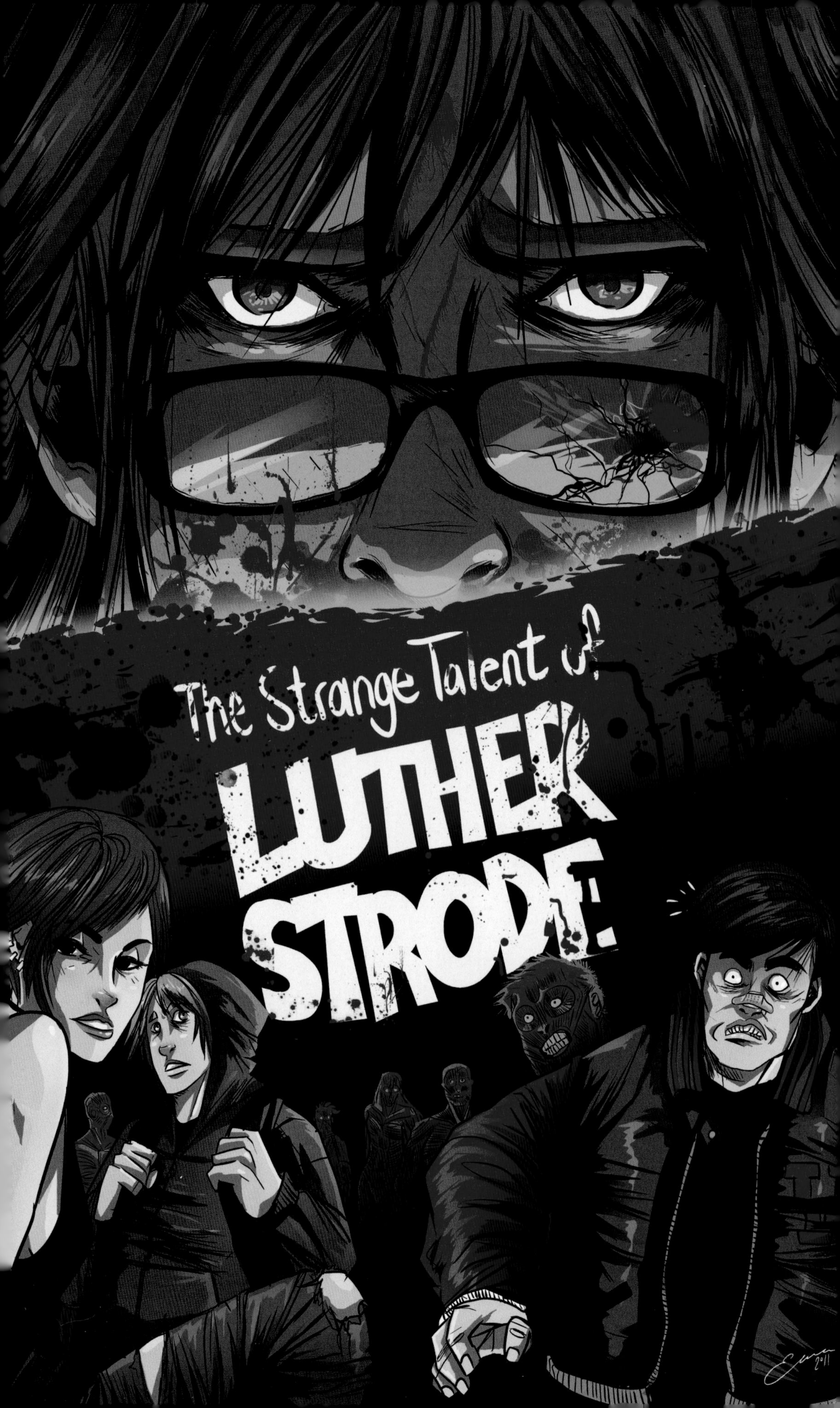
The Strange Talent of
LUTHER
STRODE

We were lucky enough to have a whole bunch of amazing artists contribute pin-ups to *The Strange Talent of Luther Strode*. So lucky, in fact, that we didn't have enough space in the individual issues to actually include all.

So, we're doing it here.

First up, we've got most of the main cast in (comparatively) happier days, done by the amazing **Eva Cabrera**.

This ad for The Hercules Method is courtesy of **Gil Agudín**.

Hugo Araújo gives us Luther doing his thing on a poor unfortunate soul.

Luther and Petra are captured after face smashery by **Mario Cau**.

Yale Stewart is responsible for this little encapsulation of the series. And yes, I realize it's not really a pin-up but it is awesome and I still giggle every time I read so I am putting it in.

Finally, we have **Nick Pitarra**'s take on everyone. Nick, if you didn't immediately recognize the art, is a frequent collaborator with **Jonathan Hickman** on books like *The Manhattan Projects* and *The Red Wing*.

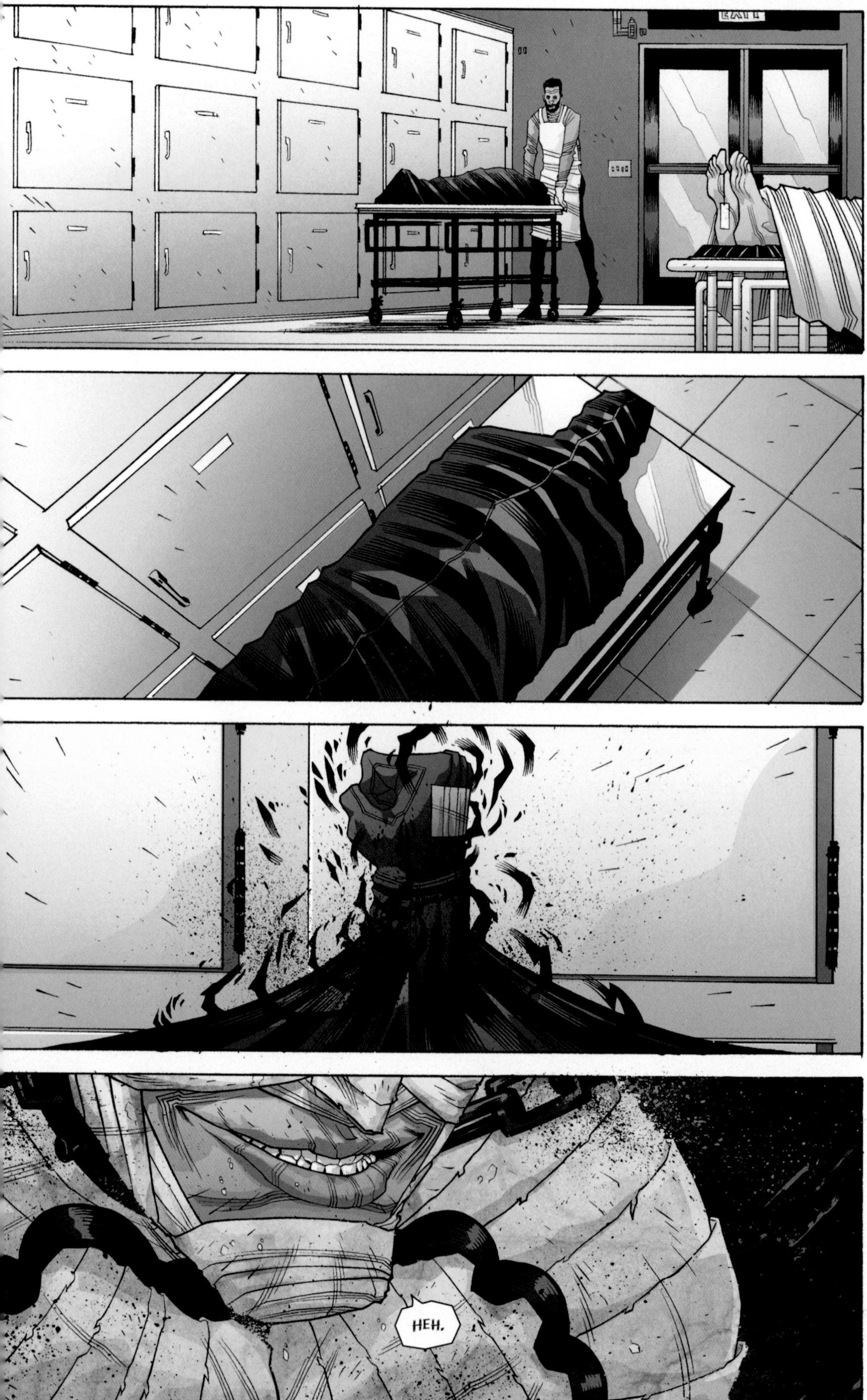
HEH.

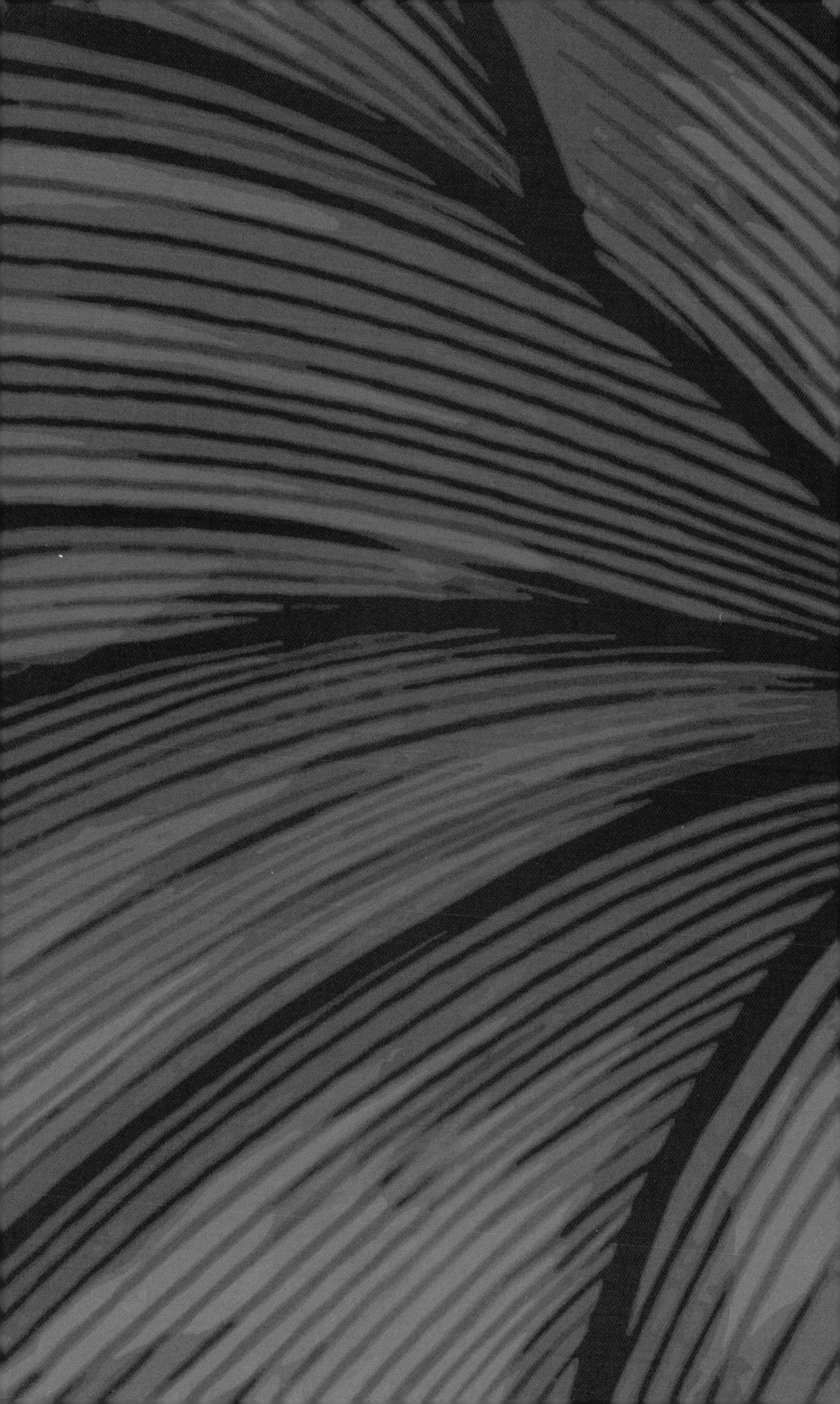

Justin Jordan's work has appeared in more than a dozen comic book anthologies, along with being a three time competitor in DC's Zuda competition. He lives in the wilds of Pennsylvania where he's occasionally mistaken for a sasquatch and is hard at work writing more comics.

Tradd Moore was born in Snellville, Georgia where he was raised solely on the teachings of *X-Men*, *Final Fantasy*, and *The Matrix*. Somewhere along the way he took up drawing and never looked back. He graduated from the Savannah College of Art and Design in 2010 and has been locked in a room drawing comic books ever since.

Felipe Sobreiro is the artist behind *The New Adventures of Sigmund Freud* and a handful of other short comics. He has been published as a colorist in Heavy Metal magazine, Image Comics' *Popgun* anthology, Alex De Campi's *Ashes* and a couple of BOOM! Studios titles. He currently lives in Brasília, Brazil's very odd capital city.

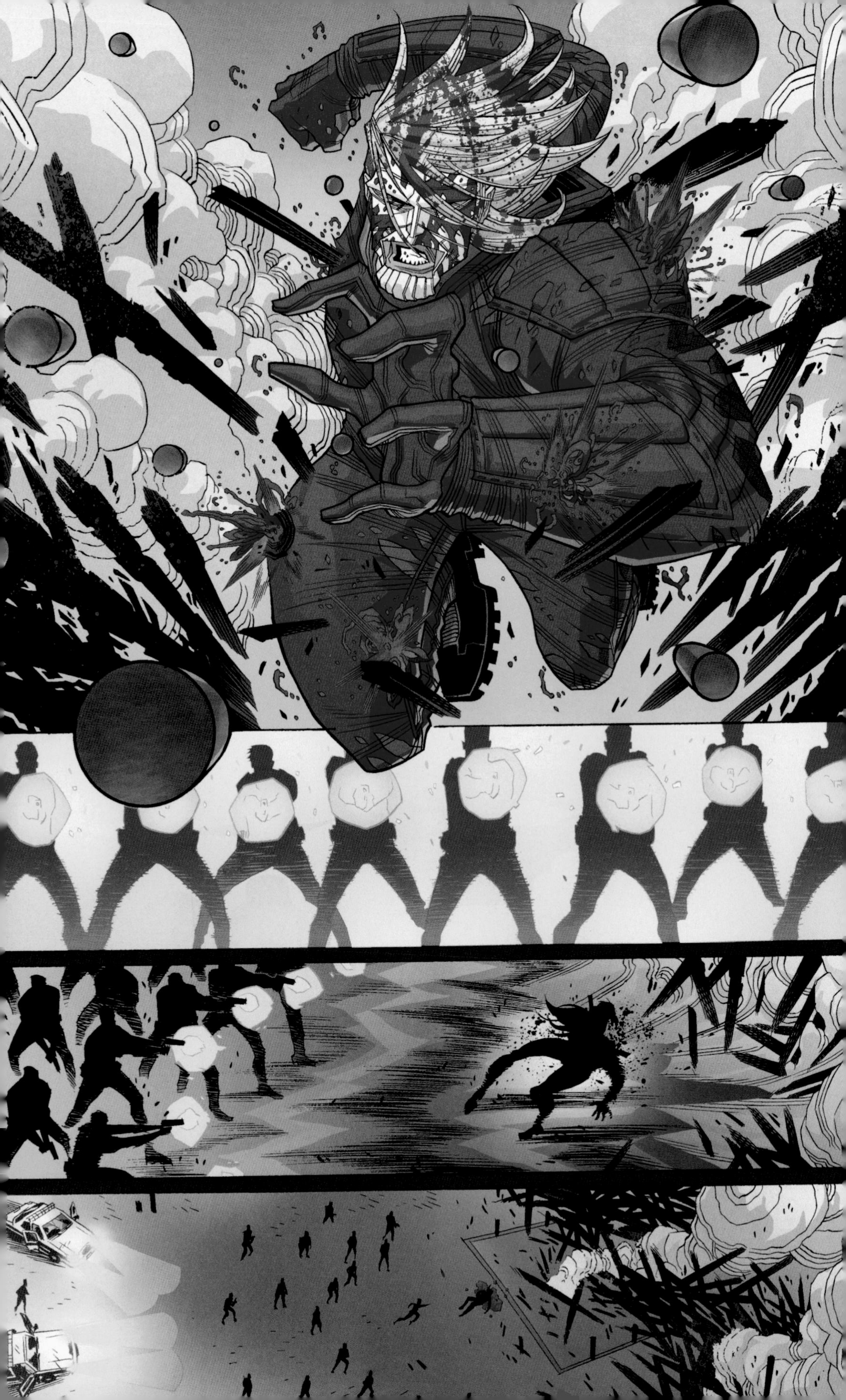

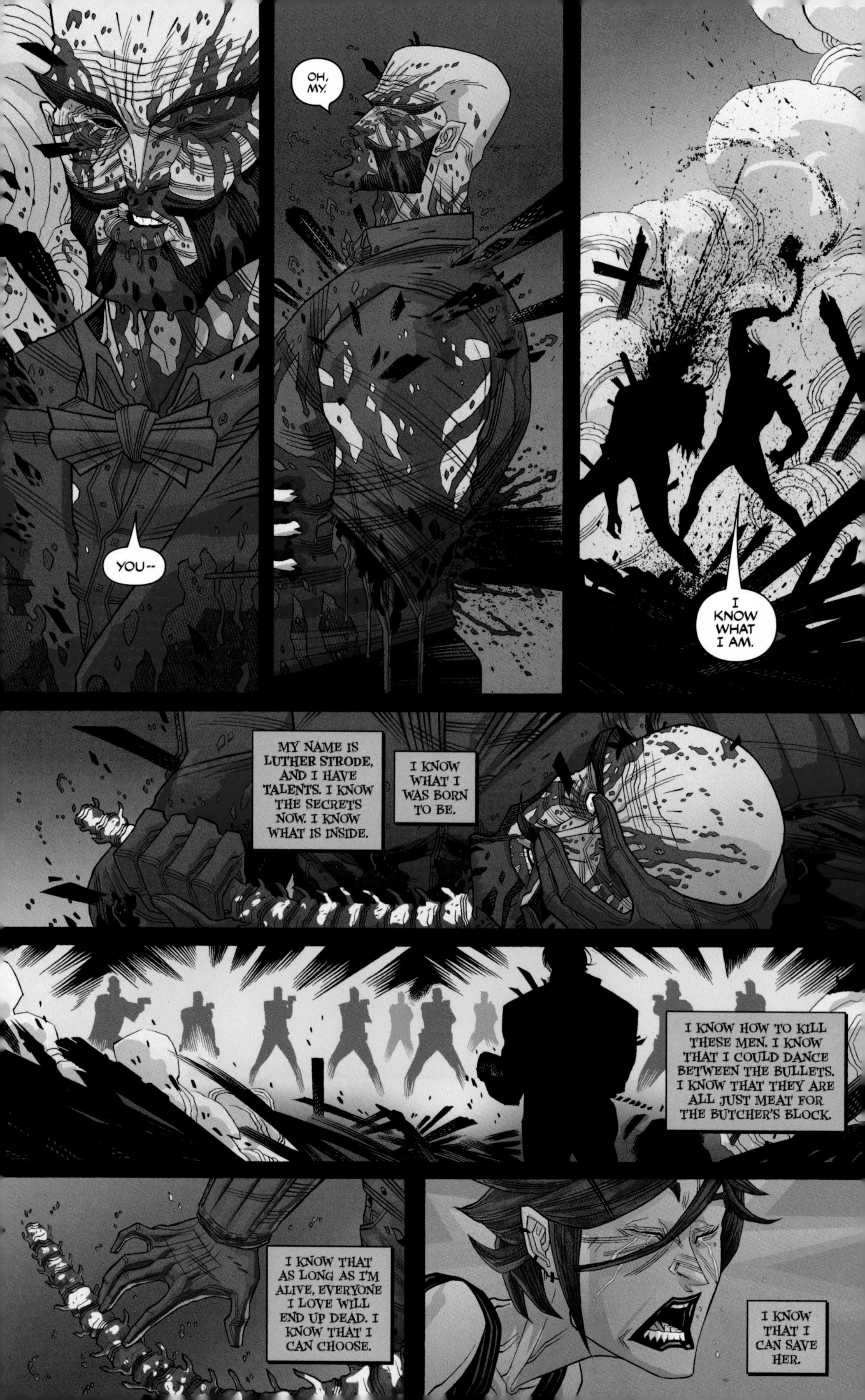
YOU--
OH, MY.
I KNOW WHAT I AM.
MY NAME IS LUTHER STRODE, AND I HAVE TALENTS. I KNOW THE SECRETS NOW. I KNOW WHAT IS INSIDE.
I KNOW WHAT I WAS BORN TO BE.
I KNOW HOW TO KILL THESE MEN. I KNOW THAT I COULD DANCE BETWEEN THE BULLETS. I KNOW THAT THEY ARE ALL JUST MEAT FOR THE BUTCHER'S BLOCK.
I KNOW THAT AS LONG AS I'M ALIVE, EVERYONE I LOVE WILL END UP DEAD. I KNOW THAT I CAN CHOOSE.
I KNOW THAT I CAN SAVE HER.

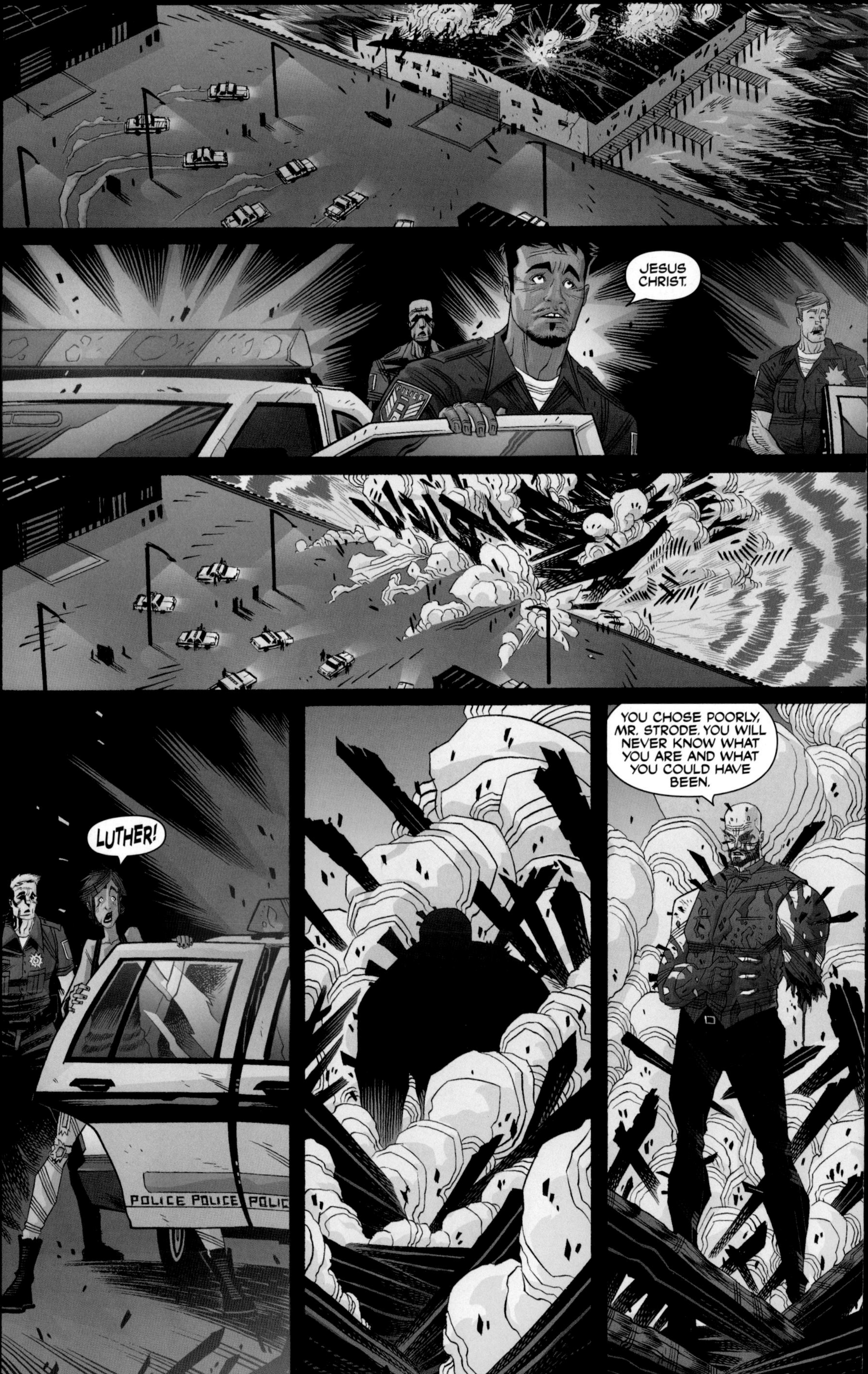
JESUS CHRIST.
LUTHER!
POLICE POLICE POLIC
YOU CHOSE POORLY, MR. STRODE. YOU WILL NEVER KNOW WHAT YOU ARE AND WHAT YOU COULD HAVE BEEN.

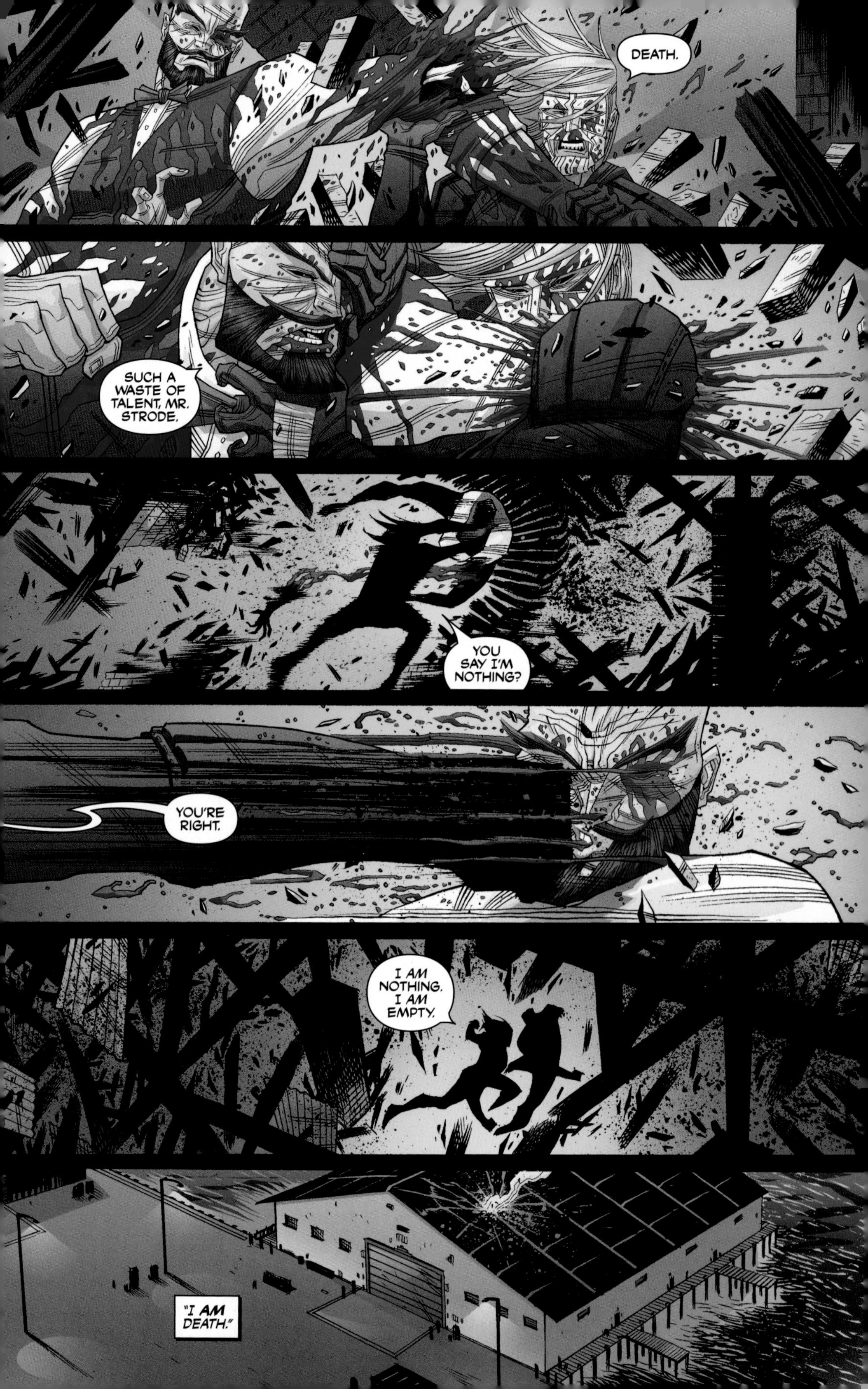
DEATH.
SUCH A WASTE OF TALENT, MR. STRODE.
YOU SAY I'M NOTHING?
YOU'RE RIGHT.
I AM NOTHING. I AM EMPTY.
"I AM DEATH."

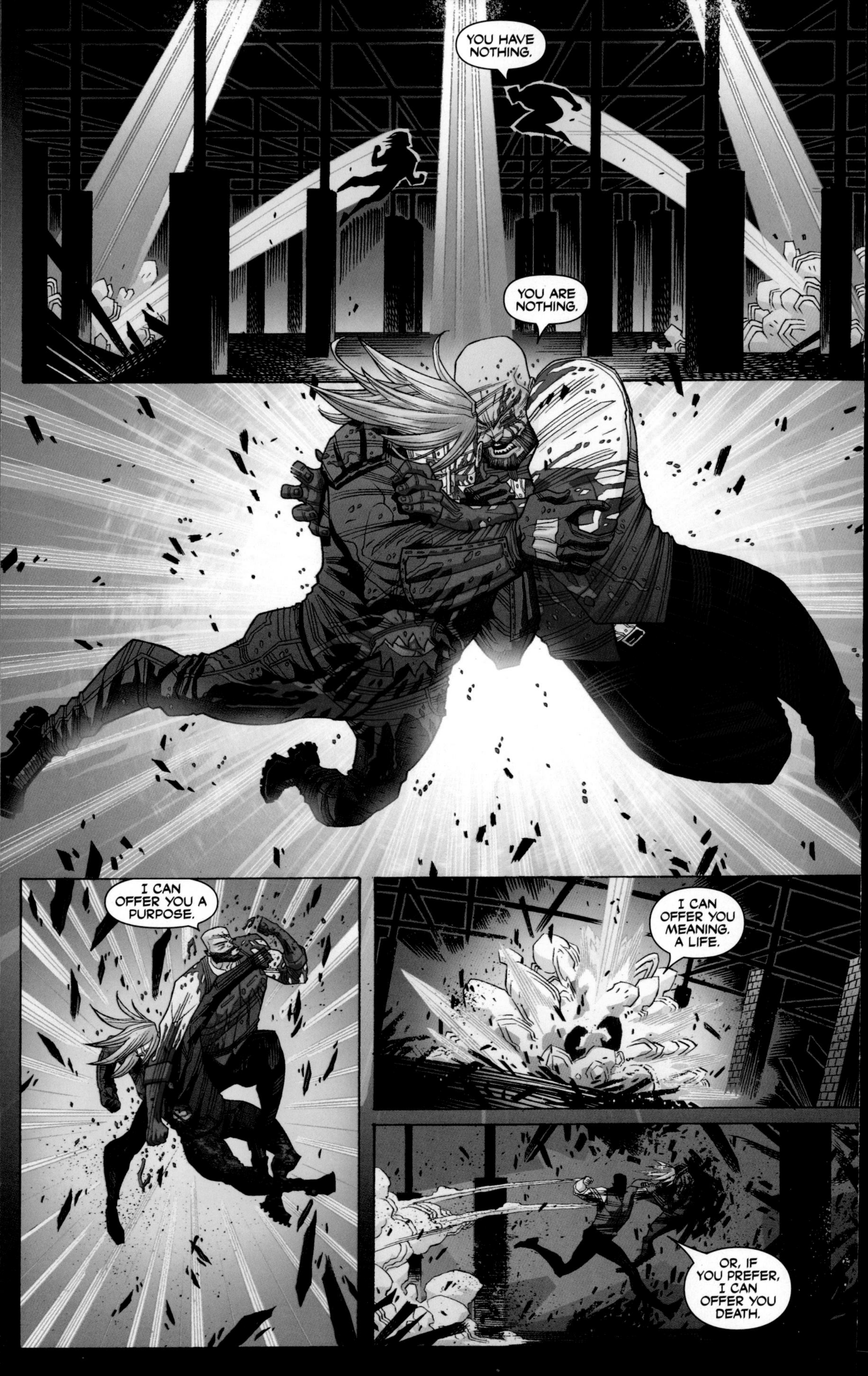
YOU HAVE NOTHING.
YOU ARE NOTHING.
I CAN OFFER YOU A PURPOSE.
I CAN OFFER YOU MEANING. A LIFE.
OR, IF YOU PREFER, I CAN OFFER YOU DEATH.

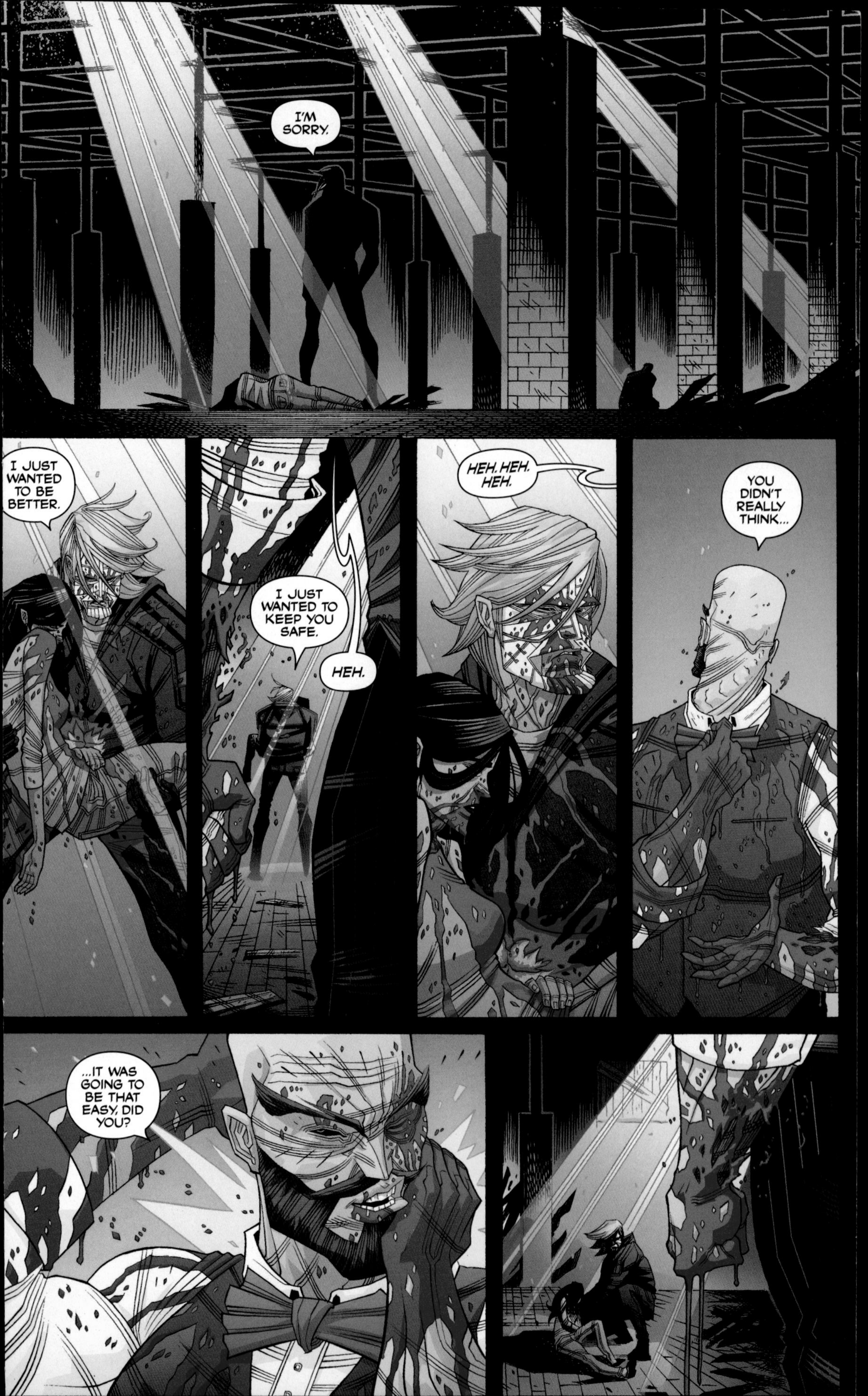
I'M SORRY.
I JUST WANTED TO BE BETTER.
I JUST WANTED TO KEEP YOU SAFE.
HEH.
HEH. HEH. HEH.
YOU DIDN'T REALLY THINK...
...IT WAS GOING TO BE THAT EASY, DID YOU?

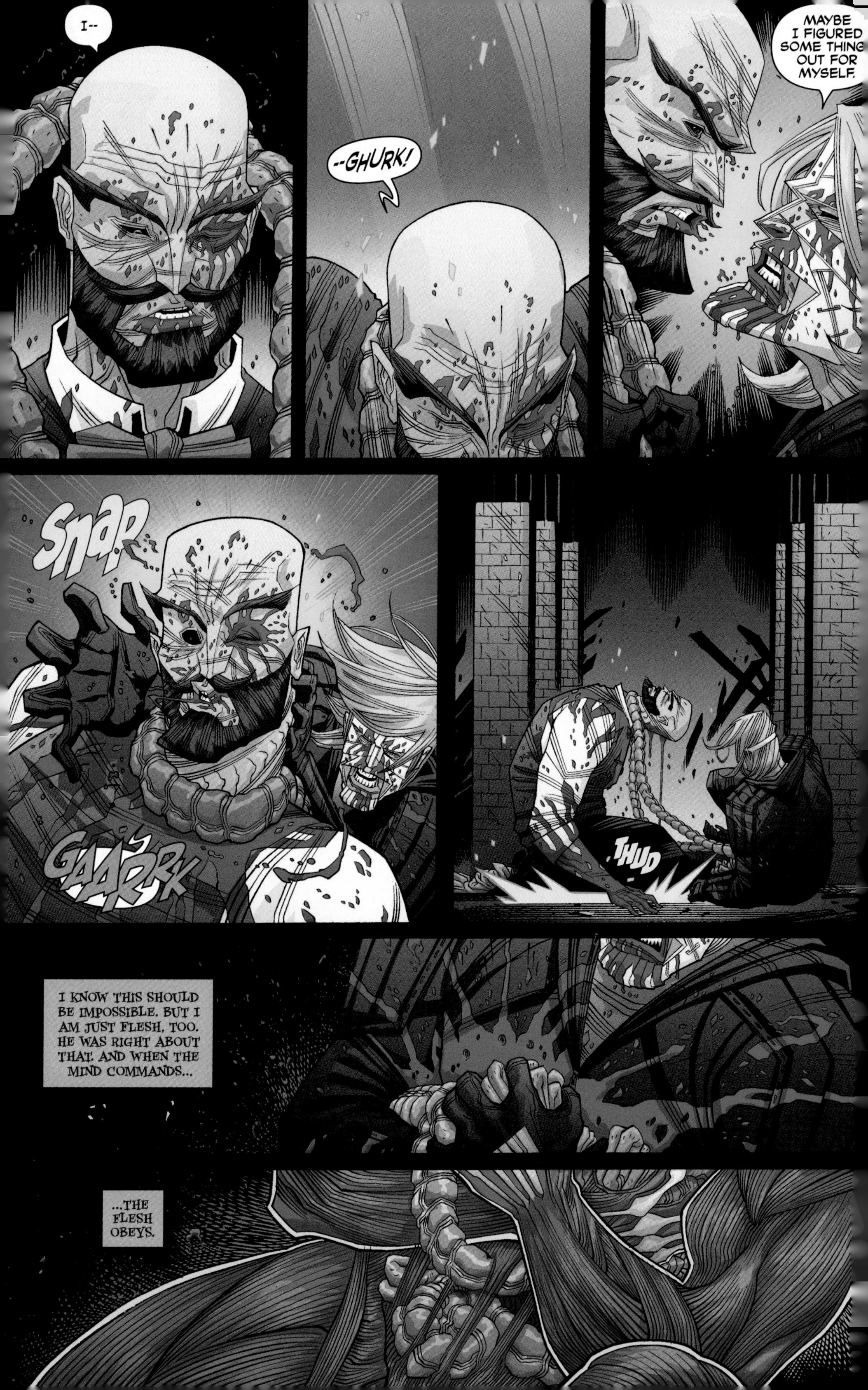
I--
--GHURK!
MAYBE I FIGURED SOME THING OUT FOR MYSELF.
SNAP
GAARRK
THUD
I KNOW THIS SHOULD BE IMPOSSIBLE. BUT I AM JUST FLESH, TOO. HE WAS RIGHT ABOUT THAT. AND WHEN THE MIND COMMANDS...
...THE FLESH OBEYS.

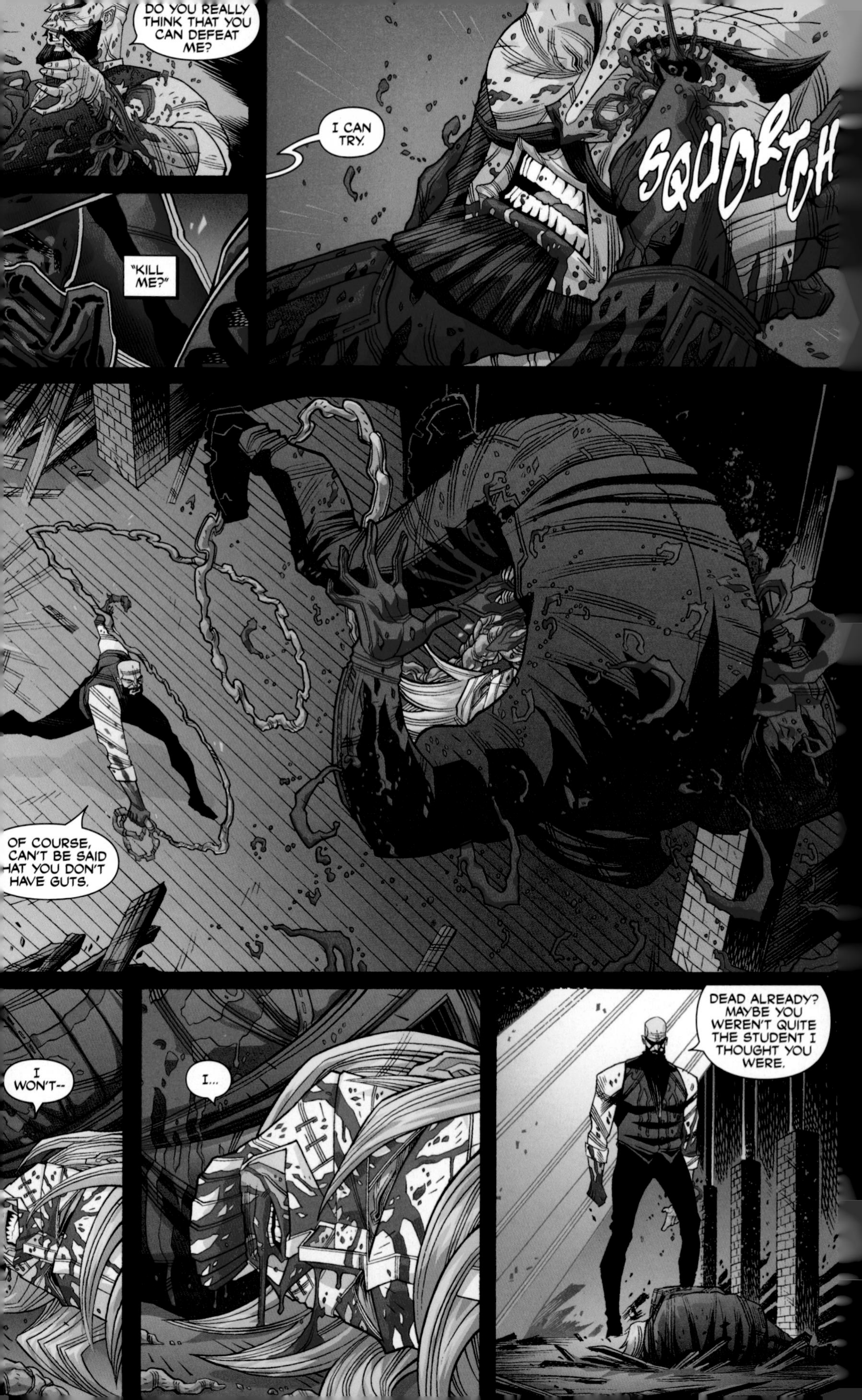
DO YOU REALLY THINK THAT YOU CAN DEFEAT ME?
I CAN TRY.
"KILL ME?"
SQUORTCH
OF COURSE, CAN'T BE SAID HAT YOU DON'T HAVE GUTS.
I WON'T--
I...
DEAD ALREADY? MAYBE YOU WEREN'T QUITE THE STUDENT I THOUGHT YOU WERE.

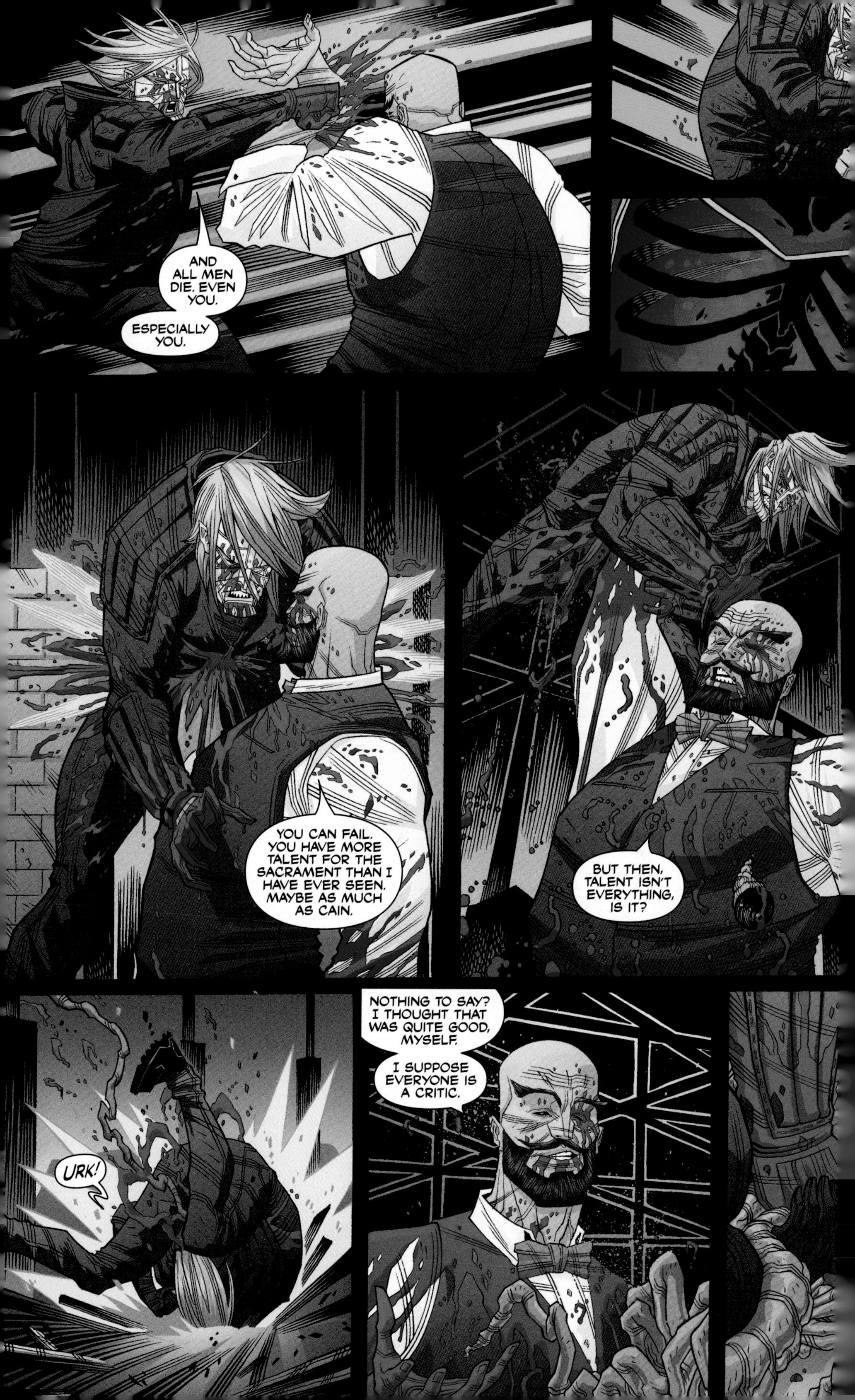
AND ALL MEN DIE. EVEN YOU.
ESPECIALLY YOU.
YOU CAN FAIL. YOU HAVE MORE TALENT FOR THE SACRAMENT THAN I HAVE EVER SEEN. MAYBE AS MUCH AS CAIN.
BUT THEN, TALENT ISN'T EVERYTHING, IS IT?
URK!
NOTHING TO SAY? I THOUGHT THAT WAS QUITE GOOD, MYSELF.
I SUPPOSE EVERYONE IS A CRITIC.

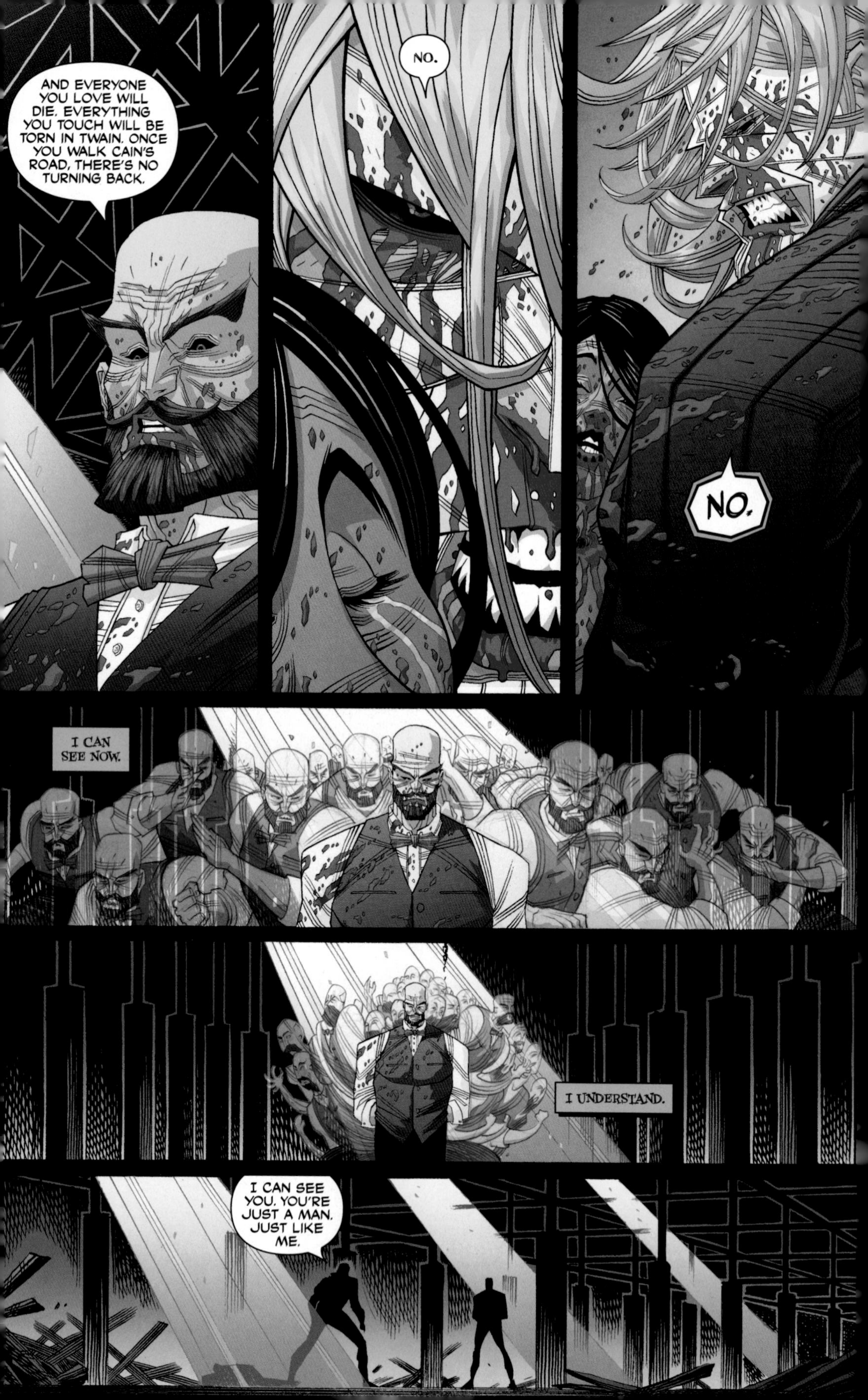
AND EVERYONE YOU LOVE WILL DIE. EVERYTHING YOU TOUCH WILL BE TORN IN TWAIN. ONCE YOU WALK CAIN'S ROAD, THERE'S NO TURNING BACK.
NO.
NO.
I CAN SEE NOW.
I UNDERSTAND.
I CAN SEE YOU. YOU'RE JUST A MAN. JUST LIKE ME.

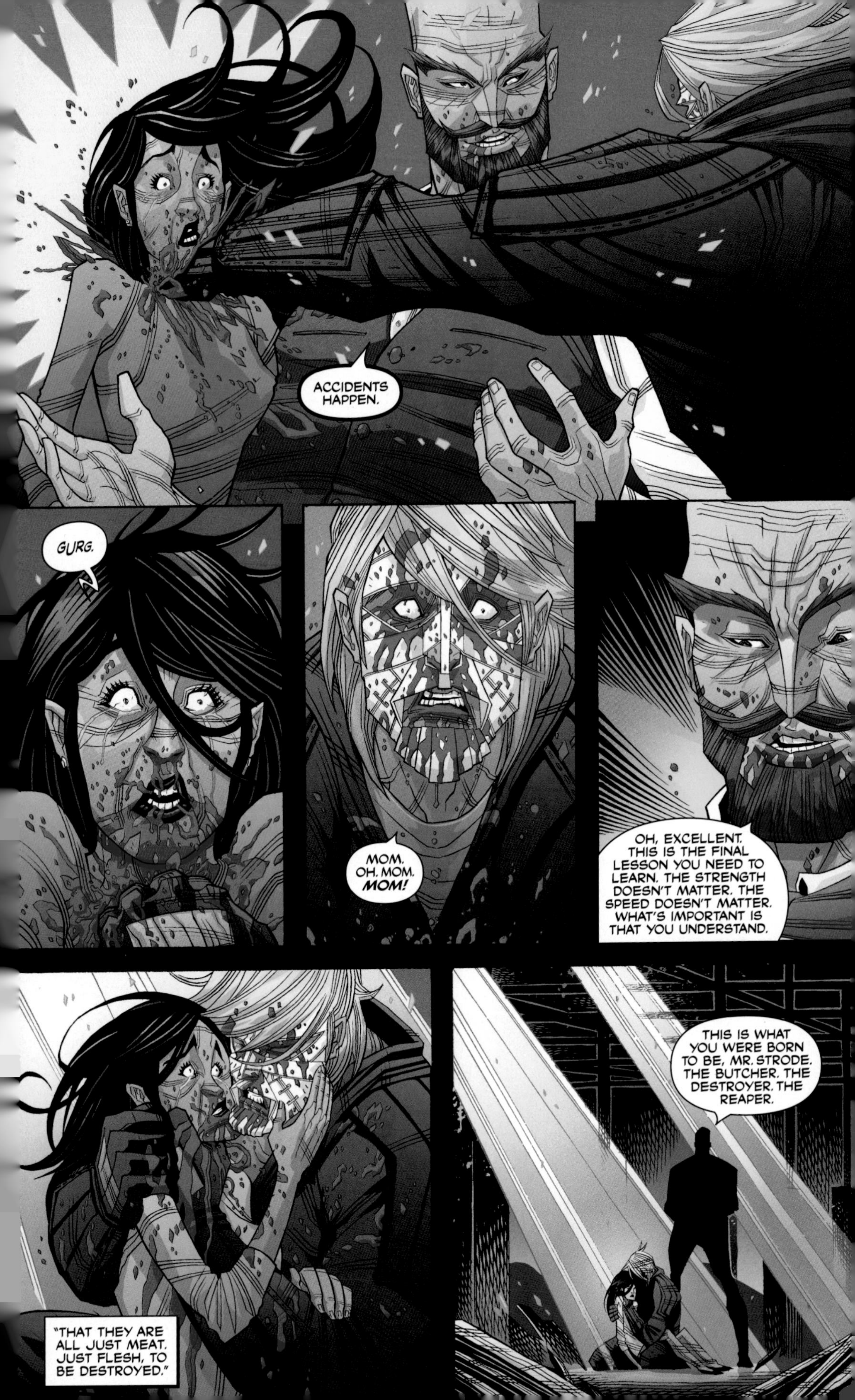
ACCIDENTS HAPPEN.
GURG.
MOM. OH, MOM. MOM!
OH, EXCELLENT. THIS IS THE FINAL LESSON YOU NEED TO LEARN. THE STRENGTH DOESN'T MATTER. THE SPEED DOESN'T MATTER. WHAT'S IMPORTANT IS THAT YOU UNDERSTAND.
"THAT THEY ARE ALL JUST MEAT. JUST FLESH, TO BE DESTROYED."
THIS IS WHAT YOU WERE BORN TO BE, MR. STRODE. THE BUTCHER. THE DESTROYER. THE REAPER.

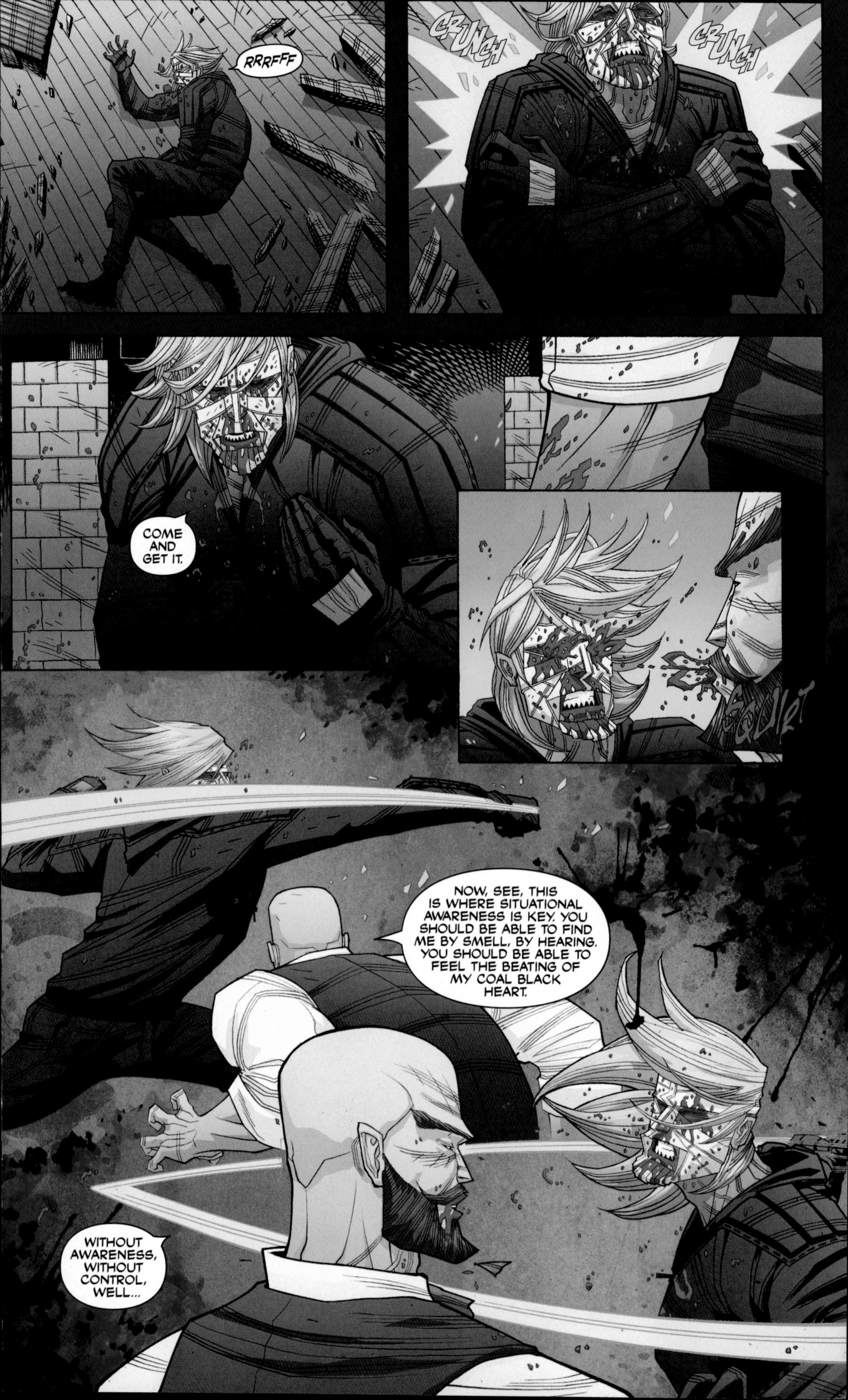
RRRFFF
CRUNCH
CRUNCH
COME AND GET IT.
SQUIRT
NOW, SEE, THIS IS WHERE SITUATIONAL AWARENESS IS KEY. YOU SHOULD BE ABLE TO FIND ME BY SMELL, BY HEARING. YOU SHOULD BE ABLE TO FEEL THE BEATING OF MY COAL BLACK HEART.
WITHOUT AWARENESS, WITHOUT CONTROL, WELL...

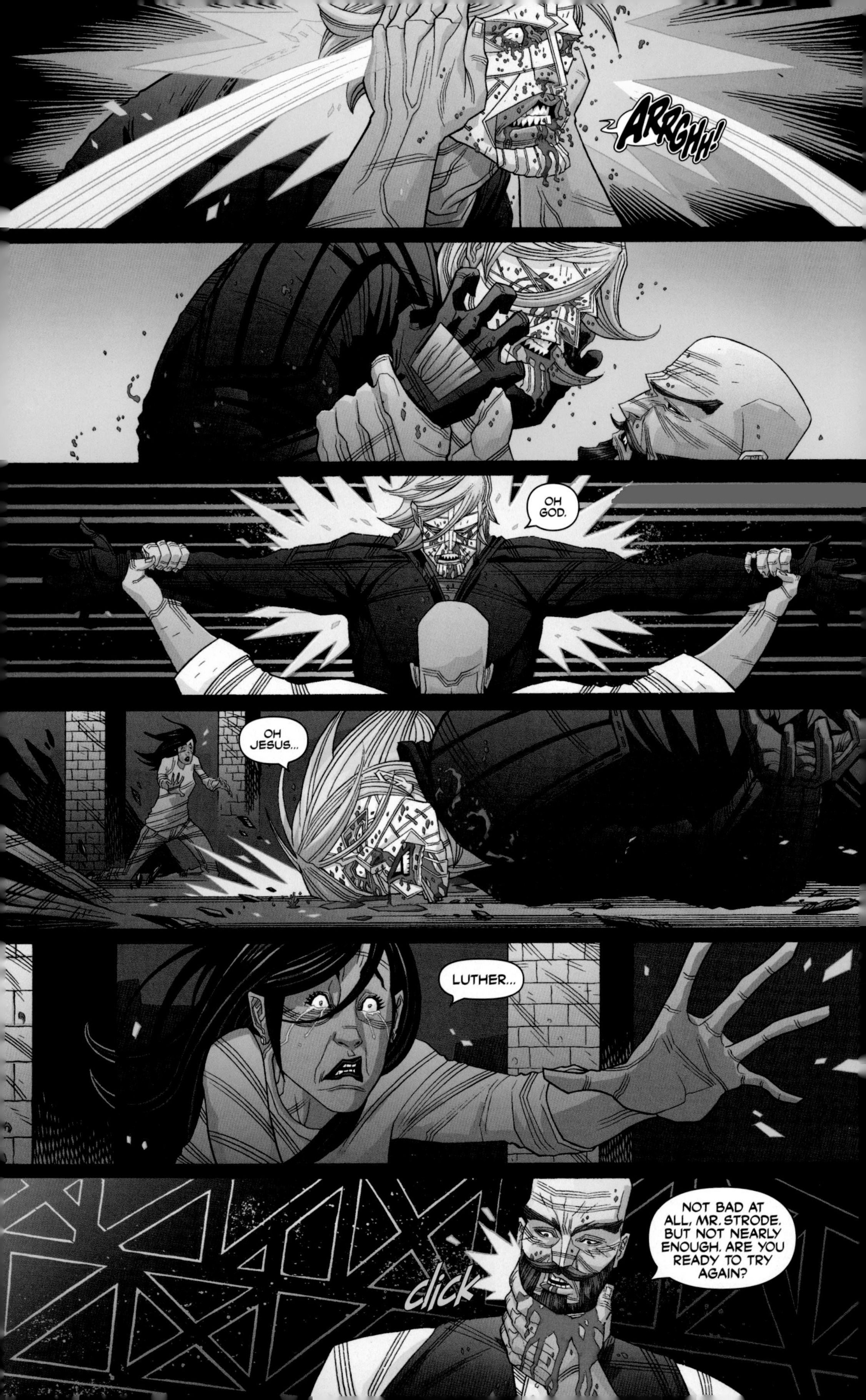
ARRGHH!
OH GOD.
OH JESUS...
LUTHER...
click
NOT BAD AT ALL, MR. STRODE. BUT NOT NEARLY ENOUGH. ARE YOU READY TO TRY AGAIN?

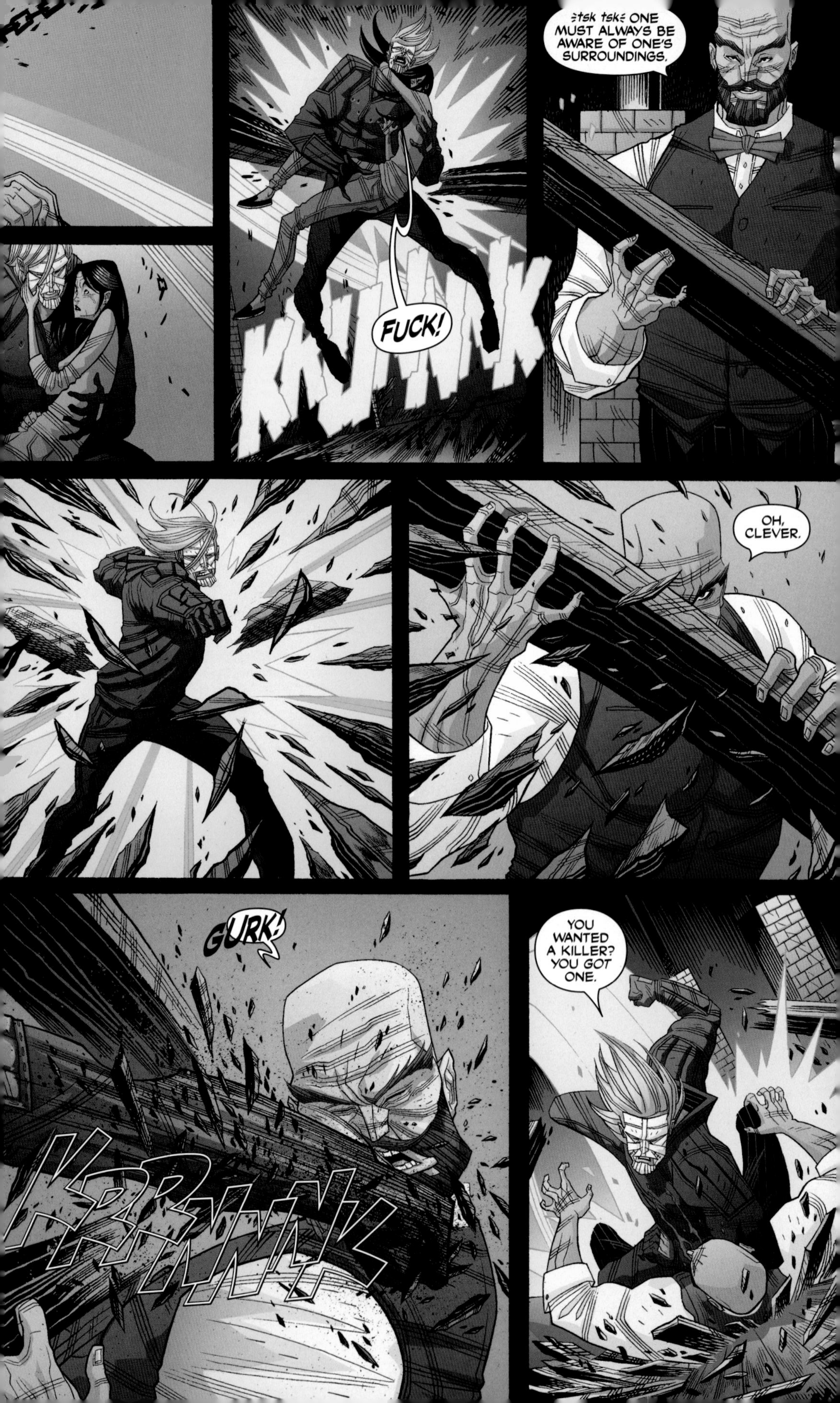
FUCK!
KRUNNK
=tsk tsk= ONE MUST ALWAYS BE AWARE OF ONE'S SURROUNDINGS.
OH, CLEVER.
GURK!
KRUNNNK
YOU WANTED A KILLER? YOU GOT ONE.

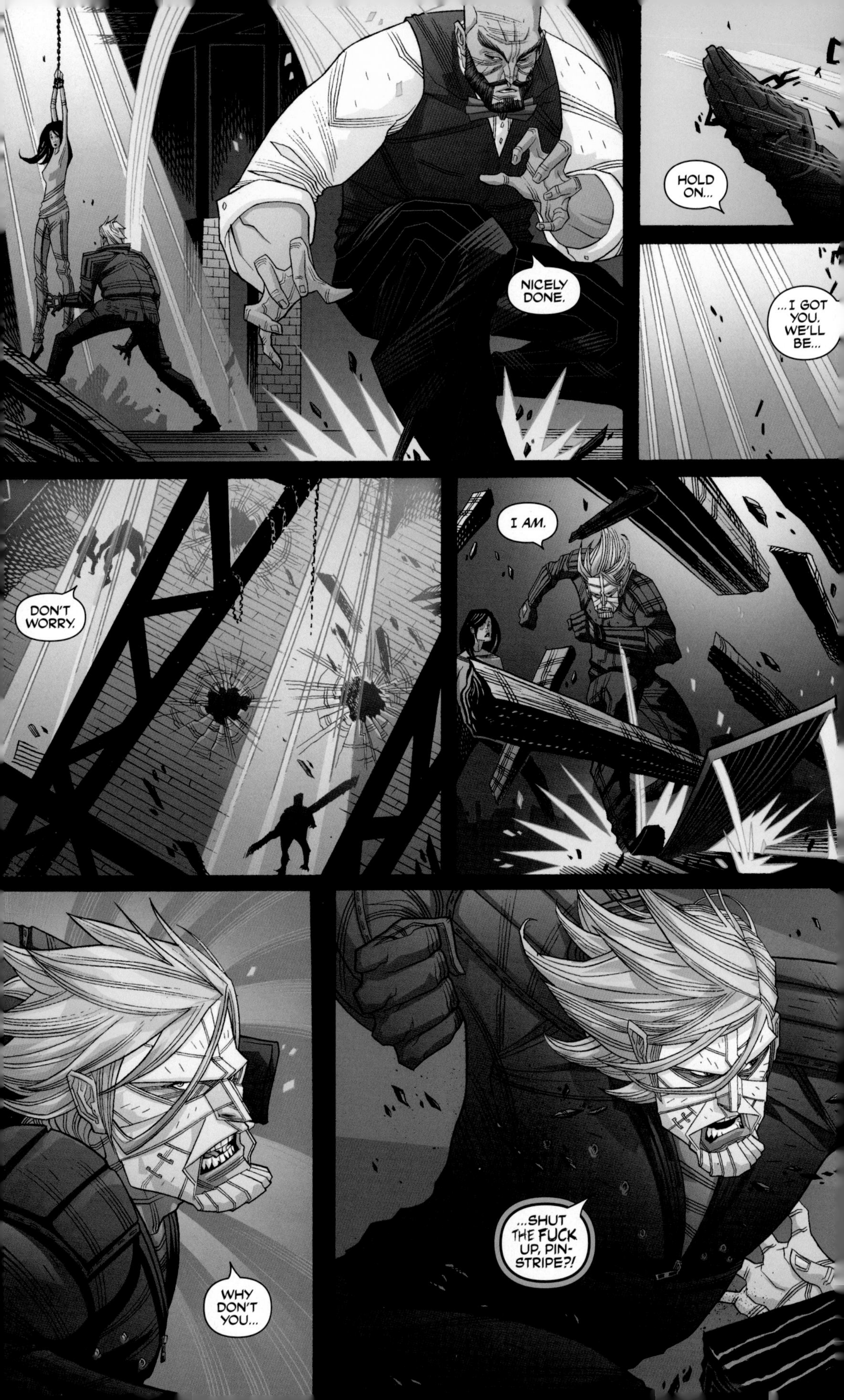
NICELY DONE.
HOLD ON...
...I GOT YOU. WE'LL BE...
DON'T WORRY.
I AM.
WHY DON'T YOU...
...SHUT THE FUCK UP, PIN-STRIPE?!

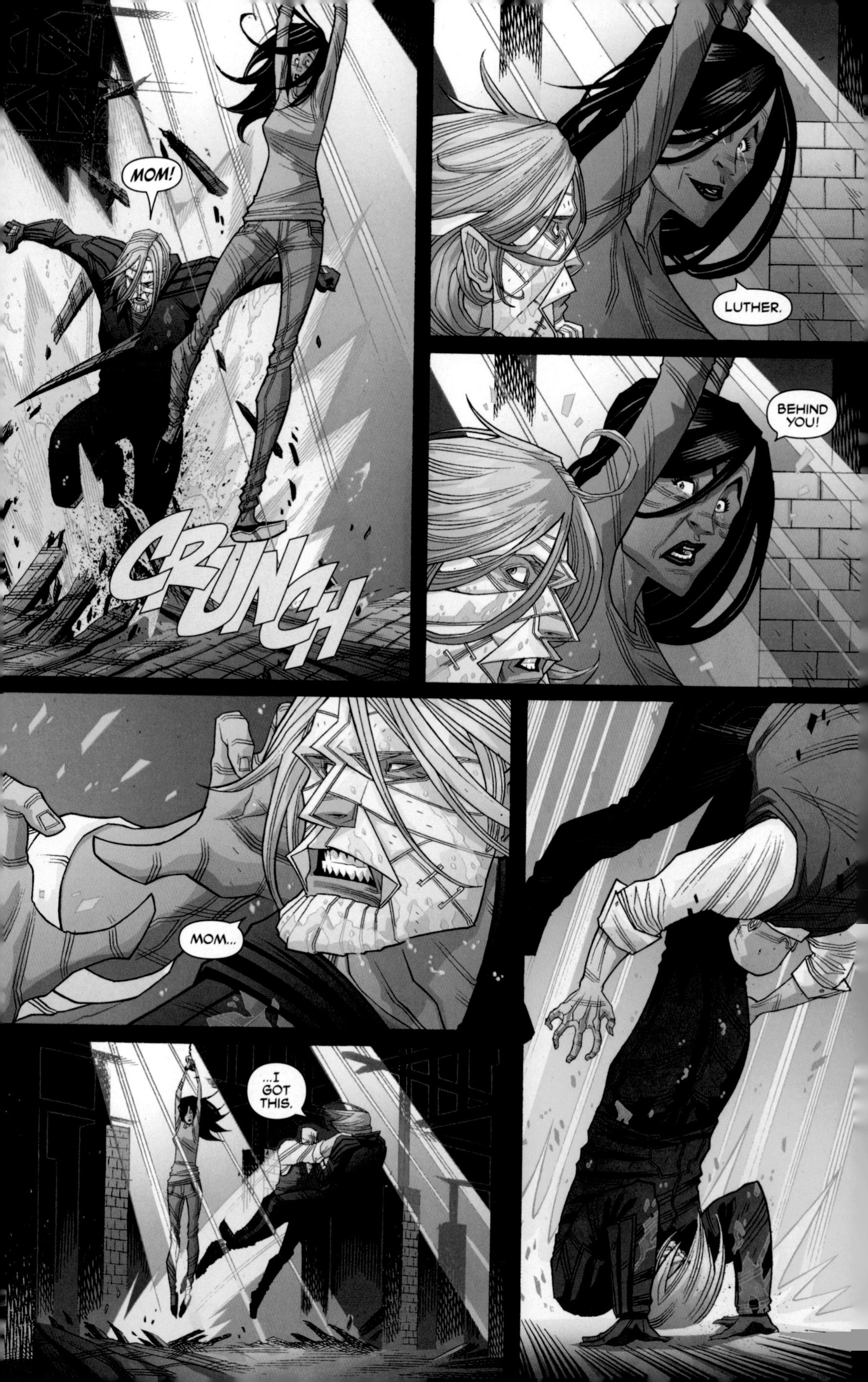
MOM!
CRUNCH
LUTHER.
BEHIND YOU!
MOM...
...I GOT THIS.

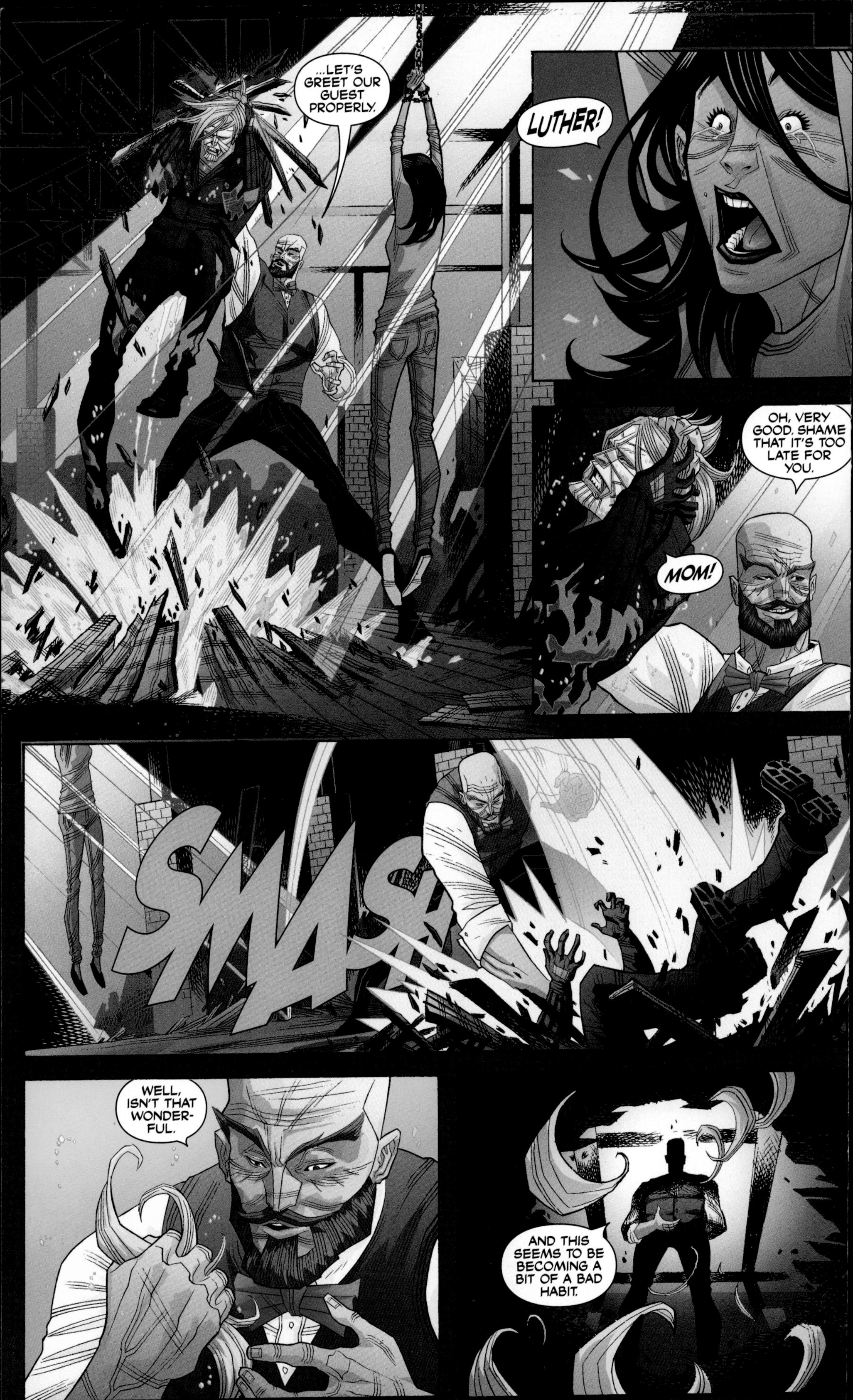
...LET'S GREET OUR GUEST PROPERLY.
LUTHER!
OH, VERY GOOD. SHAME THAT IT'S TOO LATE FOR YOU.
MOM!
SMASH
WELL, ISN'T THAT WONDER-FUL.
AND THIS SEEMS TO BE BECOMING A BIT OF A BAD HABIT.

TYPICAL. DO YOU KNOW THAT I SEND OUT THOUSANDS OF COPIES OF *THE HERCULES METHOD* EACH YEAR?

I EVEN [P]UT IT OUT ON [TH]E "INTERNET", [A]S MUCH [A]S I DISLIKE [T]HAT CURSED THING.

AND YET THE NUMBER OF PEOPLE IN THE LAST DECADE WHO HAVE LEARNED TO DO *THIS*, WHICH IS LITTLE MORE THAN A SIMPLE PARLOR TRICK?

[N]ONE.

[O]Y YOUR SON. WHICH IS, OF [C]OURSE, WHY CAIN [S]ENT ME HERE. [C]ERTAINLY COULDN'T [C]OME HIMSELF. [T]HERE'D HARDLY BE A CITY LEFT, AFTER.

AND I MUST TELL YOU, HE'S GONE FURTHER THAN I COULD HAVE EVER EXPECTED. A BIT SOFT, OF COURSE, BUT SO MUCH RAW TALENT.

SPEAKING OF WHICH...

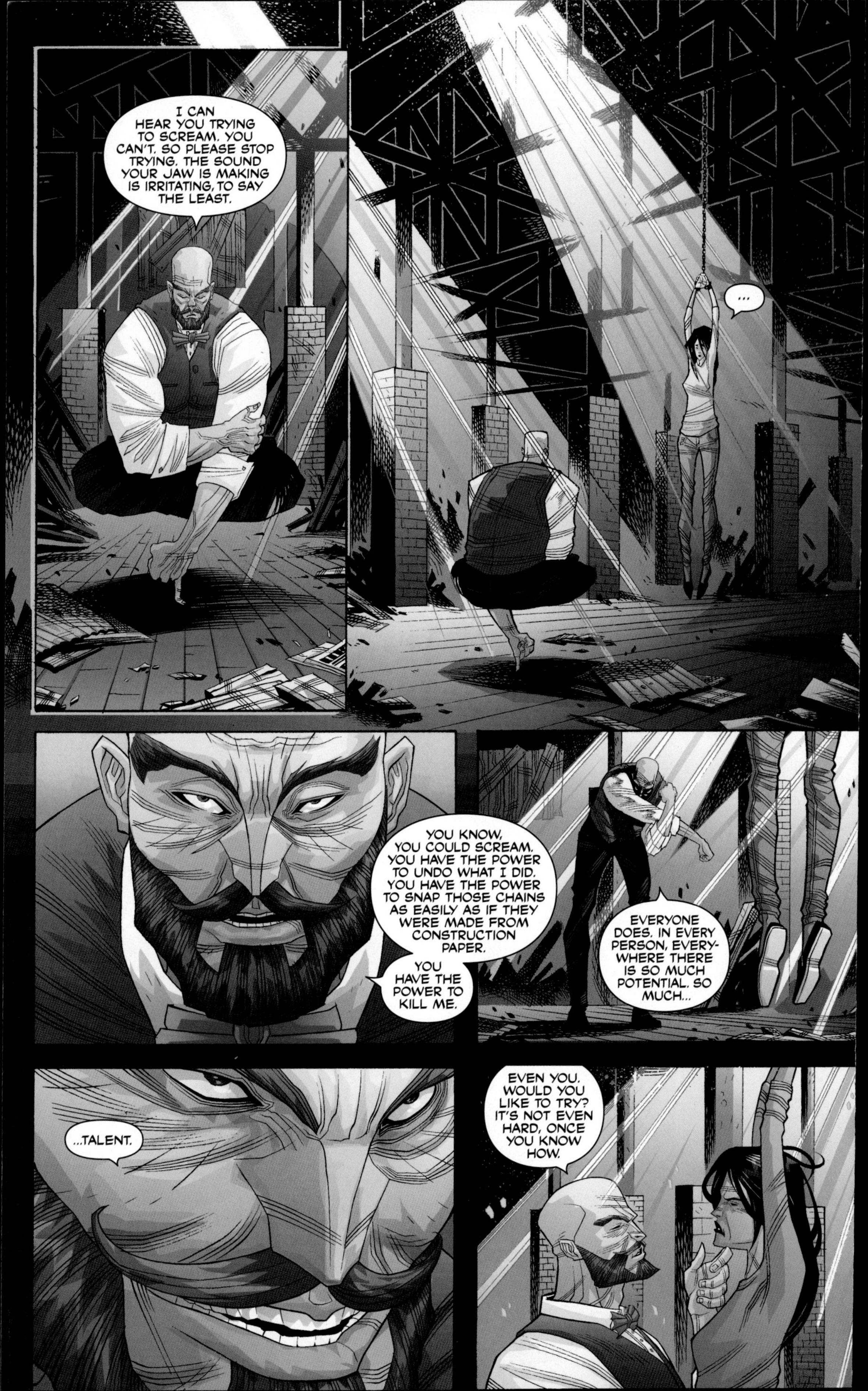
I CAN HEAR YOU TRYING TO SCREAM. YOU CAN'T, SO PLEASE STOP TRYING. THE SOUND YOUR JAW IS MAKING IS IRRITATING, TO SAY THE LEAST.
...
YOU KNOW, YOU COULD SCREAM. YOU HAVE THE POWER TO UNDO WHAT I DID. YOU HAVE THE POWER TO SNAP THOSE CHAINS AS EASILY AS IF THEY WERE MADE FROM CONSTRUCTION PAPER.
YOU HAVE THE POWER TO KILL ME.
EVERYONE DOES. IN EVERY PERSON, EVERY-WHERE THERE IS SO MUCH POTENTIAL. SO MUCH...
...TALENT.
EVEN YOU. WOULD YOU LIKE TO TRY? IT'S NOT EVEN HARD, ONCE YOU KNOW HOW.

JUST... DON'T.

LUTHER, THE POLICE.

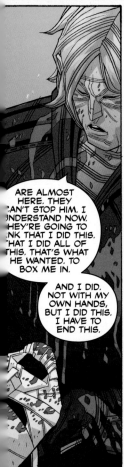

...ARE ALMOST HERE. THEY CAN'T STOP HIM. I UNDERSTAND NOW. THEY'RE GOING TO THINK THAT I DID THIS. THAT I DID ALL OF THIS. THAT'S WHAT HE WANTED. TO BOX ME IN.

AND I DID. NOT WITH MY OWN HANDS, BUT I DID THIS. I HAVE TO END THIS.

LUTHER, I DON'T UNDERSTAND. WHO DID THIS? WHAT THE FUCK ARE YOU TALKING ABOUT!?

WHEN THE POLICE COME, TELL THEM...

TELL THEM WHATEVER YOU WANT. THEY CAN'T STOP ME. THEY CAN'T STOP HIM.

BUT I CAN.

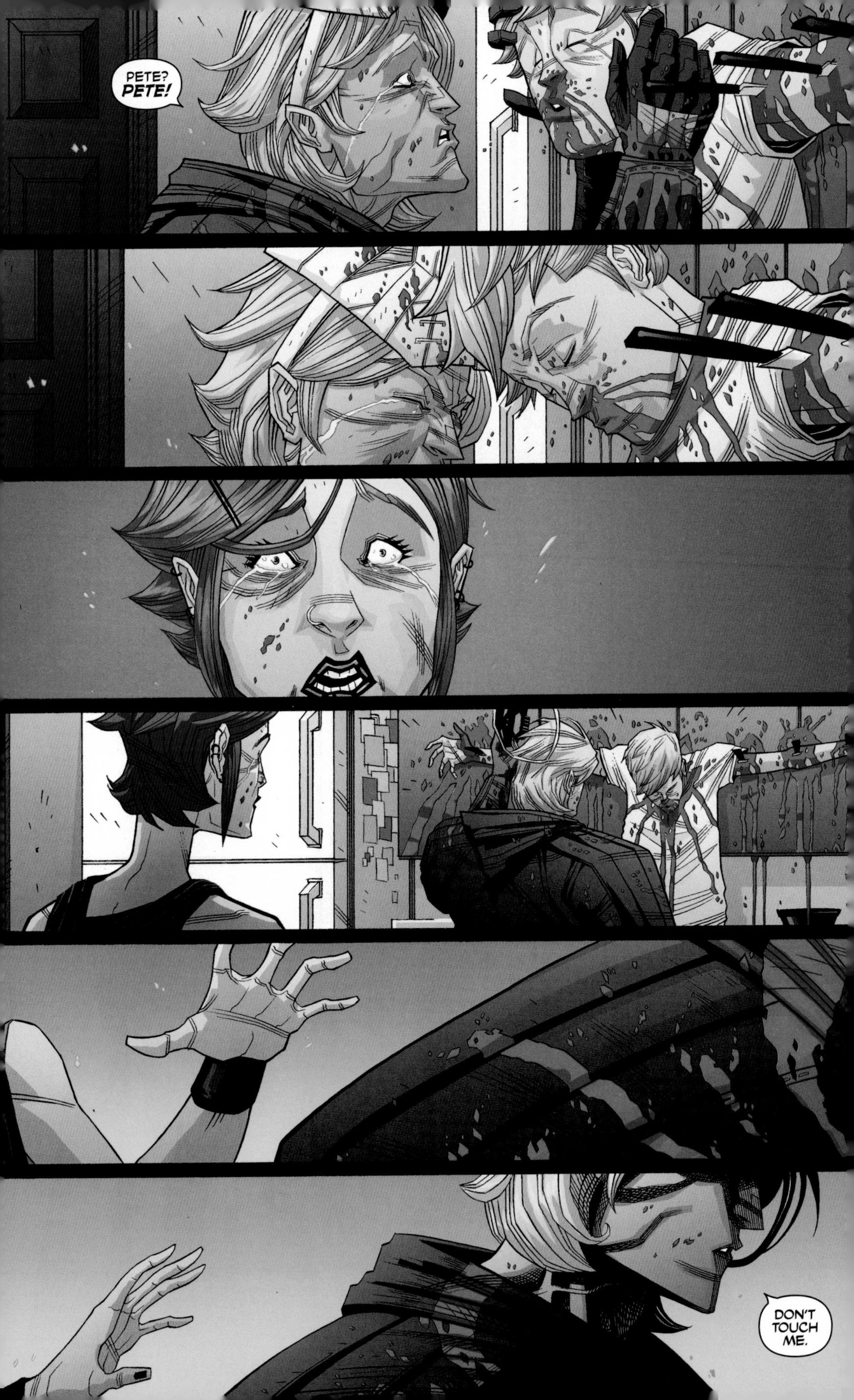
PETE? PETE!
DON'T TOUCH ME.

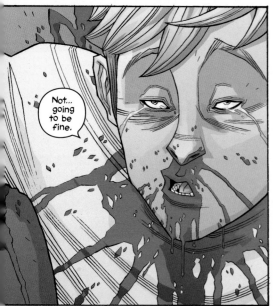

Not... going to be fine.

PETE, JUST TRY TO STAY STILL. THE AMBULANCE...

I'm sorry, dude. I tried... protect her.

I KNOW, I...

He has her. He...said... docks.

'm srrry...

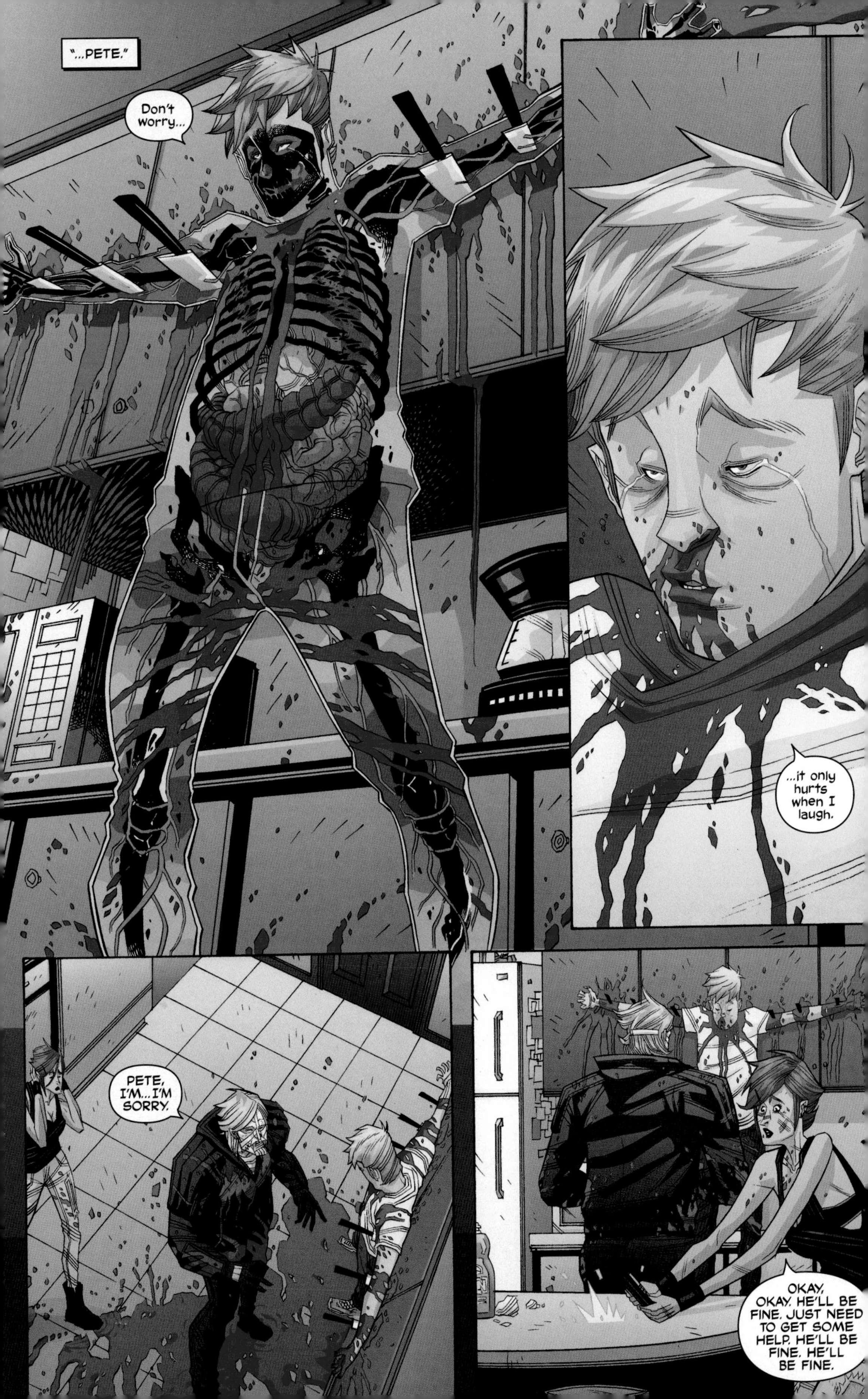
"...PETE."
Don't worry...
...it only hurts when I laugh.
PETE, I'M... I'M SORRY.
OKAY, OKAY. HE'LL BE FINE. JUST NEED TO GET SOME HELP. HE'LL BE FINE. HE'LL BE FINE.

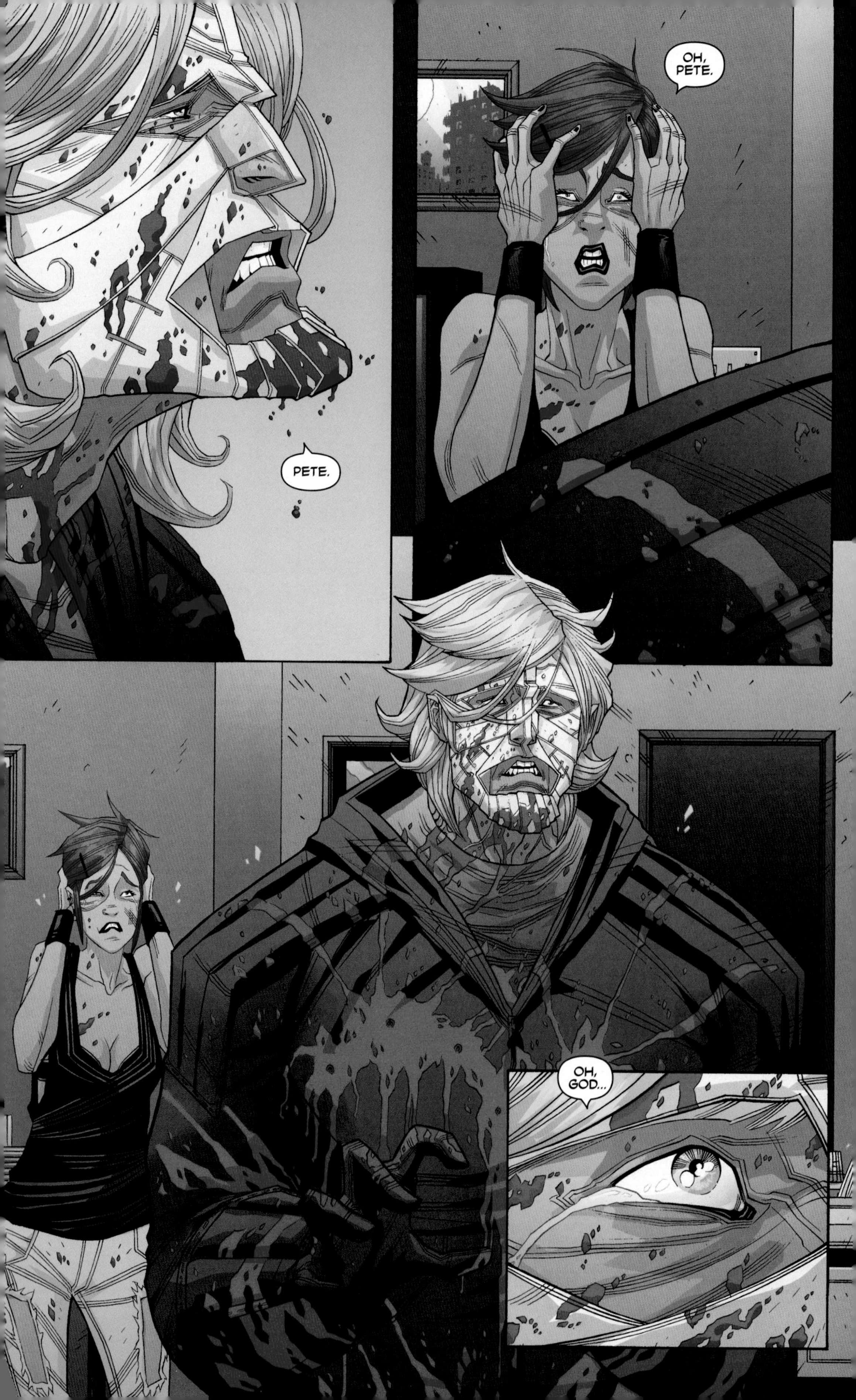
PETE.
OH, PETE.
OH, GOD...

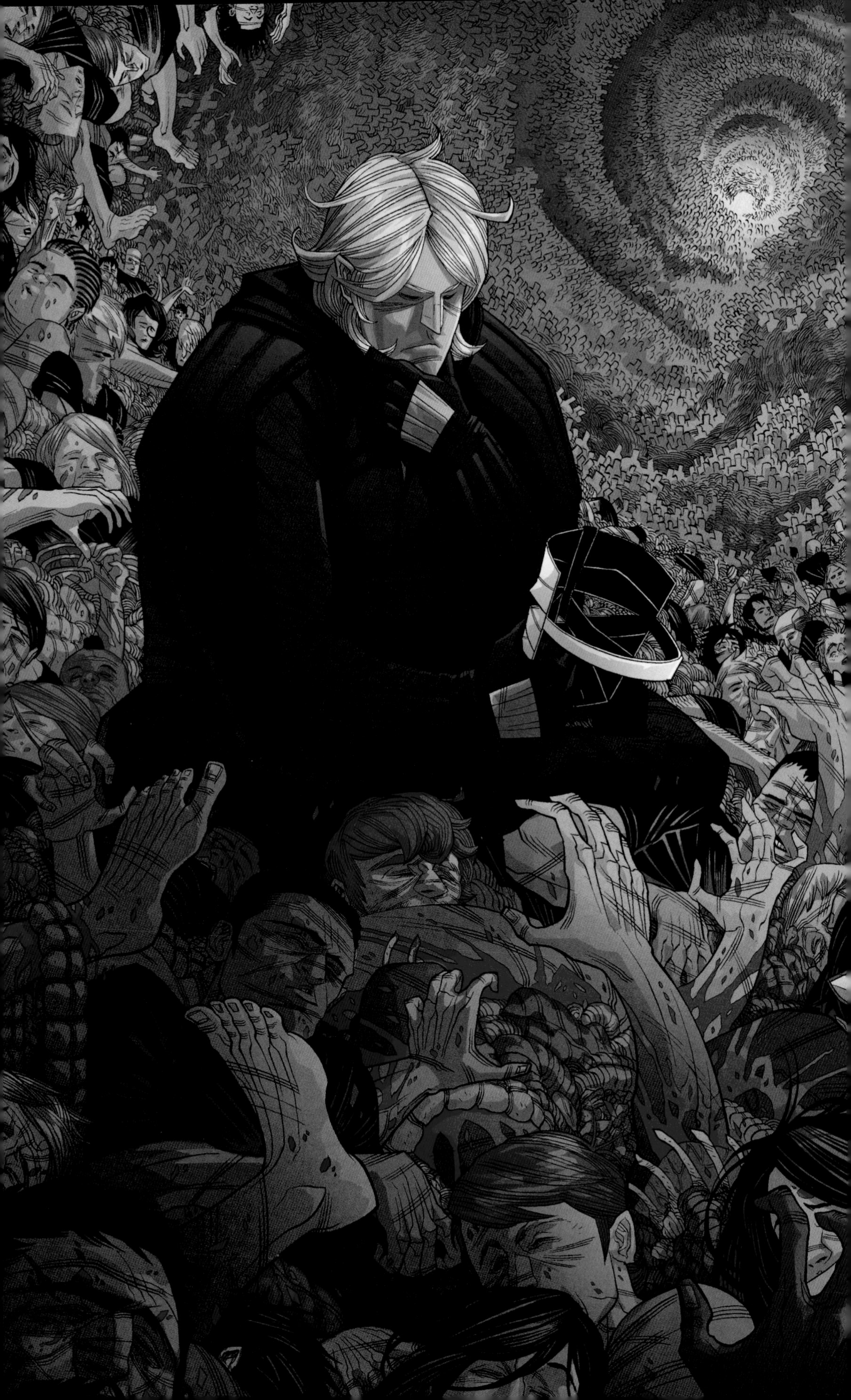

DUDE!!

where the hell were you today? I mean, I assume you were out doing the BOW CHIKA WOW WOW with Petra, but your mom has ~~totally~~ totally been blowing up my phone all afternoon. I'm going to swing by and try to slow down the crazy. BUT if you get this before you see me, **CALL MY ASS.** Also if you tapped that Russian ass, I want deets.

- teh Pete

SUPER LUTHER

jealous of my drawing skills? thought so.

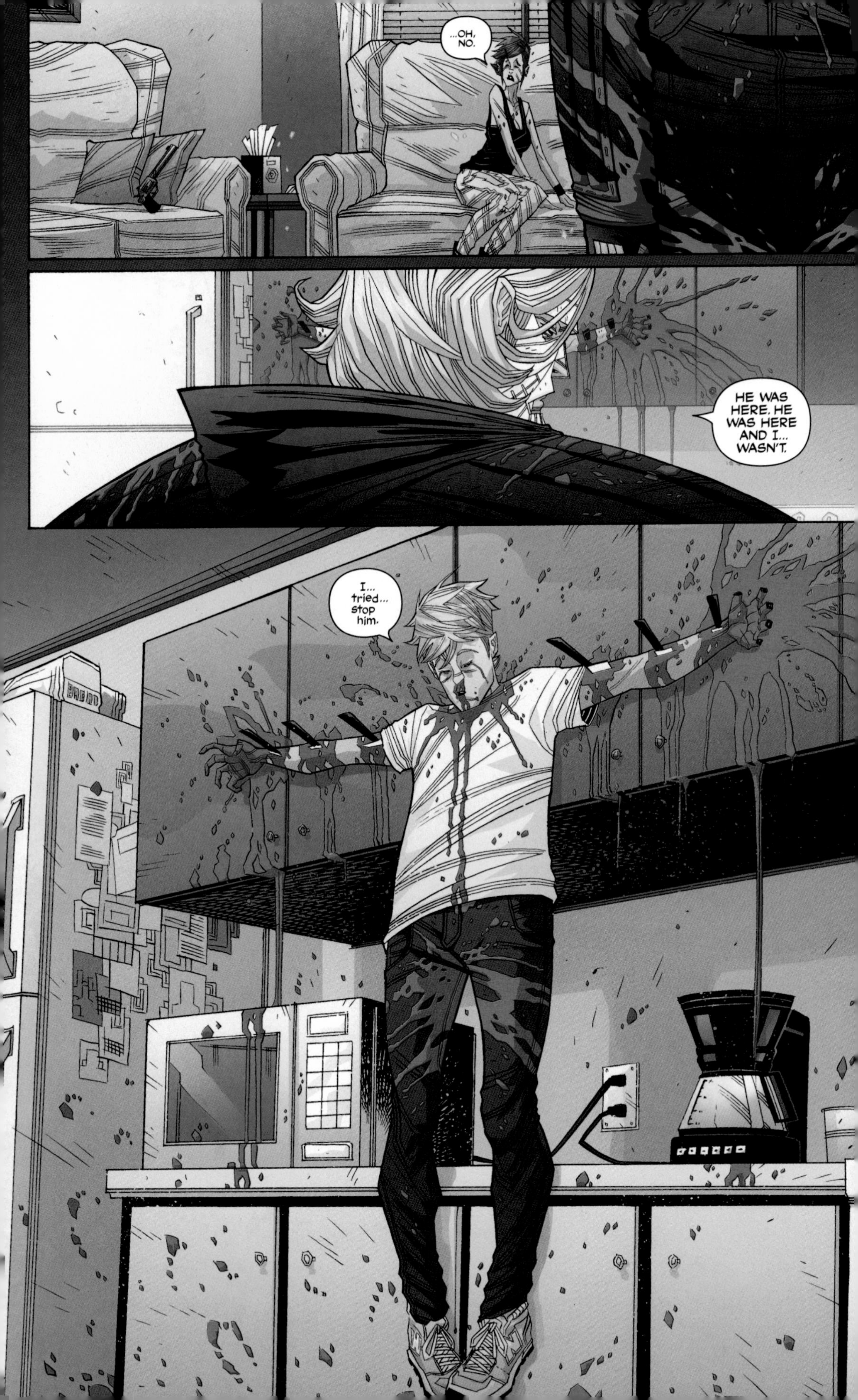
...OH, NO.
HE WAS HERE. HE WAS HERE AND I... WASN'T.
I... tried... stop him.

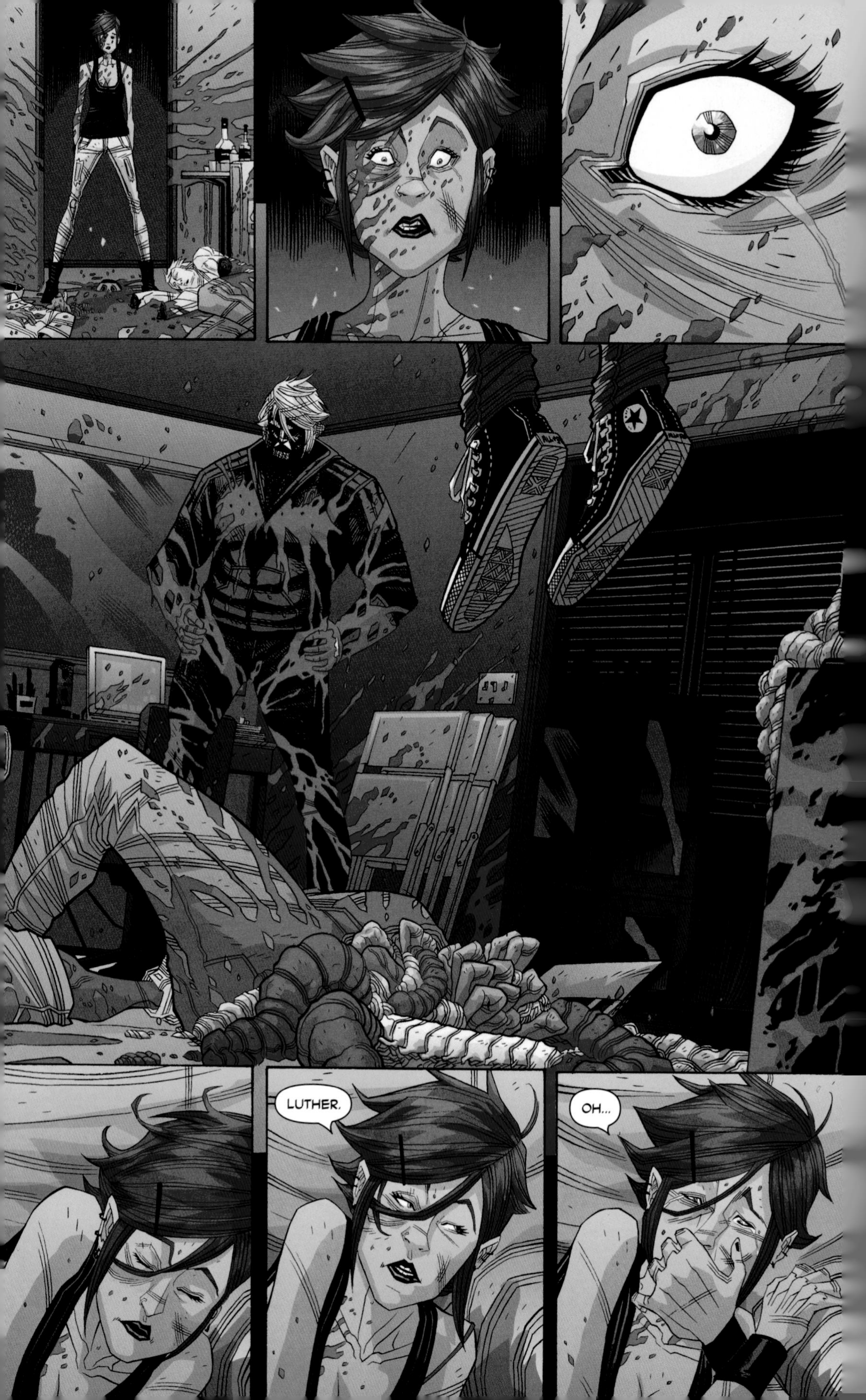
LUTHER.
OH...

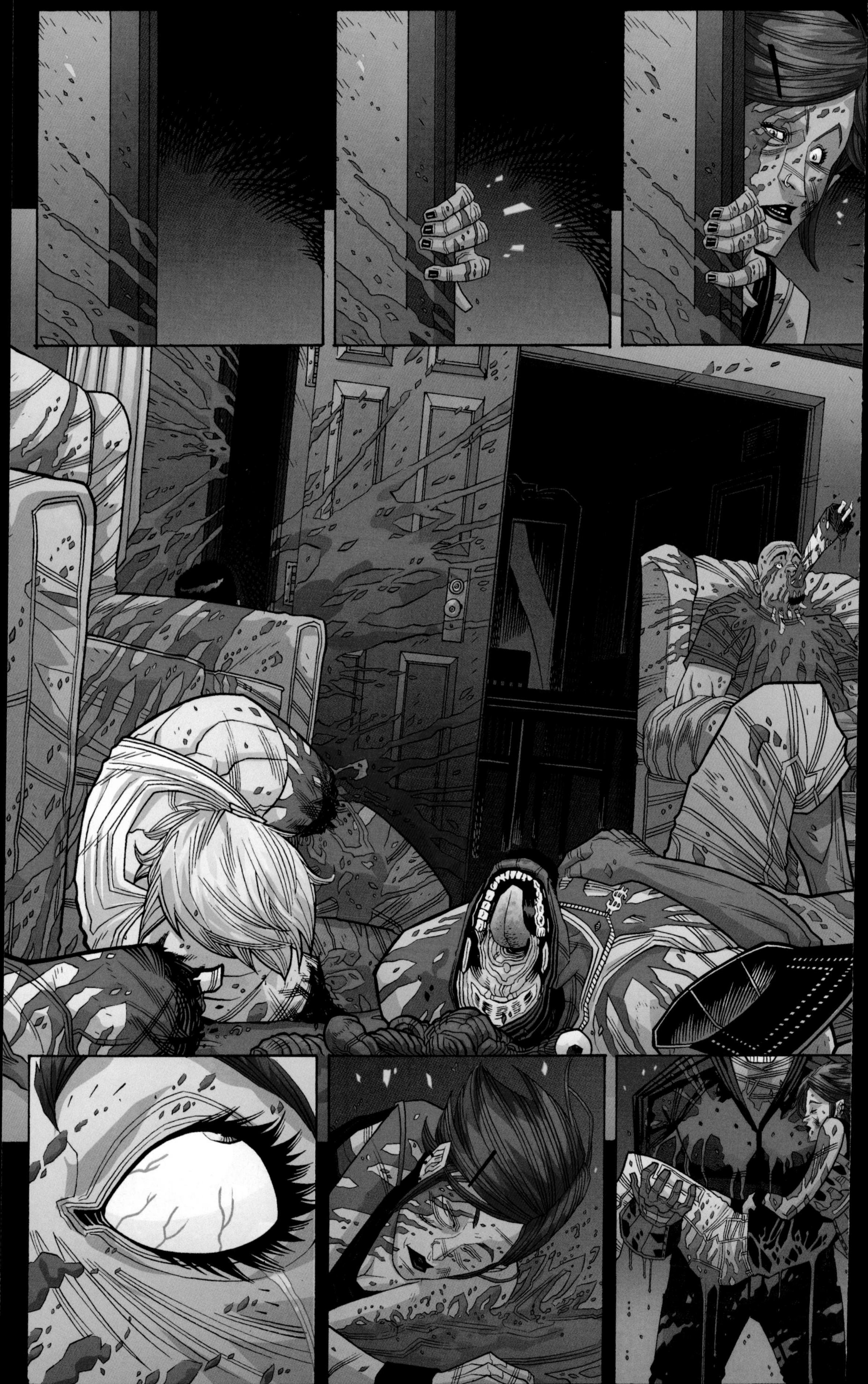

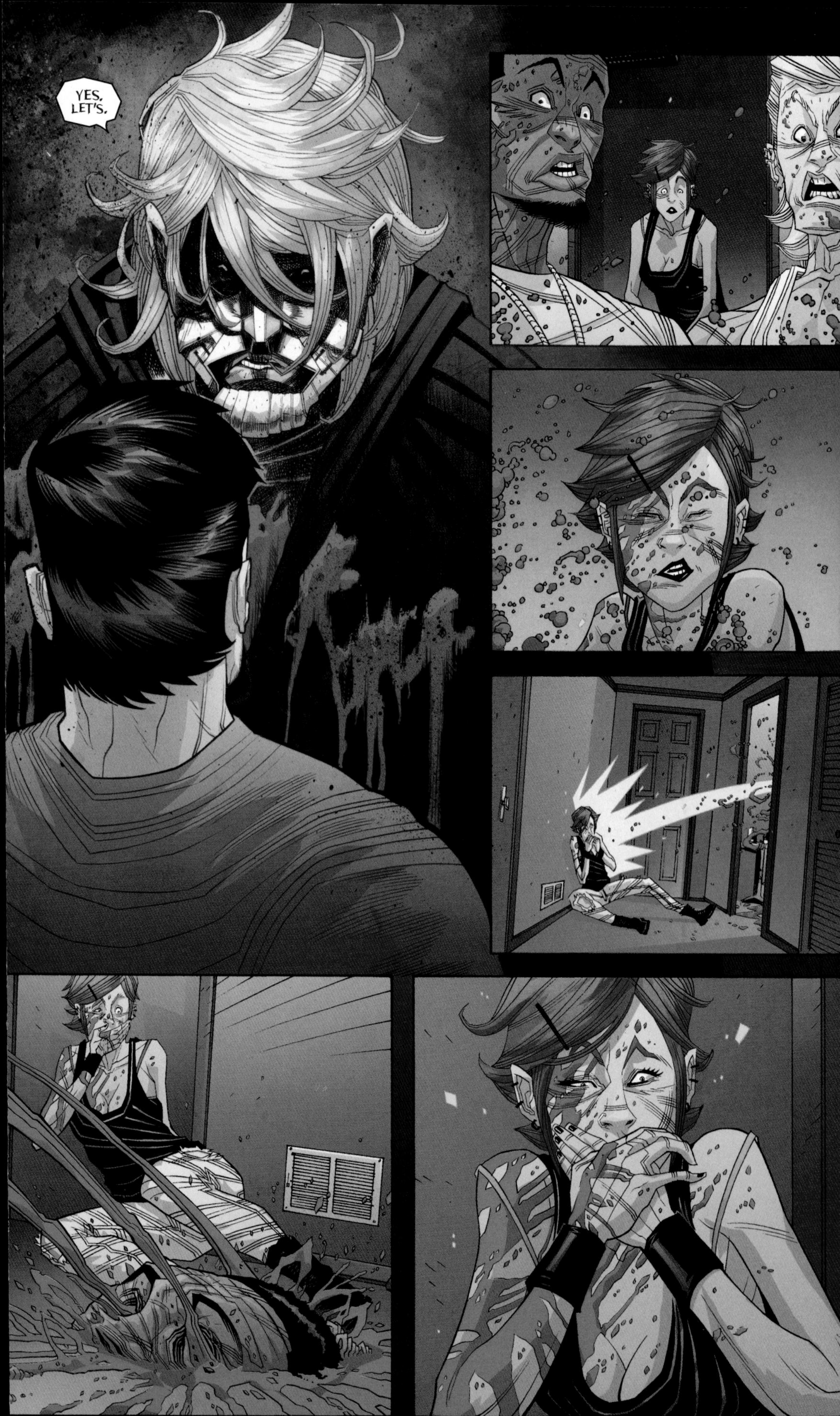
YES, LET'S.

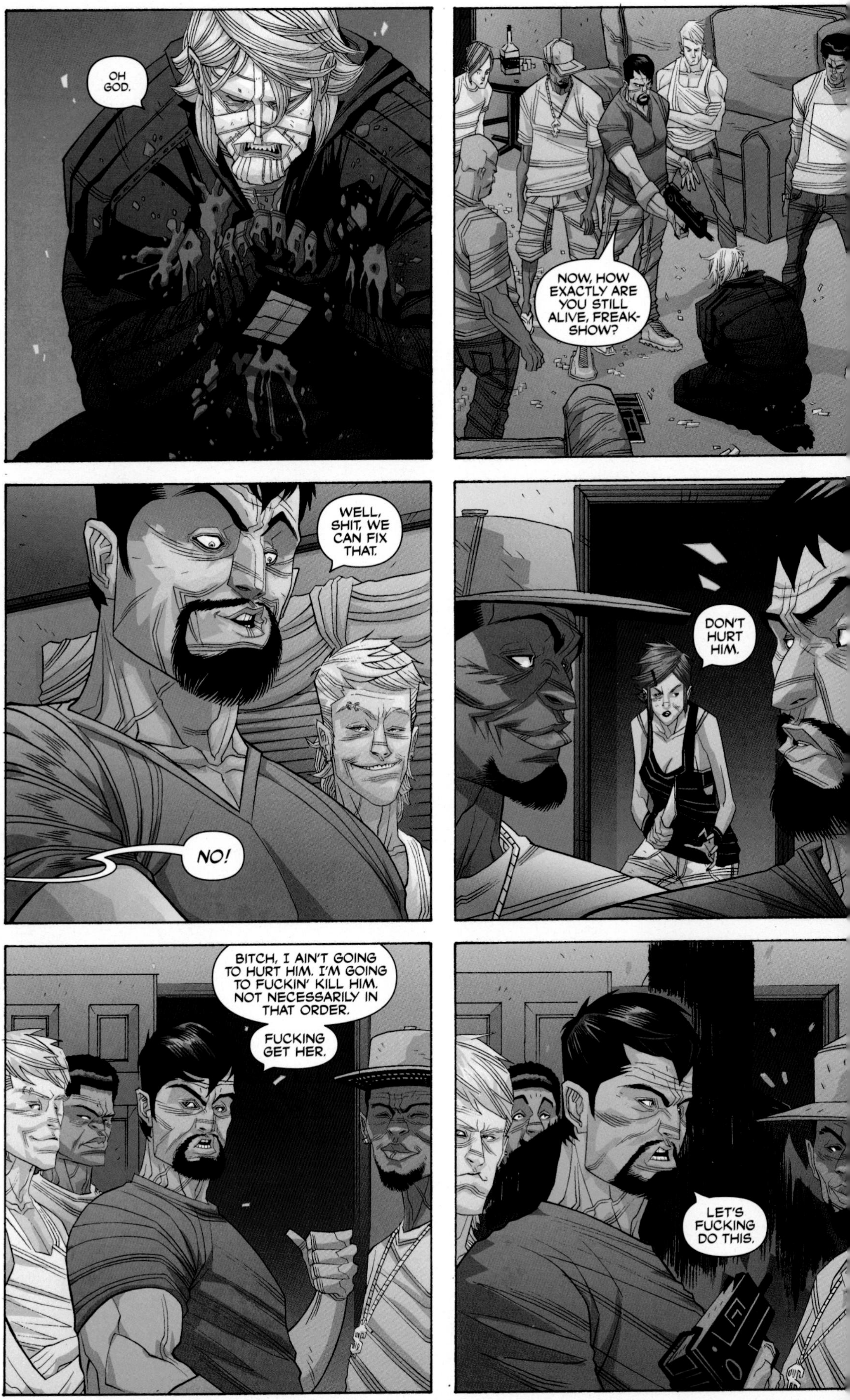
OH GOD.
NOW, HOW EXACTLY ARE YOU STILL ALIVE, FREAK-SHOW?
WELL, SHIT, WE CAN FIX THAT.
NO!
DON'T HURT HIM.
BITCH, I AIN'T GOING TO HURT HIM. I'M GOING TO FUCKIN' KILL HIM. NOT NECESSARILY IN THAT ORDER.
FUCKING GET HER.
LET'S FUCKING DO THIS.

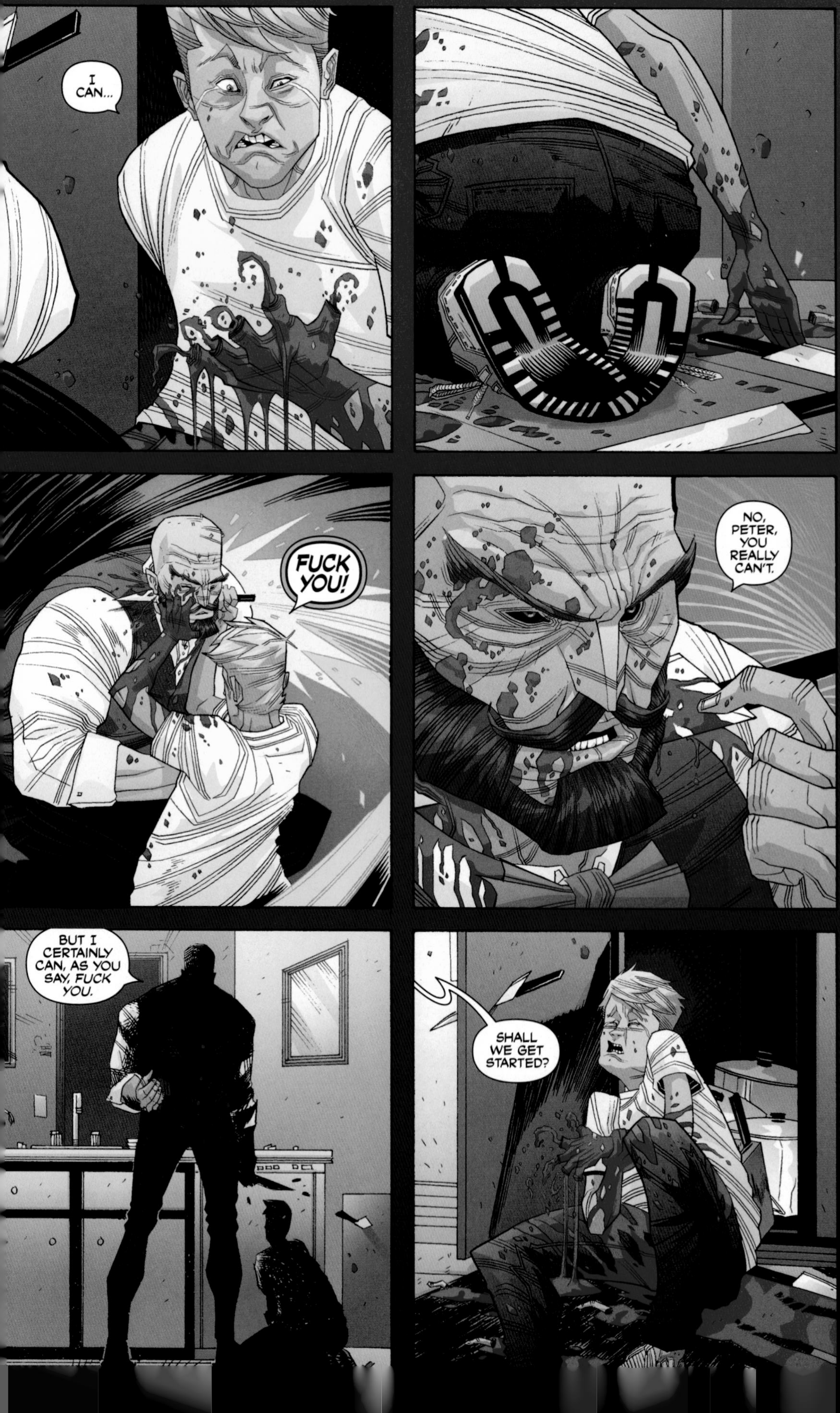
I CAN...
FUCK YOU!
NO, PETER, YOU REALLY CAN'T.
BUT I CERTAINLY CAN, AS YOU SAY, FUCK YOU.
SHALL WE GET STARTED?

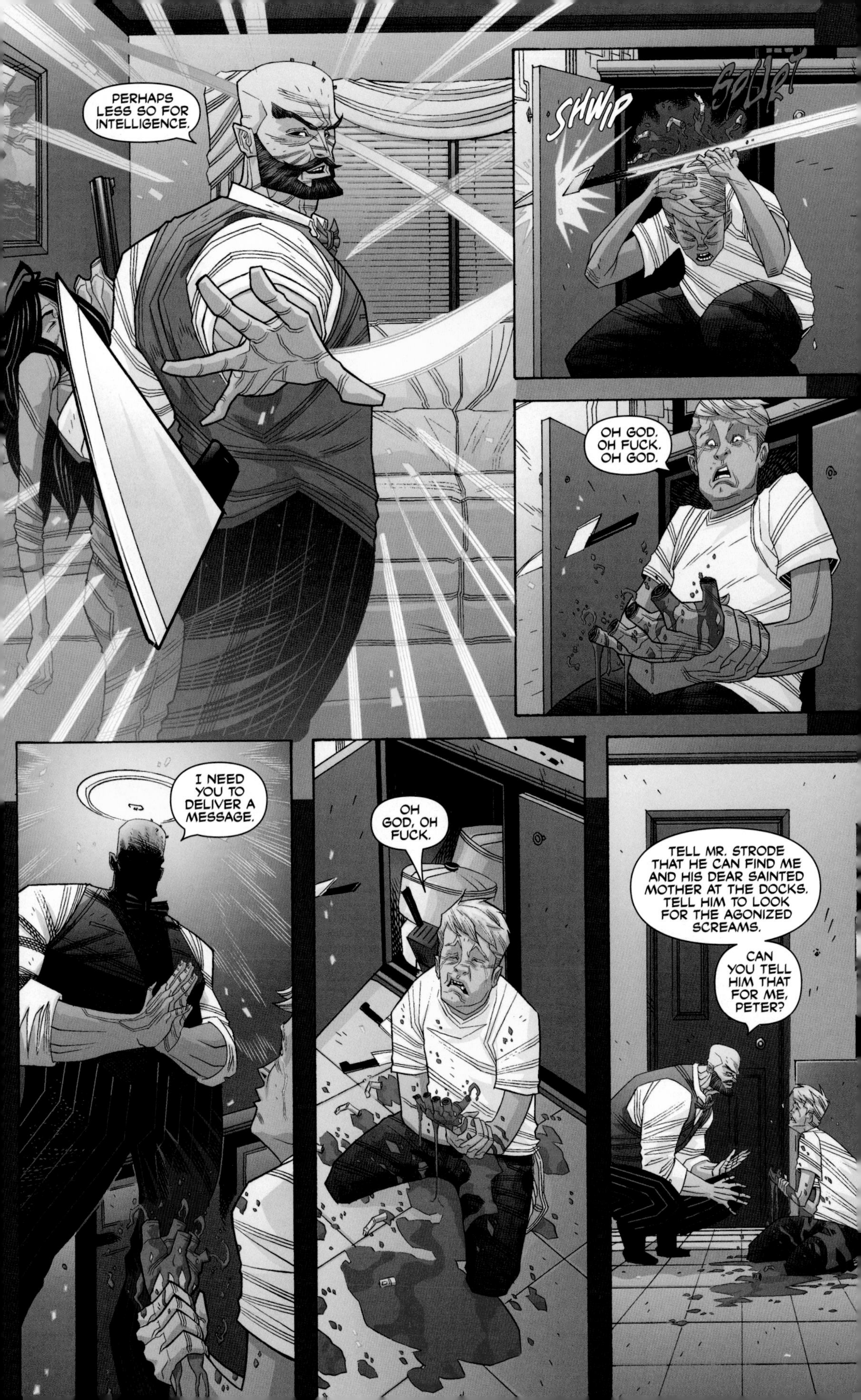
PERHAPS LESS SO FOR INTELLIGENCE.
SHWIP
SPURT
OH GOD. OH FUCK. OH GOD.
I NEED YOU TO DELIVER A MESSAGE.
OH GOD, OH FUCK.
TELL MR. STRODE THAT HE CAN FIND ME AND HIS DEAR SAINTED MOTHER AT THE DOCKS. TELL HIM TO LOOK FOR THE AGONIZED SCREAMS.
CAN YOU TELL HIM THAT FOR ME, PETER?

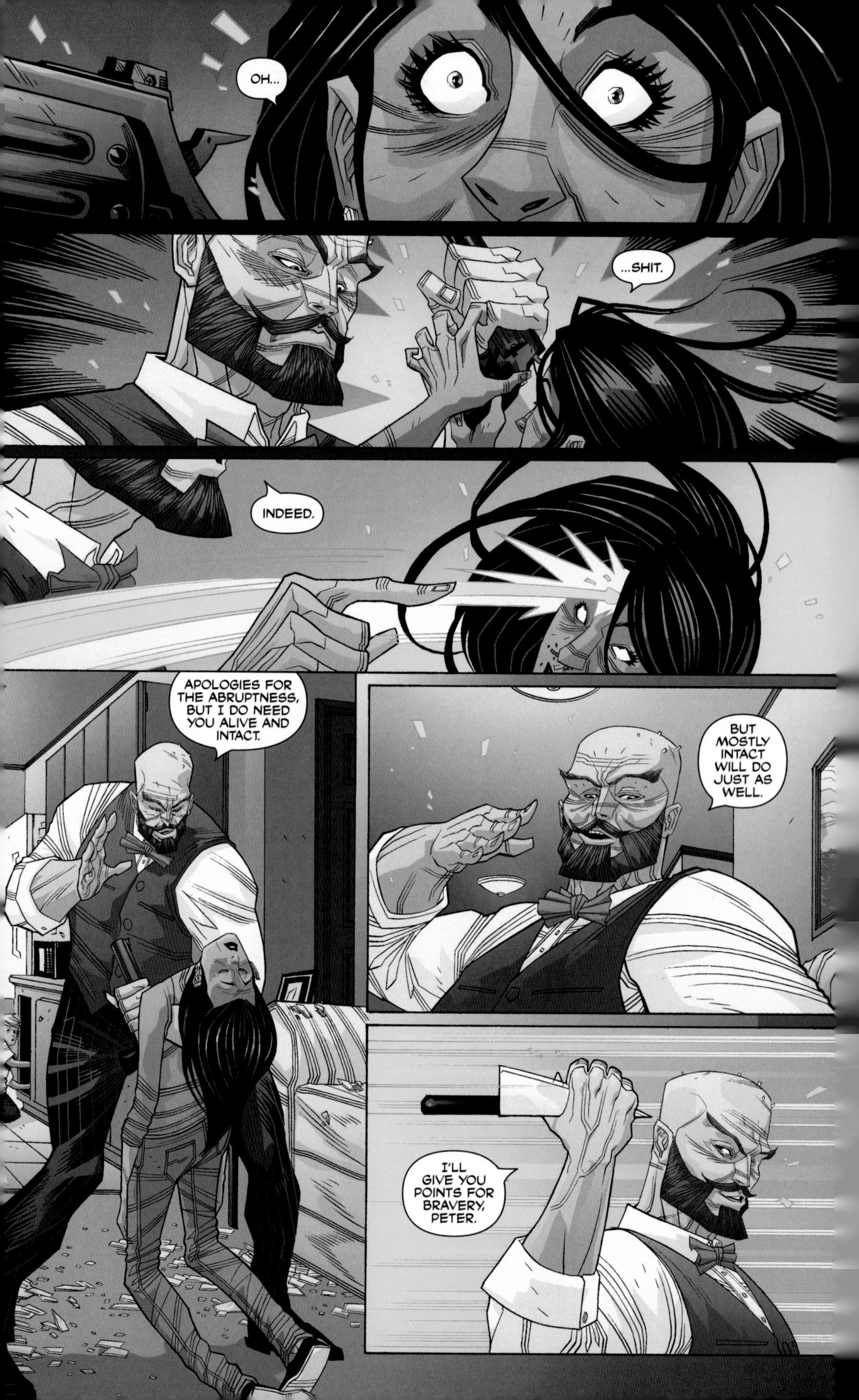
OH...
...SHIT.
INDEED.
APOLOGIES FOR THE ABRUPTNESS, BUT I DO NEED YOU ALIVE AND INTACT.
BUT MOSTLY INTACT WILL DO JUST AS WELL.
I'LL GIVE YOU POINTS FOR BRAVERY, PETER.

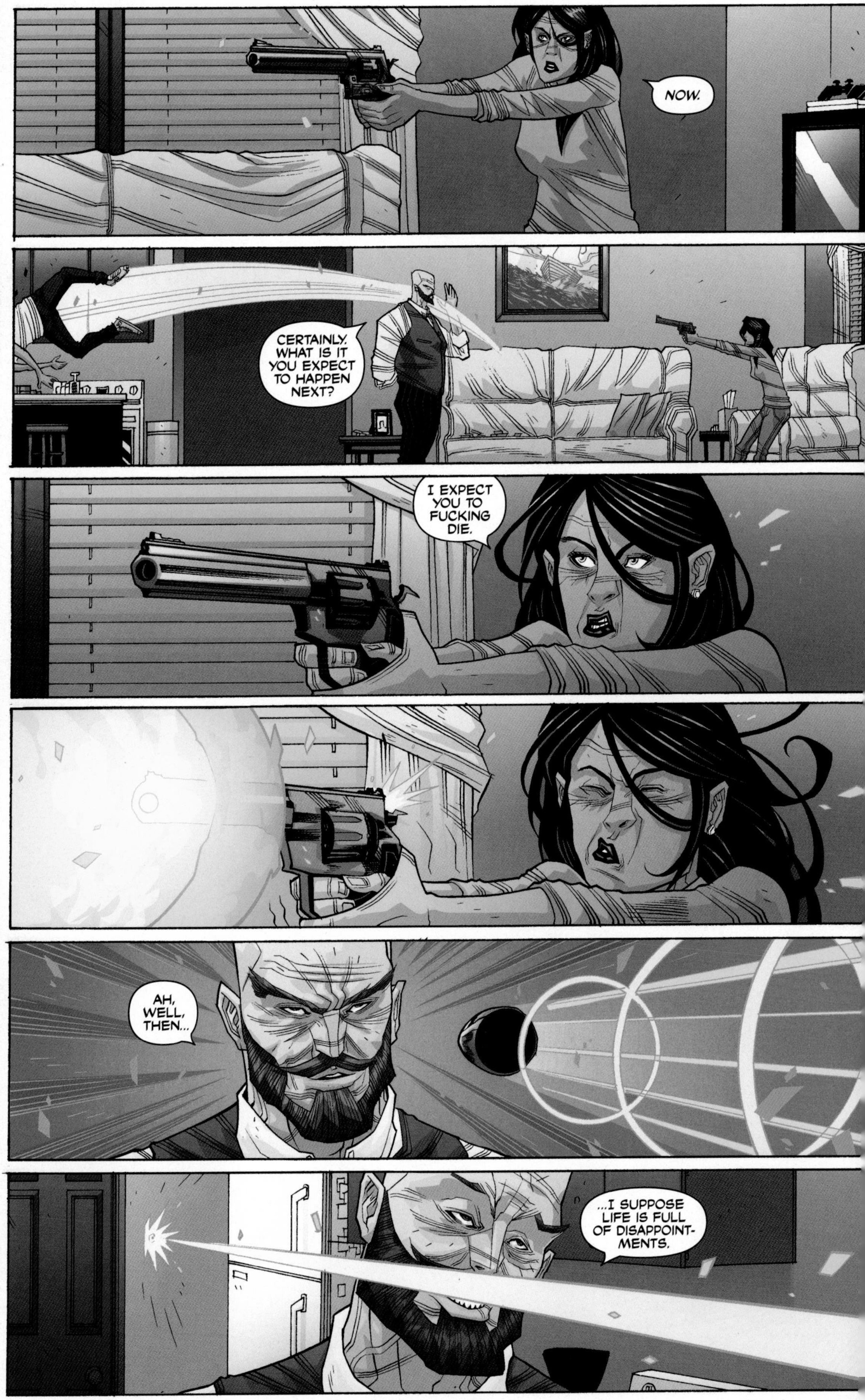
NOW.
CERTAINLY. WHAT IS IT YOU EXPECT TO HAPPEN NEXT?
I EXPECT YOU TO FUCKING DIE.
AH, WELL, THEN...
...I SUPPOSE LIFE IS FULL OF DISAPPOINT-MENTS.

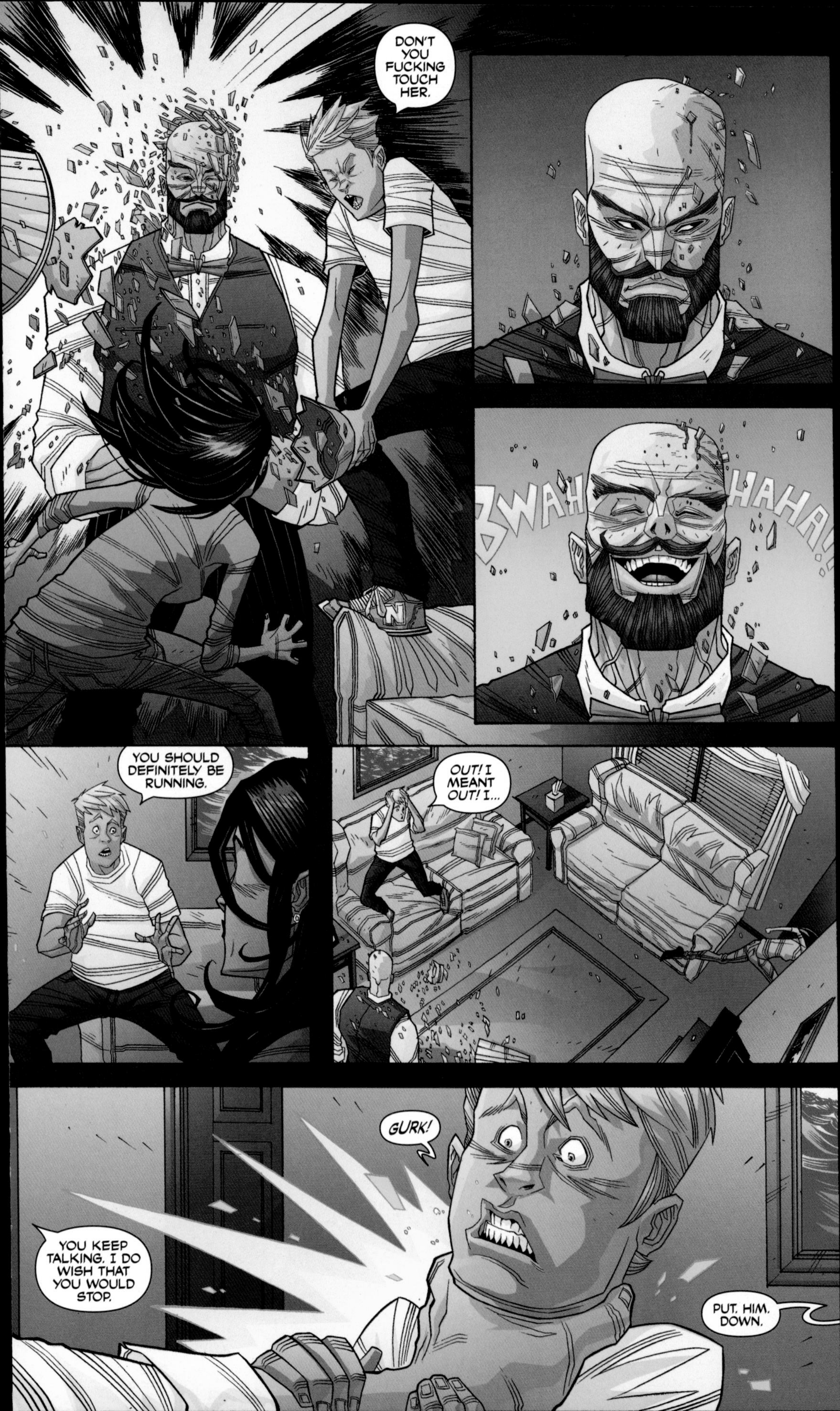
DON'T YOU FUCKING TOUCH HER.
BWAH
HAHA!
YOU SHOULD DEFINITELY BE RUNNING.
OUT! I MEANT OUT! I...
GURK!
YOU KEEP TALKING. I DO WISH THAT YOU WOULD STOP.
PUT. HIM. DOWN.

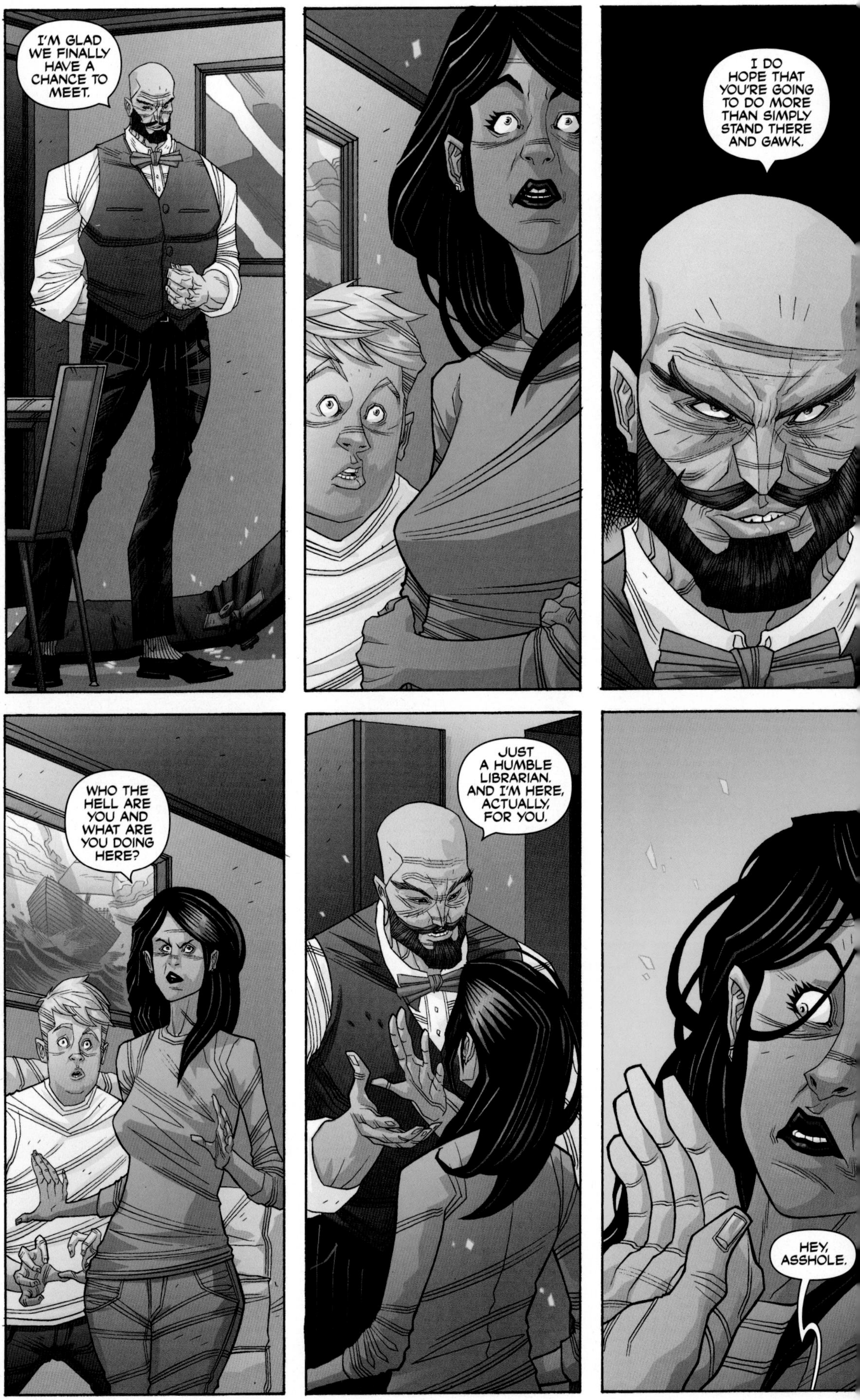
I'M GLAD WE FINALLY HAVE A CHANCE TO MEET.
I DO HOPE THAT YOU'RE GOING TO DO MORE THAN SIMPLY STAND THERE AND GAWK.
WHO THE HELL ARE YOU AND WHAT ARE YOU DOING HERE?
JUST A HUMBLE LIBRARIAN. AND I'M HERE, ACTUALLY, FOR YOU.
HEY, ASSHOLE.

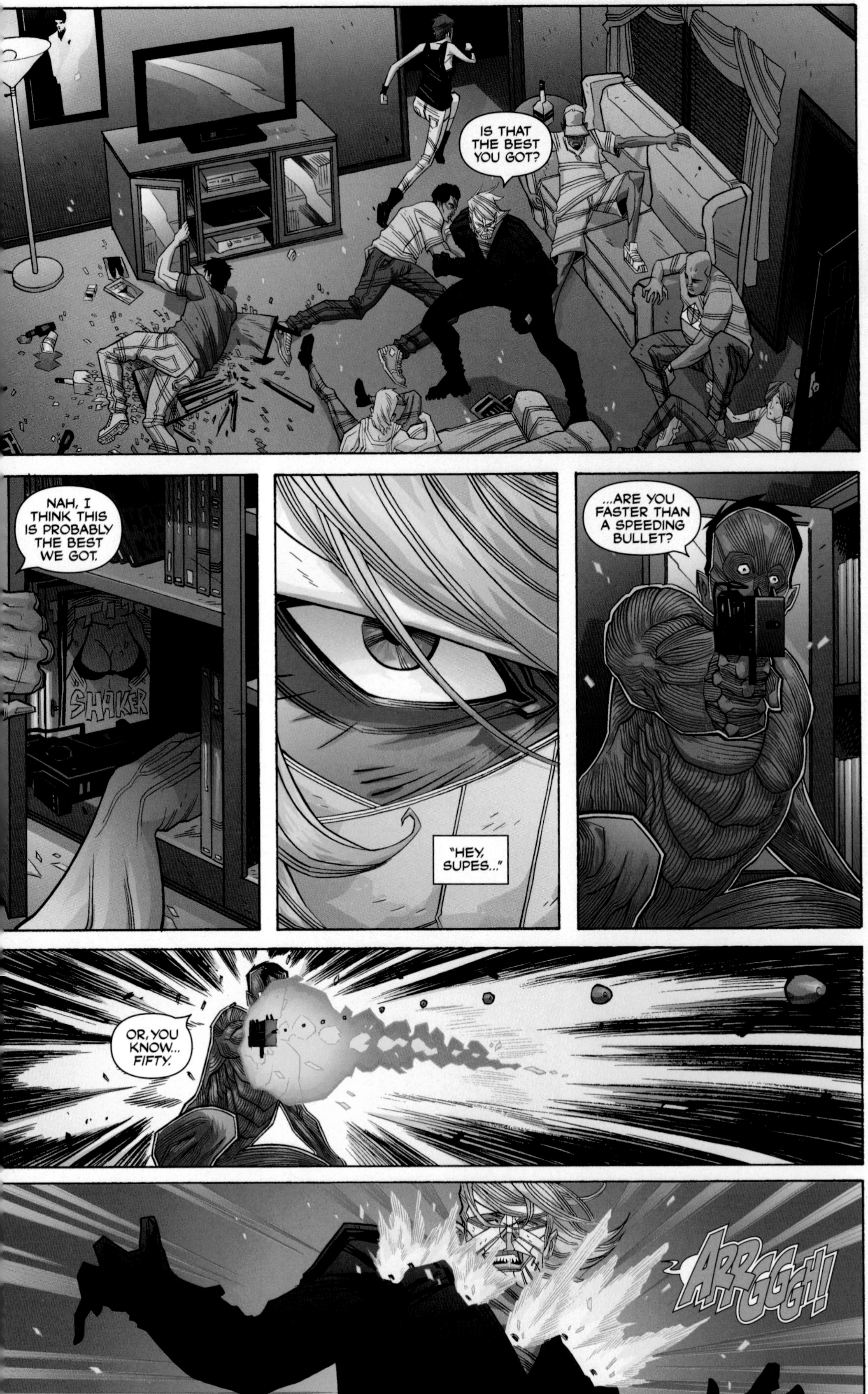
IS THAT THE BEST YOU GOT?
NAH, I THINK THIS IS PROBABLY THE BEST WE GOT.
SHAKER
"HEY, SUPES..."
...ARE YOU FASTER THAN A SPEEDING BULLET?
OR, YOU KNOW... FIFTY.
ARRGGGH!

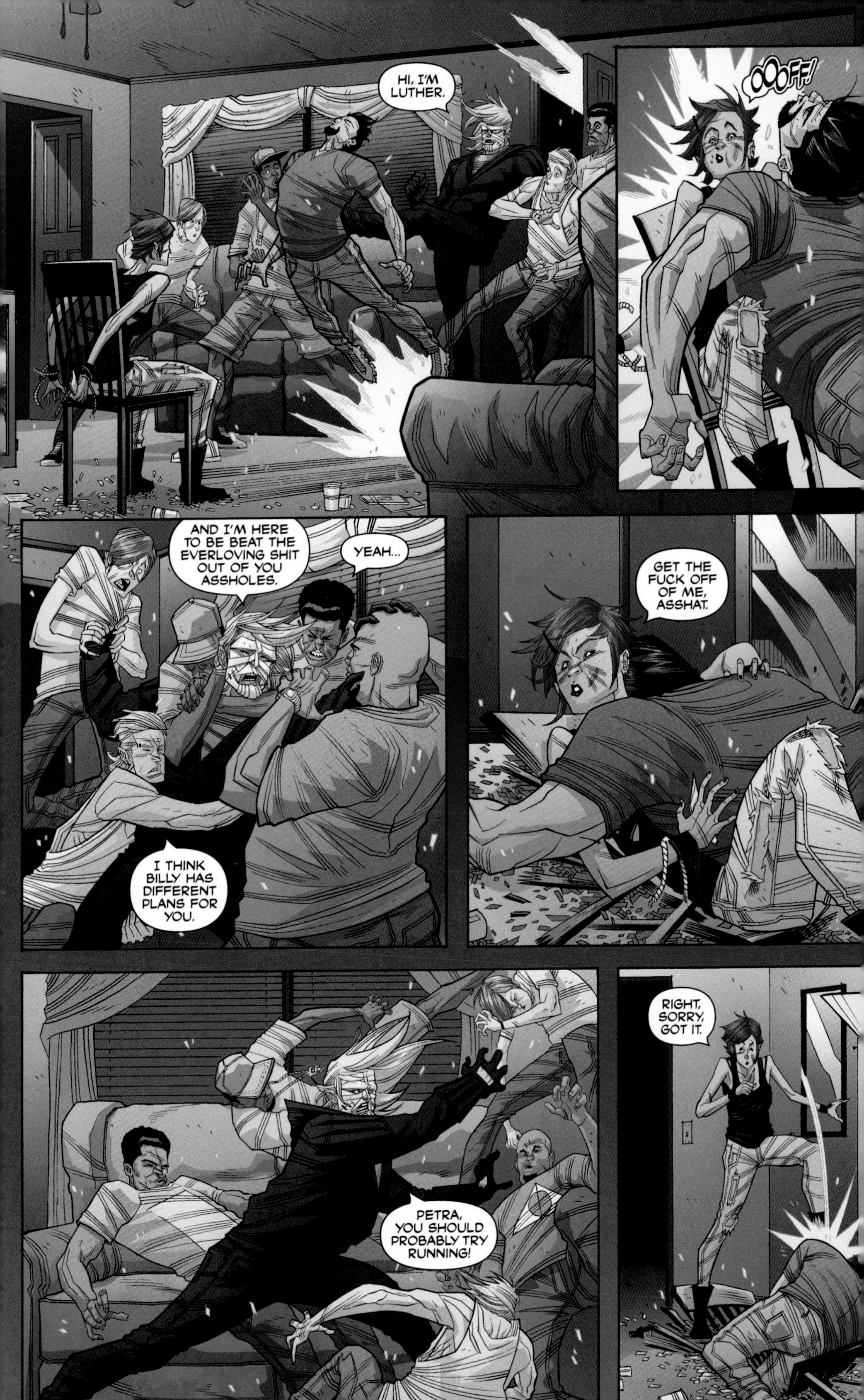
HI, I'M LUTHER.
OOOFF!
AND I'M HERE TO BE BEAT THE EVERLOVING SHIT OUT OF YOU ASSHOLES.
YEAH...
I THINK BILLY HAS DIFFERENT PLANS FOR YOU.
GET THE FUCK OFF OF ME, ASSHAT.
PETRA, YOU SHOULD PROBABLY TRY RUNNING!
RIGHT, SORRY, GOT IT.

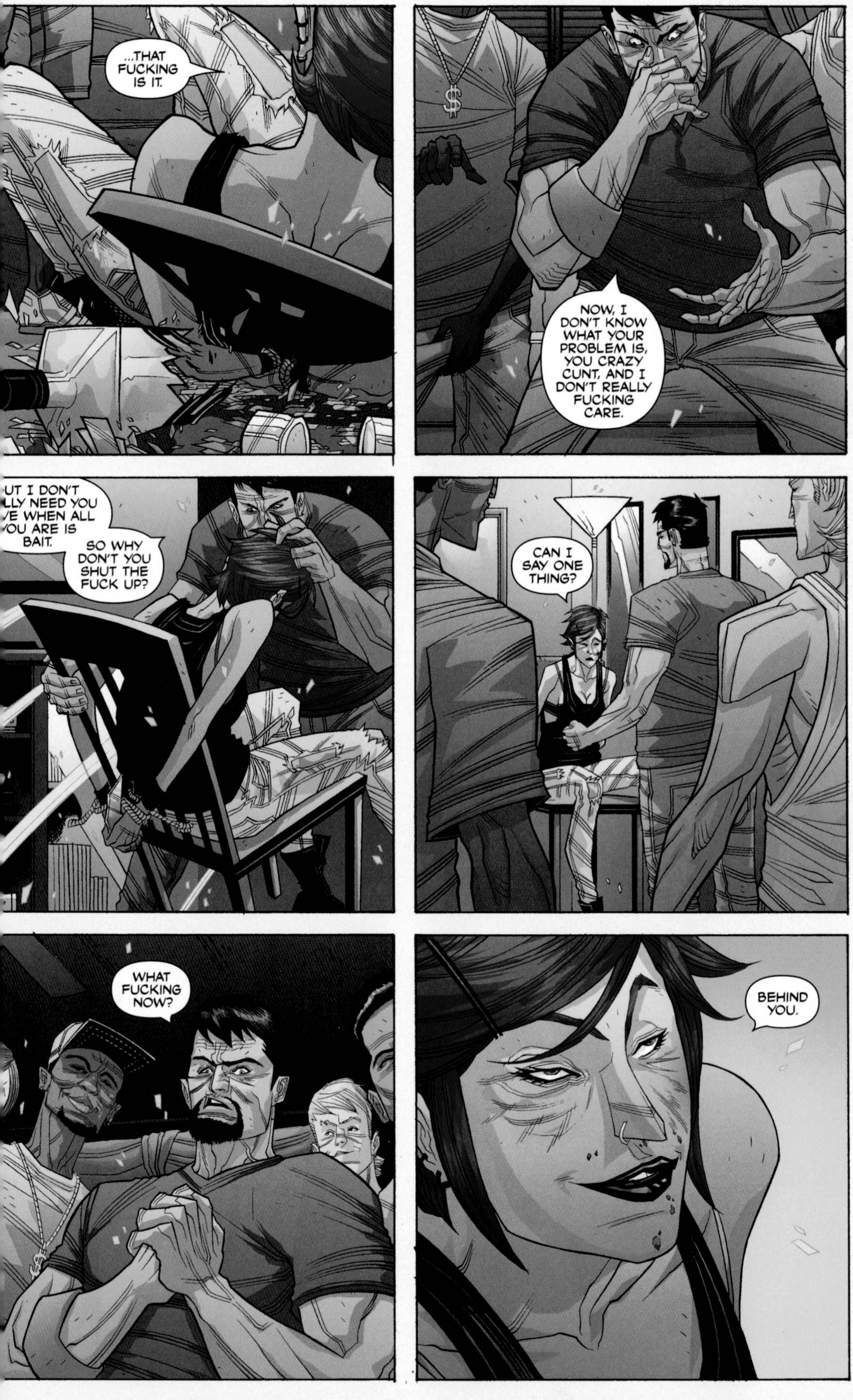
...THAT FUCKING IS IT.
NOW, I DON'T KNOW WHAT YOUR PROBLEM IS, YOU CRAZY CUNT, AND I DON'T REALLY FUCKING CARE.
UT I DON'T LLY NEED YOU E WHEN ALL OU ARE IS BAIT.
SO WHY DON'T YOU SHUT THE FUCK UP?
CAN I SAY ONE THING?
WHAT FUCKING NOW?
BEHIND YOU.

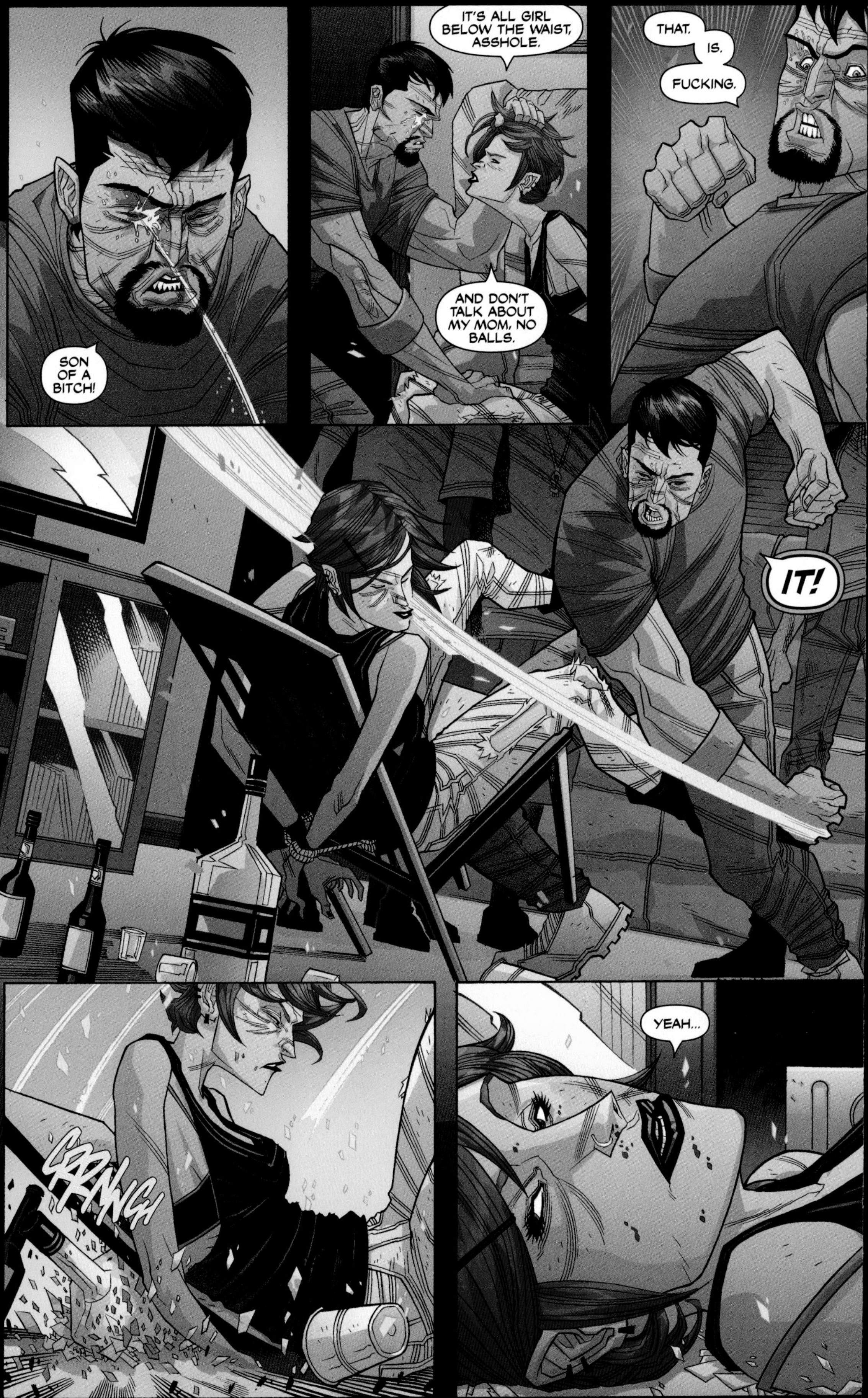
SON OF A BITCH!
IT'S ALL GIRL BELOW THE WAIST, ASSHOLE.
AND DON'T TALK ABOUT MY MOM, NO BALLS.
THAT.
IS.
FUCKING.
IT!
CRRNNCH
YEAH...

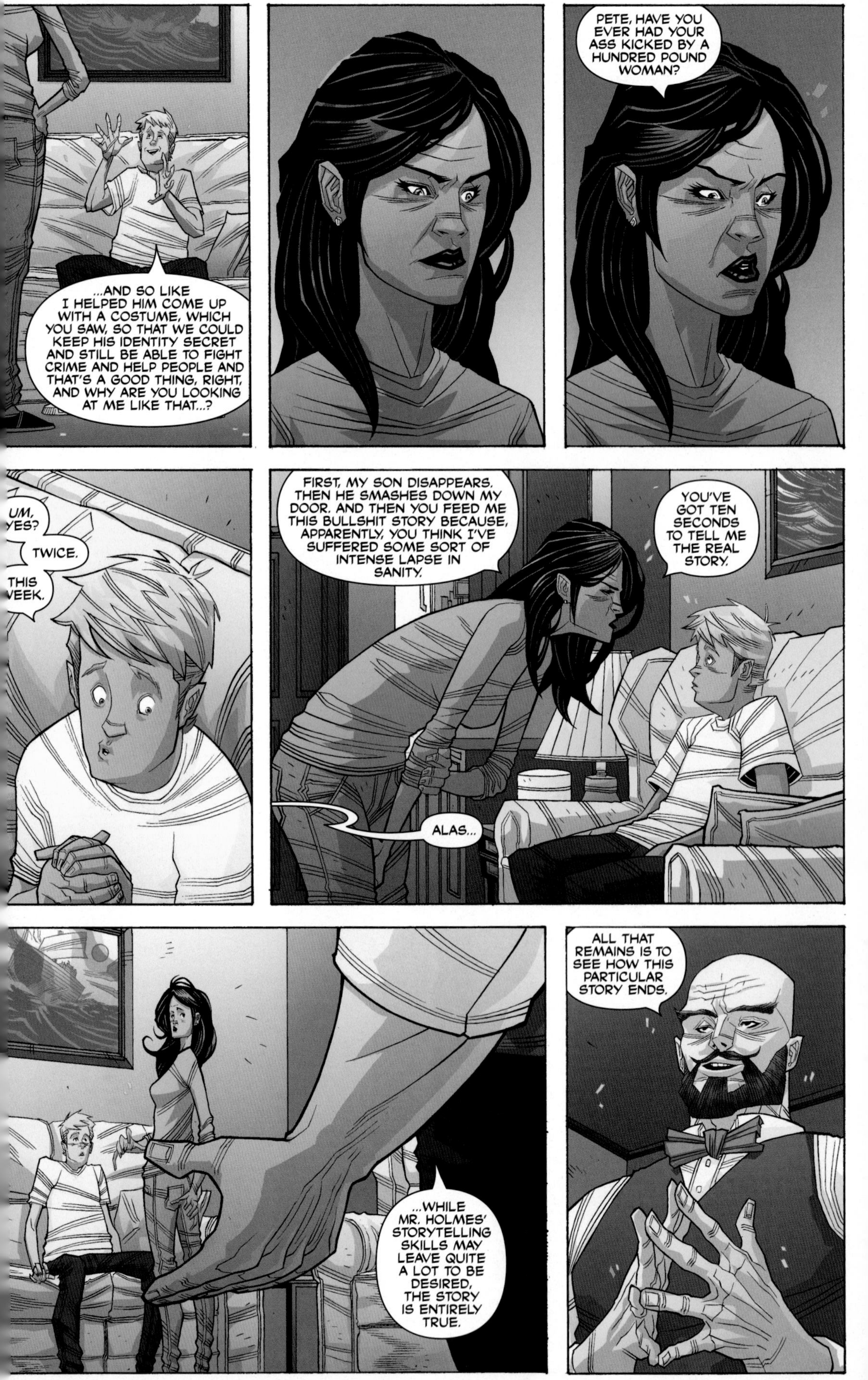
...AND SO LIKE I HELPED HIM COME UP WITH A COSTUME, WHICH YOU SAW, SO THAT WE COULD KEEP HIS IDENTITY SECRET AND STILL BE ABLE TO FIGHT CRIME AND HELP PEOPLE AND THAT'S A GOOD THING, RIGHT, AND WHY ARE YOU LOOKING AT ME LIKE THAT...?
PETE, HAVE YOU EVER HAD YOUR ASS KICKED BY A HUNDRED POUND WOMAN?
UM, YES?
TWICE.
THIS WEEK.
FIRST, MY SON DISAPPEARS. THEN HE SMASHES DOWN MY DOOR. AND THEN YOU FEED ME THIS BULLSHIT STORY BECAUSE, APPARENTLY, YOU THINK I'VE SUFFERED SOME SORT OF INTENSE LAPSE IN SANITY.
YOU'VE GOT TEN SECONDS TO TELL ME THE REAL STORY.
ALAS...
...WHILE MR. HOLMES' STORYTELLING SKILLS MAY LEAVE QUITE A LOT TO BE DESIRED, THE STORY IS ENTIRELY TRUE.
ALL THAT REMAINS IS TO SEE HOW THIS PARTICULAR STORY ENDS.

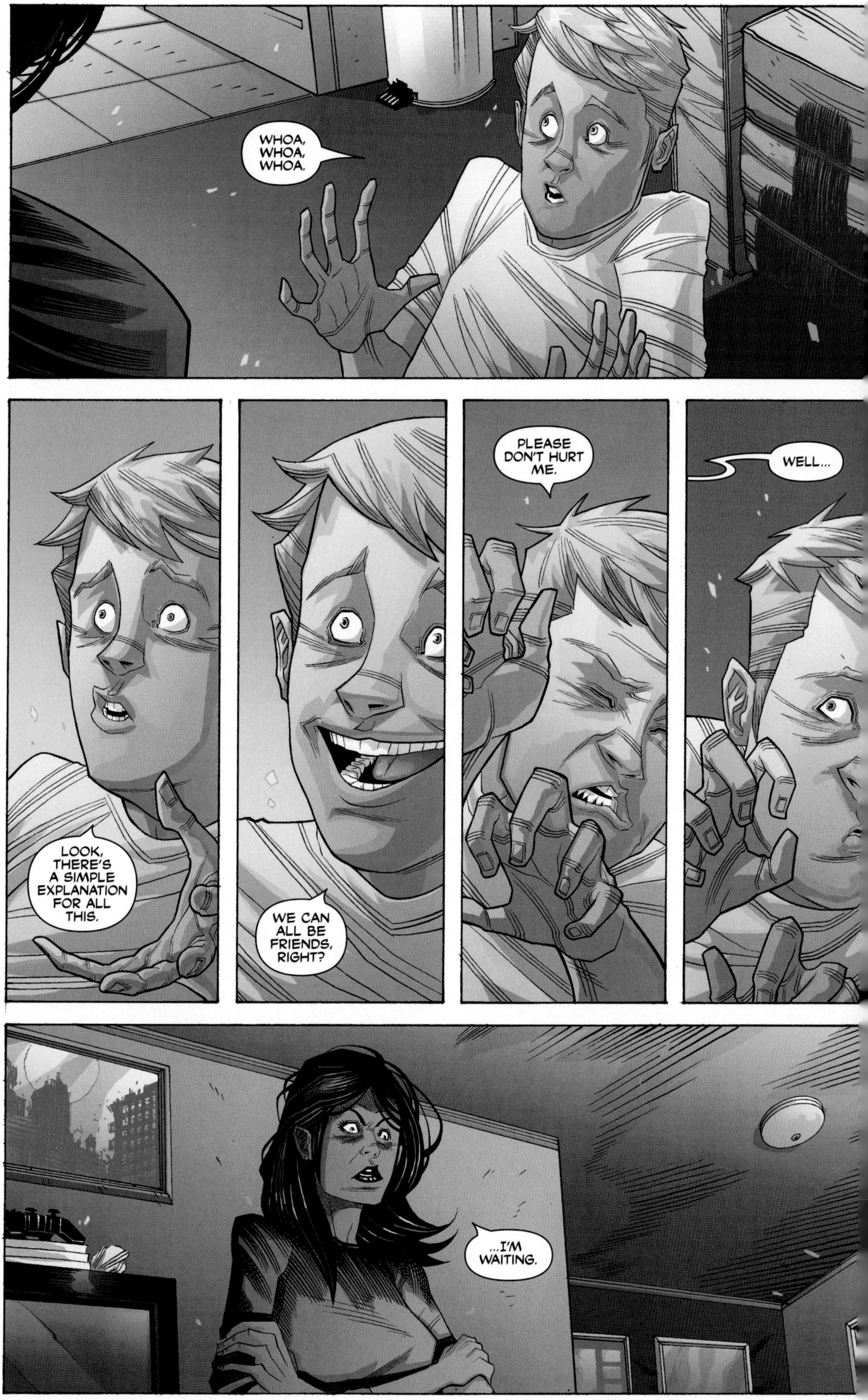
WHOA, WHOA, WHOA.
LOOK, THERE'S A SIMPLE EXPLANATION FOR ALL THIS.
WE CAN ALL BE FRIENDS, RIGHT?
PLEASE DON'T HURT ME.
WELL...
...I'M WAITING.

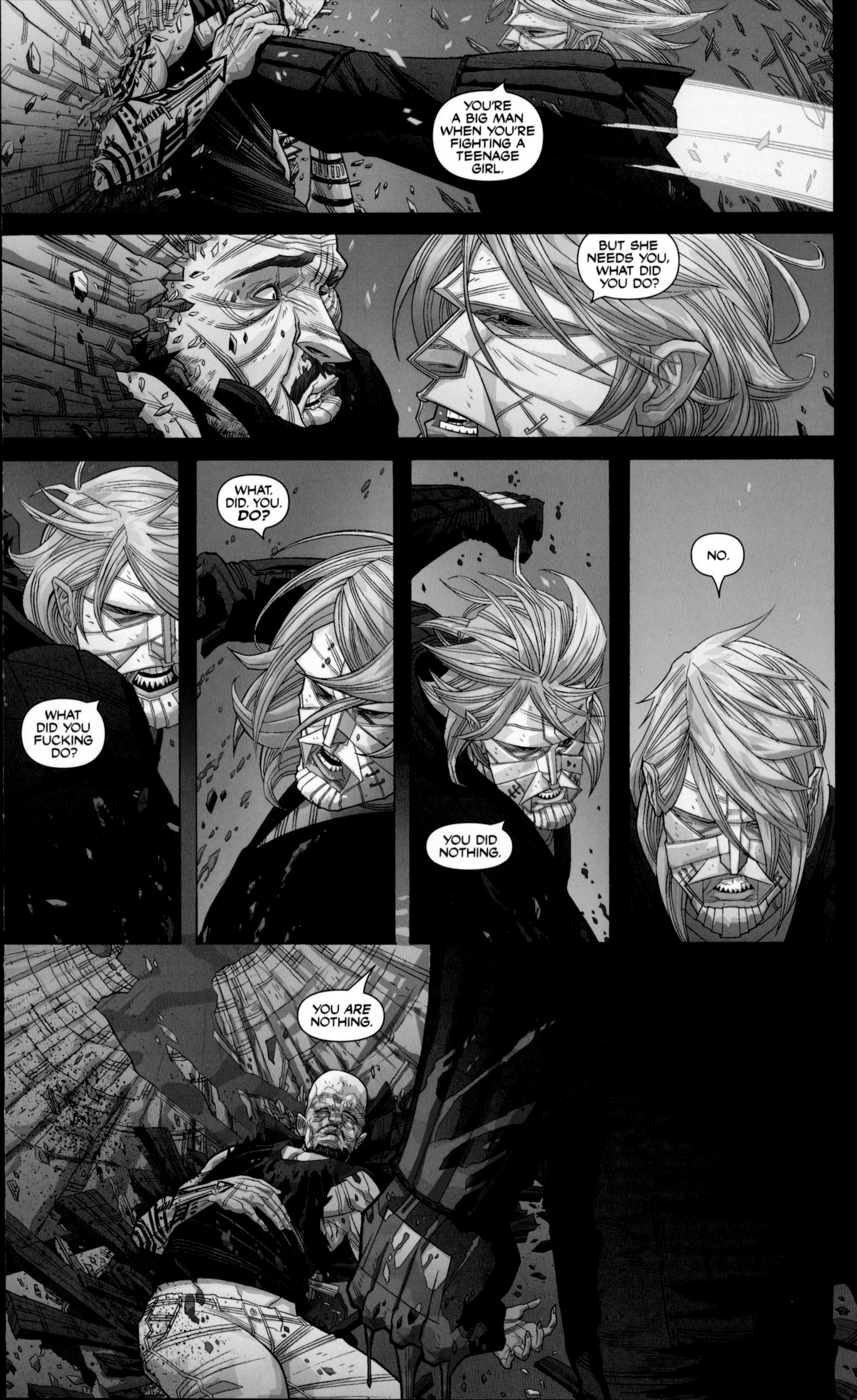
YOU'RE A BIG MAN WHEN YOU'RE FIGHTING A TEENAGE GIRL.
BUT SHE NEEDS YOU, WHAT DID YOU DO?
WHAT DID YOU FUCKING DO?
WHAT. DID. YOU. DO?
YOU DID NOTHING.
NO.
YOU ARE NOTHING.

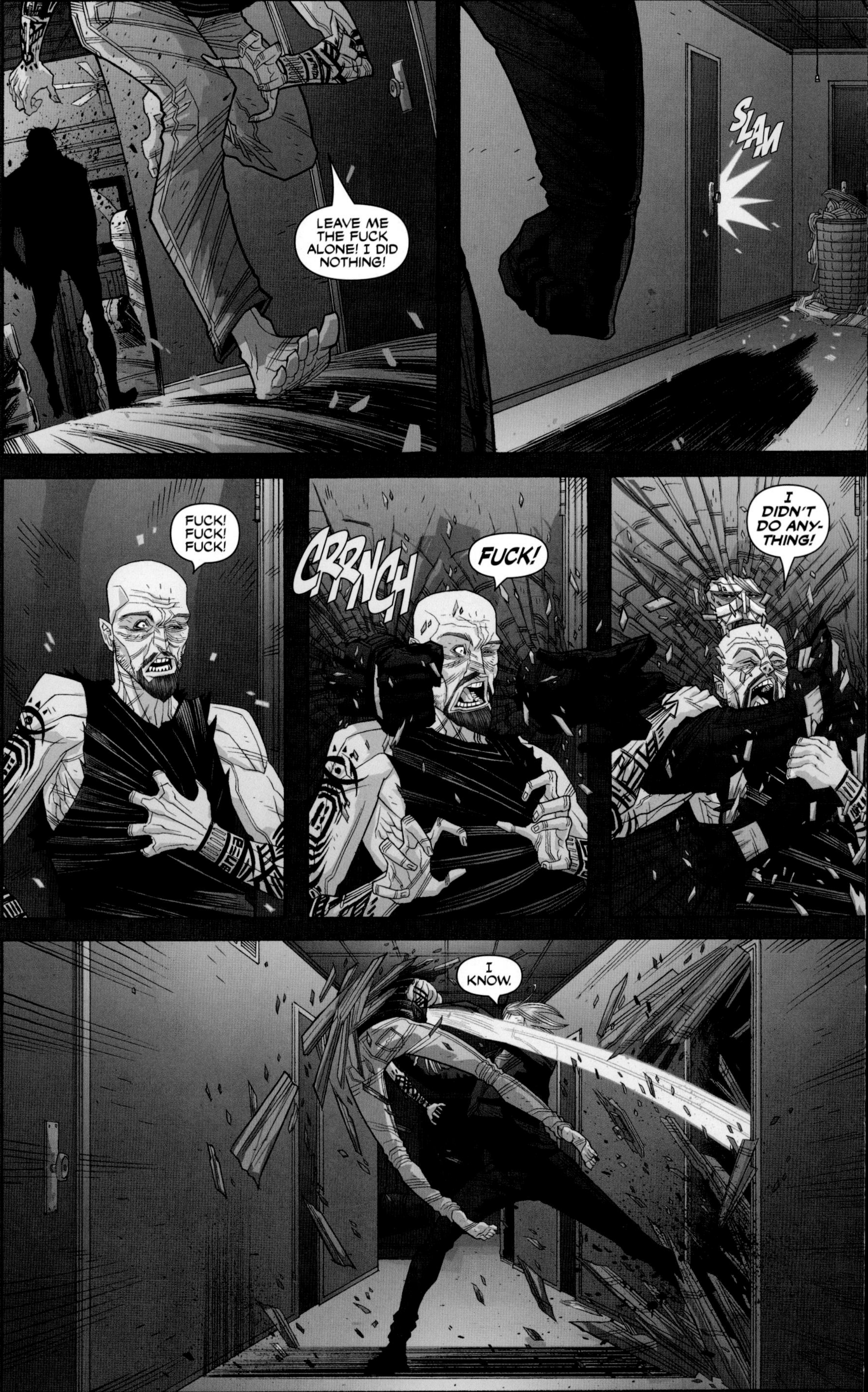
LEAVE ME THE FUCK ALONE! I DID NOTHING!
SLAM
FUCK! FUCK! FUCK!
CRRNCH
FUCK!
I DIDN'T DO ANY-THING!
I KNOW.

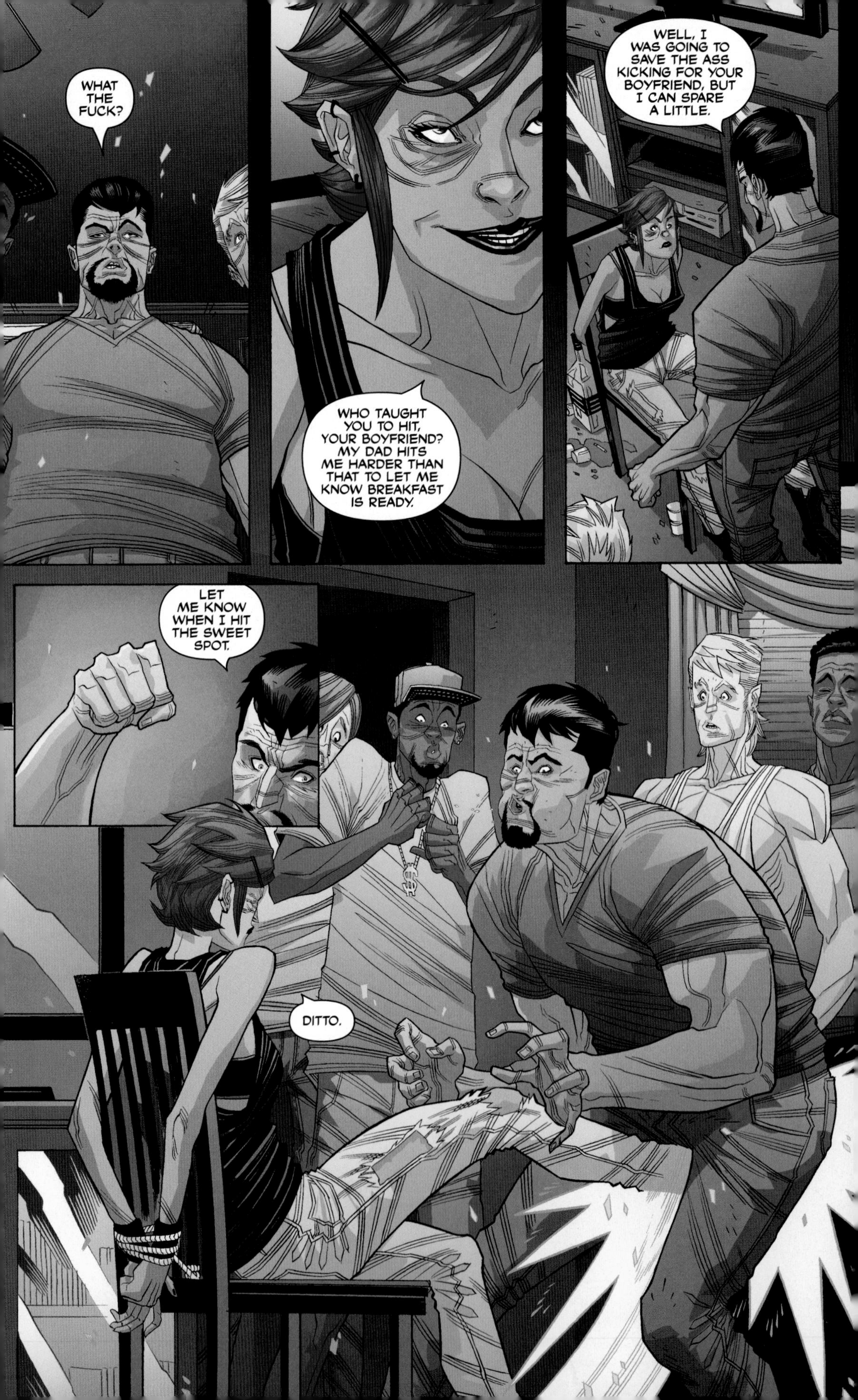
WHAT THE FUCK?
WHO TAUGHT YOU TO HIT, YOUR BOYFRIEND? MY DAD HITS ME HARDER THAN THAT TO LET ME KNOW BREAKFAST IS READY.
WELL, I WAS GOING TO SAVE THE ASS KICKING FOR YOUR BOYFRIEND, BUT I CAN SPARE A LITTLE.
LET ME KNOW WHEN I HIT THE SWEET SPOT.
DITTO.

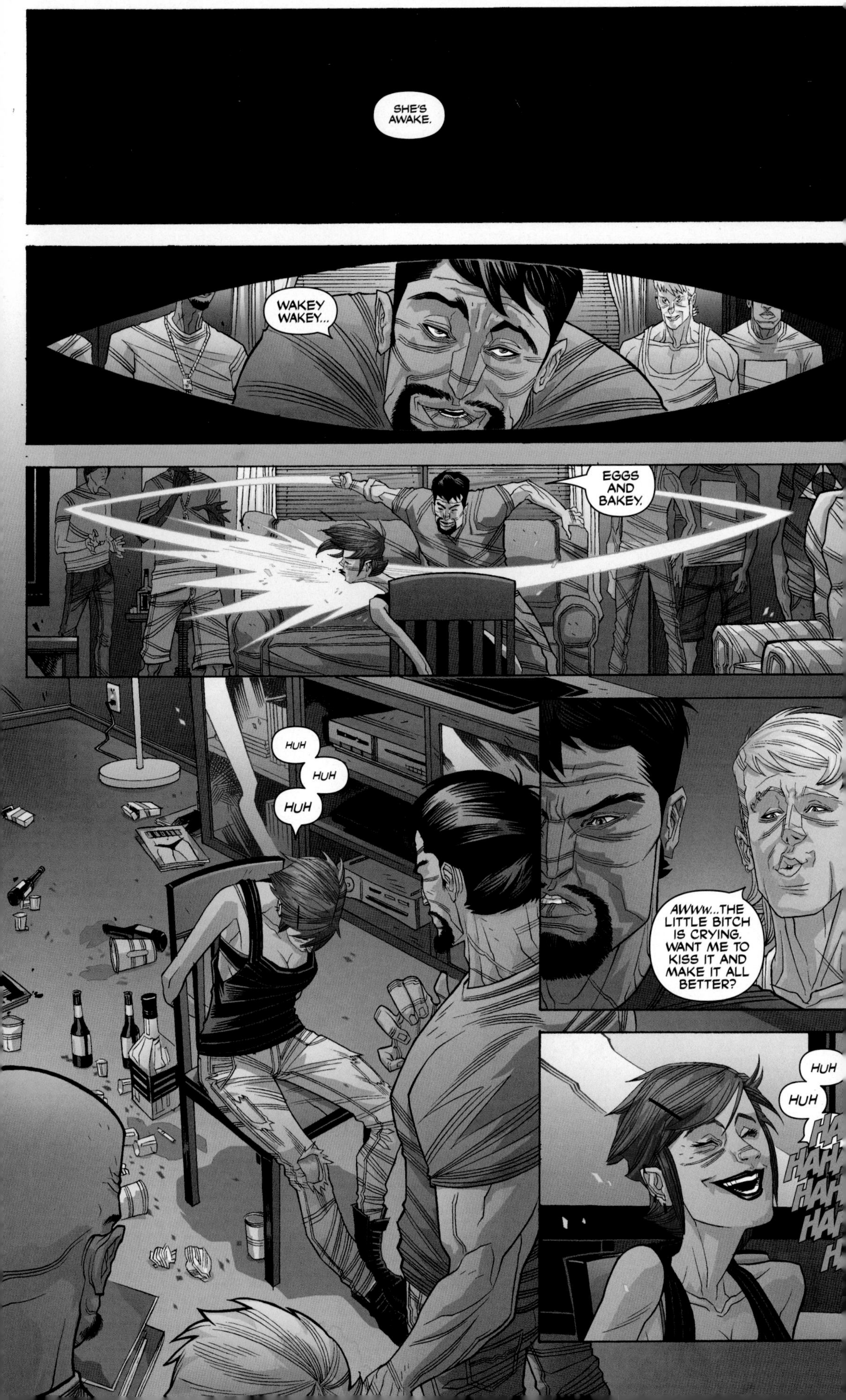
SHE'S AWAKE.
WAKEY WAKEY...
EGGS AND BAKEY.
HUH
HUH
HUH
AWWW...THE LITTLE BITCH IS CRYING. WANT ME TO KISS IT AND MAKE IT ALL BETTER?
HUH
HUH

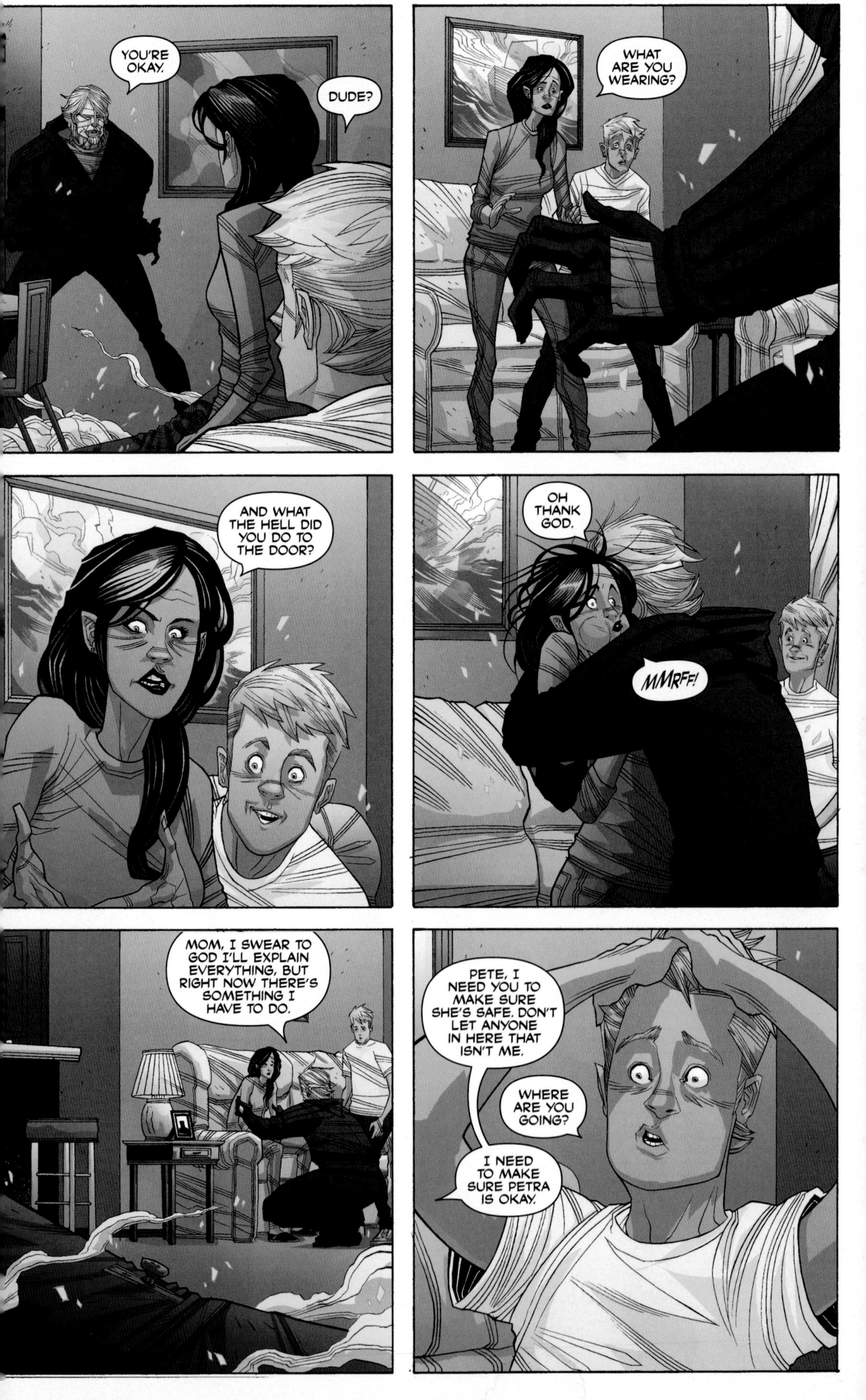
YOU'RE OKAY.
DUDE?
WHAT ARE YOU WEARING?
AND WHAT THE HELL DID YOU DO TO THE DOOR?
OH THANK GOD.
MMRFF!
MOM, I SWEAR TO GOD I'LL EXPLAIN EVERYTHING, BUT RIGHT NOW THERE'S SOMETHING I HAVE TO DO.
PETE, I NEED YOU TO MAKE SURE SHE'S SAFE. DON'T LET ANYONE IN HERE THAT ISN'T ME.
WHERE ARE YOU GOING?
I NEED TO MAKE SURE PETRA IS OKAY.

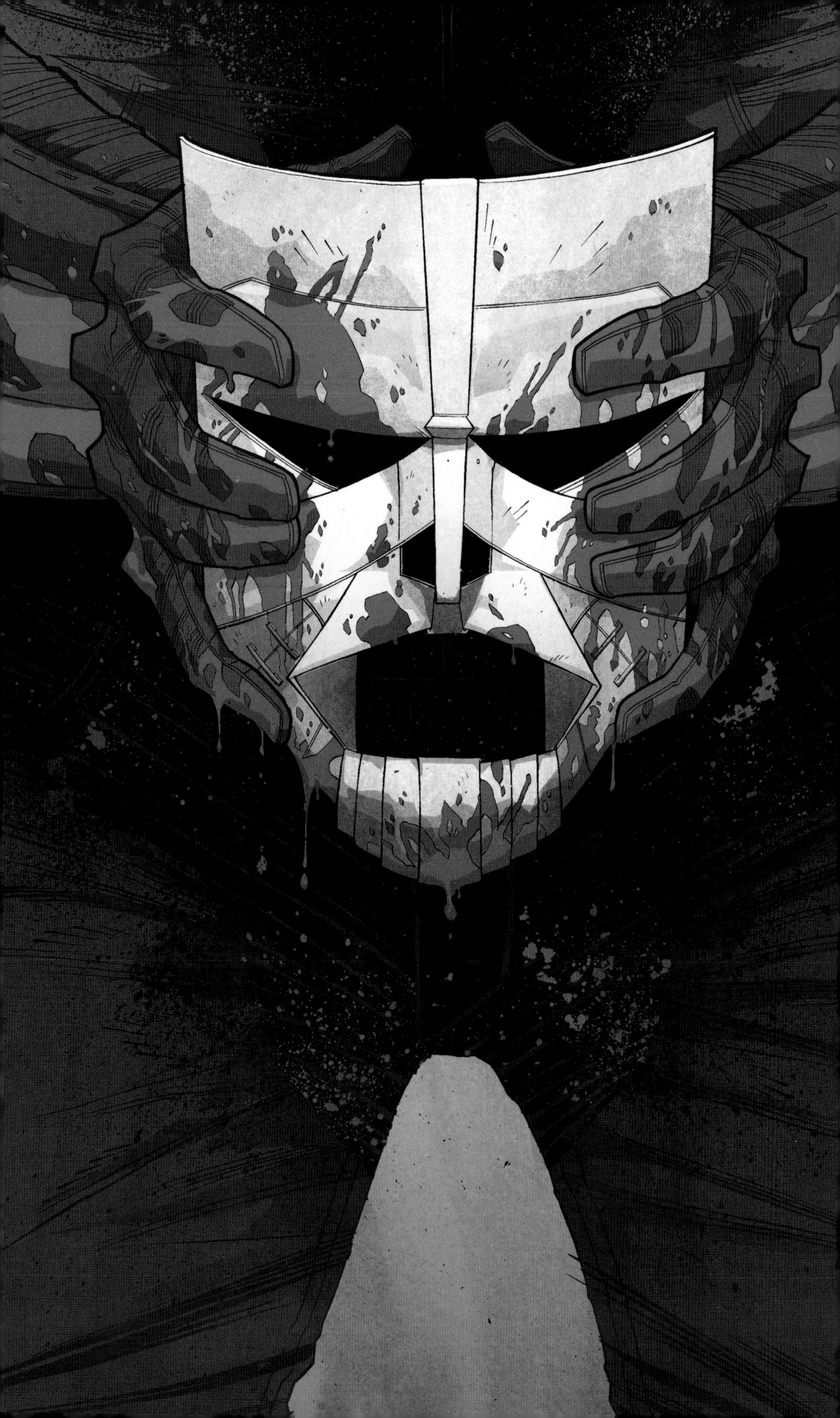

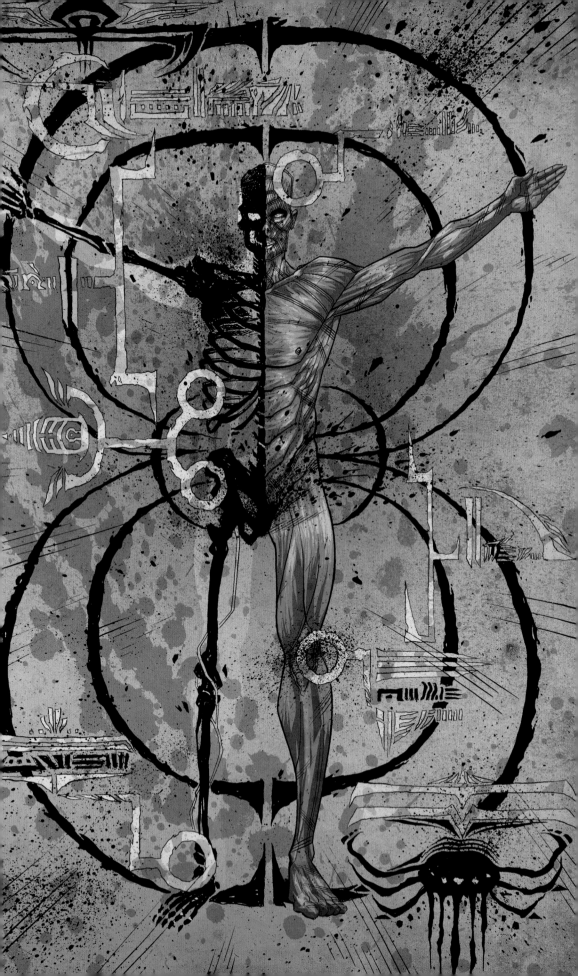

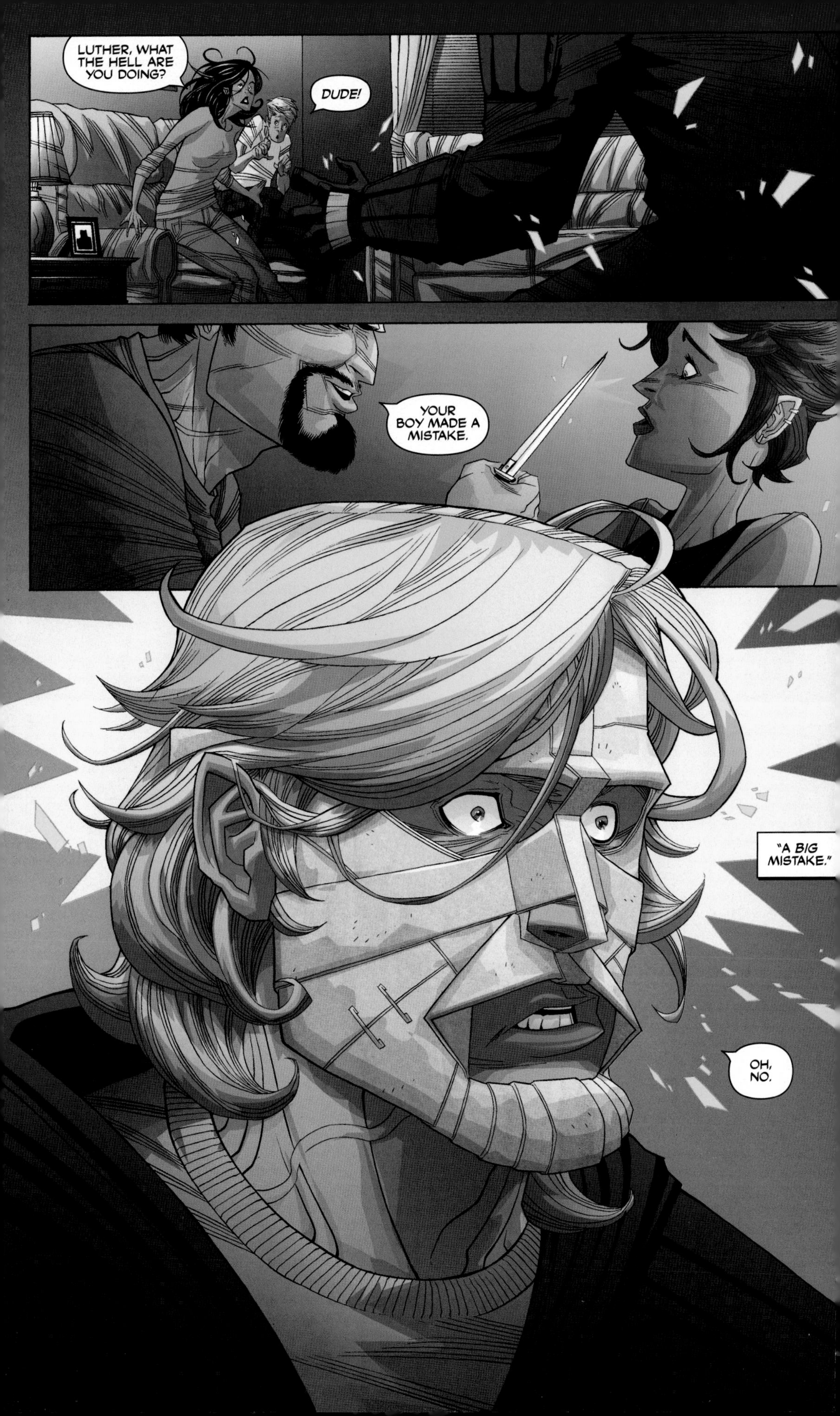
LUTHER, WHAT THE HELL ARE YOU DOING?
DUDE!
YOUR BOY MADE A MISTAKE.
"A BIG MISTAKE."
OH, NO.

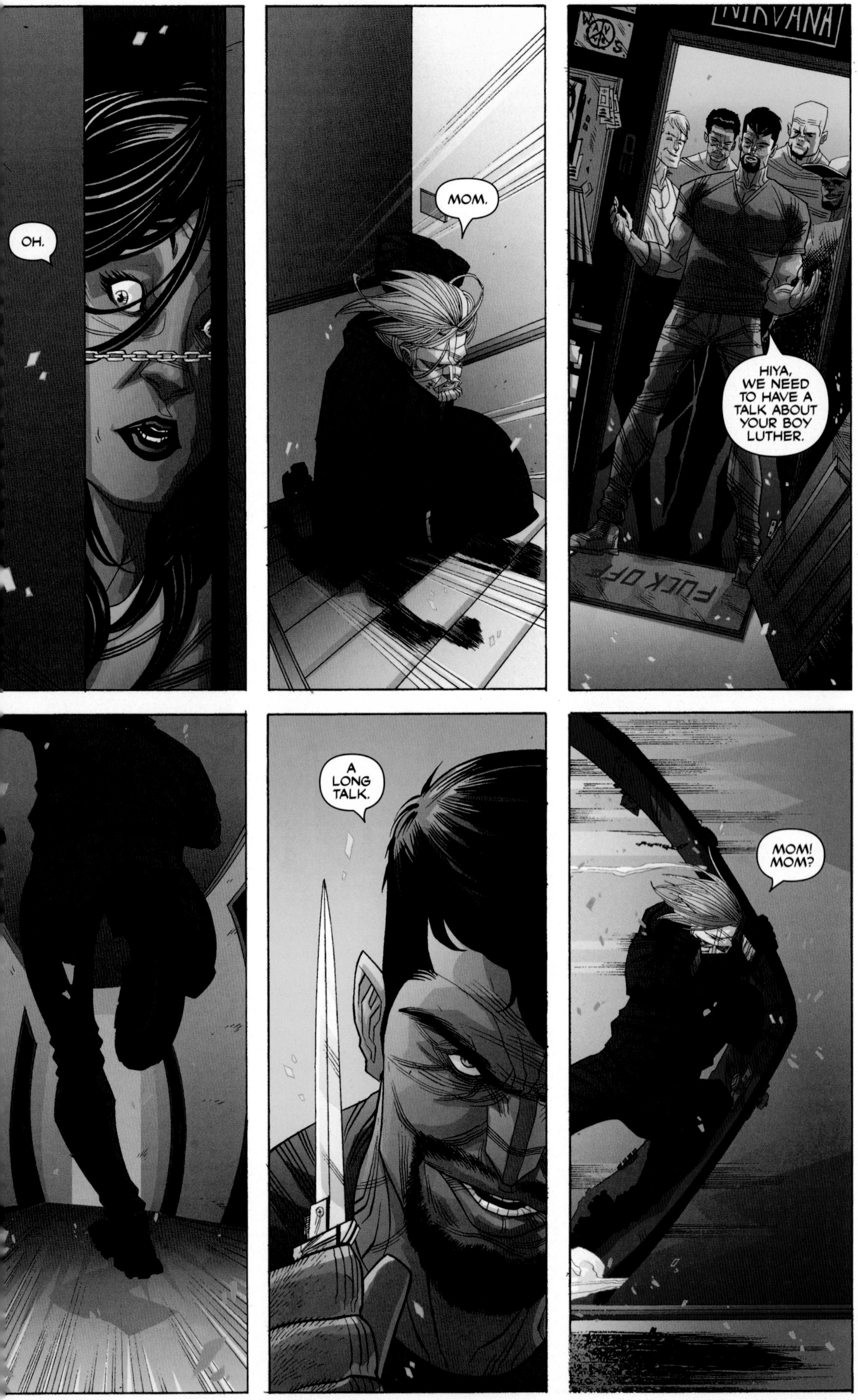
OH.
MOM.
NIRVANA
HIYA, WE NEED TO HAVE A TALK ABOUT YOUR BOY LUTHER.
FUCK OFF
A LONG TALK.
MOM! MOM?

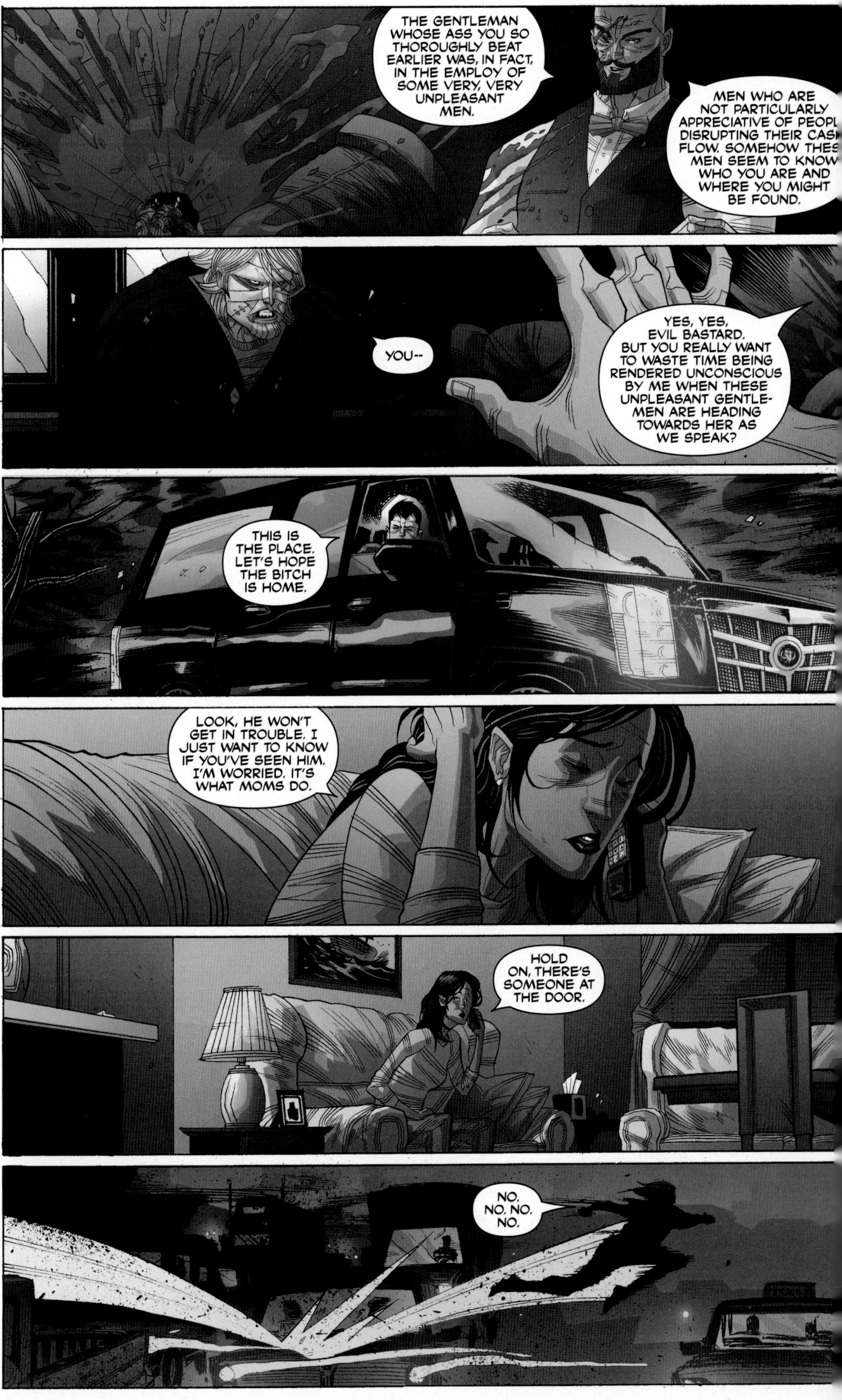
THE GENTLEMAN WHOSE ASS YOU SO THOROUGHLY BEAT EARLIER WAS, IN FACT, IN THE EMPLOY OF SOME VERY, VERY UNPLEASANT MEN.
MEN WHO ARE NOT PARTICULARLY APPRECIATIVE OF PEOPL DISRUPTING THEIR CAS FLOW. SOMEHOW THES MEN SEEM TO KNOW WHO YOU ARE AND WHERE YOU MIGHT BE FOUND.
YOU--
YES, YES, EVIL BASTARD. BUT YOU REALLY WANT TO WASTE TIME BEING RENDERED UNCONSCIOUS BY ME WHEN THESE UNPLEASANT GENTLE-MEN ARE HEADING TOWARDS HER AS WE SPEAK?
THIS IS THE PLACE. LET'S HOPE THE BITCH IS HOME.
LOOK, HE WON'T GET IN TROUBLE. I JUST WANT TO KNOW IF YOU'VE SEEN HIM. I'M WORRIED. IT'S WHAT MOMS DO.
HOLD ON, THERE'S SOMEONE AT THE DOOR.
NO. NO, NO, NO.

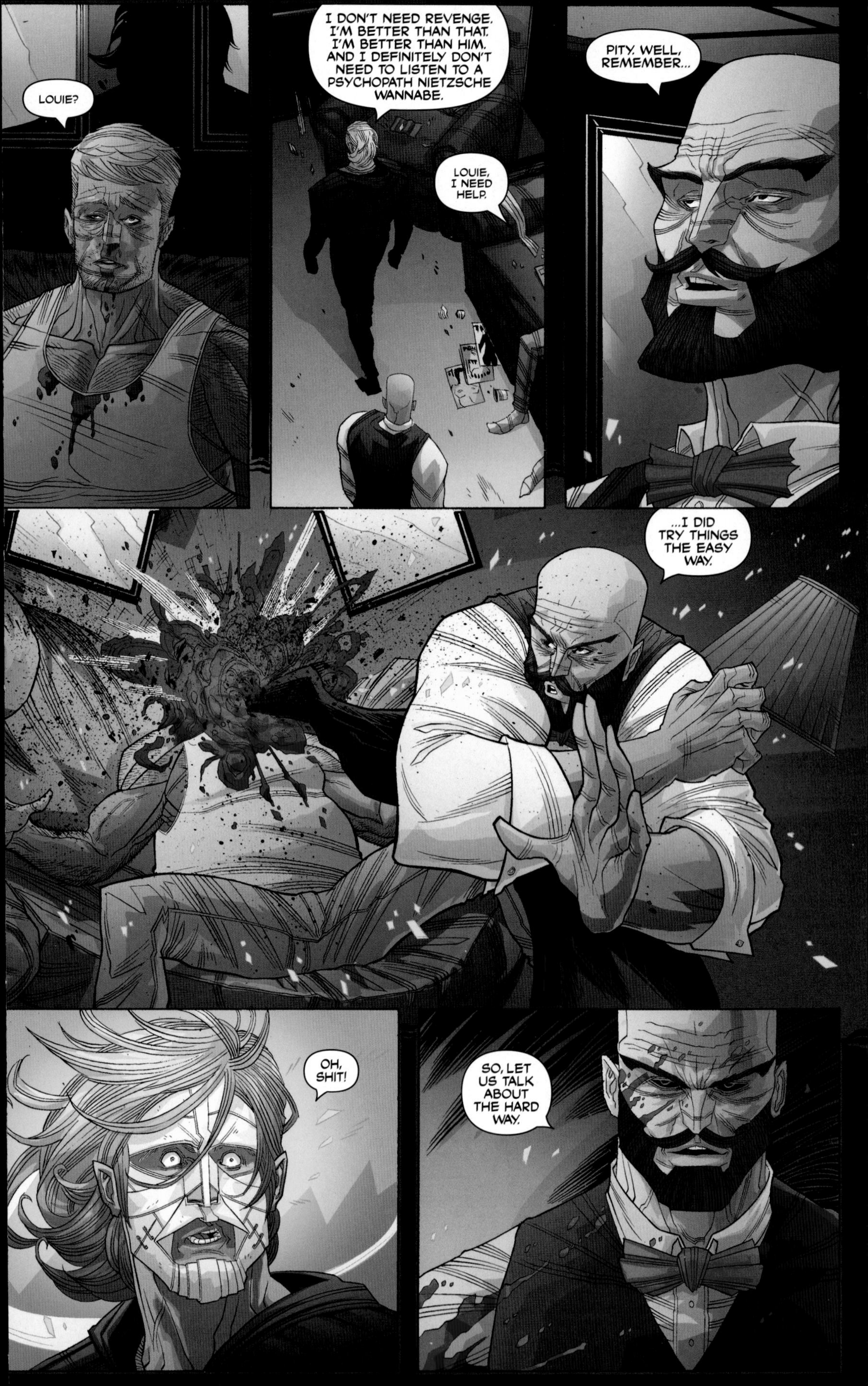
LOUIE?
I DON'T NEED REVENGE. I'M BETTER THAN THAT. I'M BETTER THAN HIM. AND I DEFINITELY DON'T NEED TO LISTEN TO A PSYCHOPATH NIETZSCHE WANNABE.
LOUIE, I NEED HELP.
PITY. WELL, REMEMBER...
...I DID TRY THINGS THE EASY WAY.
OH, SHIT!
SO, LET US TALK ABOUT THE HARD WAY.

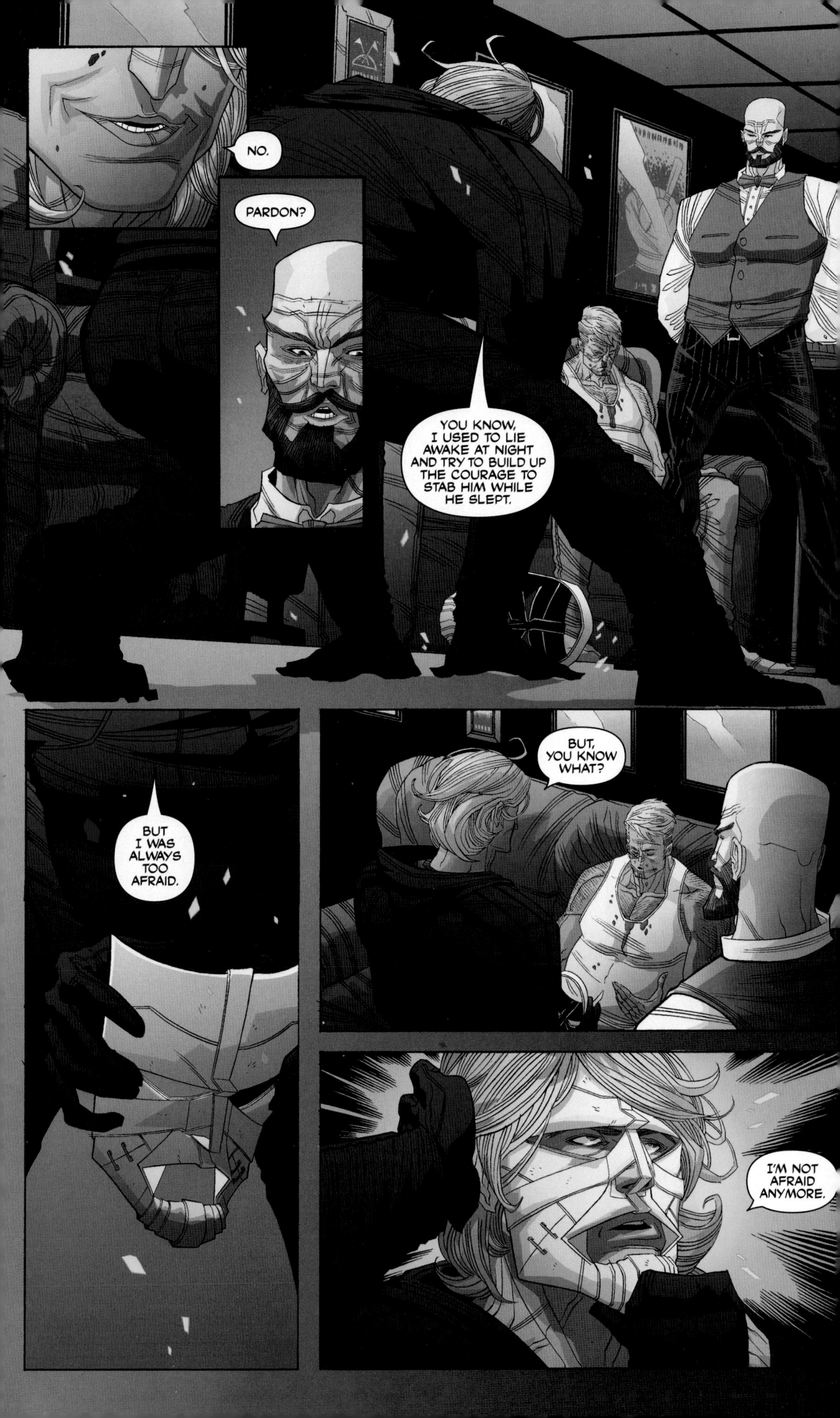
NO.
PARDON?
YOU KNOW, I USED TO LIE AWAKE AT NIGHT AND TRY TO BUILD UP THE COURAGE TO STAB HIM WHILE HE SLEPT.
BUT I WAS ALWAYS TOO AFRAID.
BUT, YOU KNOW WHAT?
I'M NOT AFRAID ANYMORE.

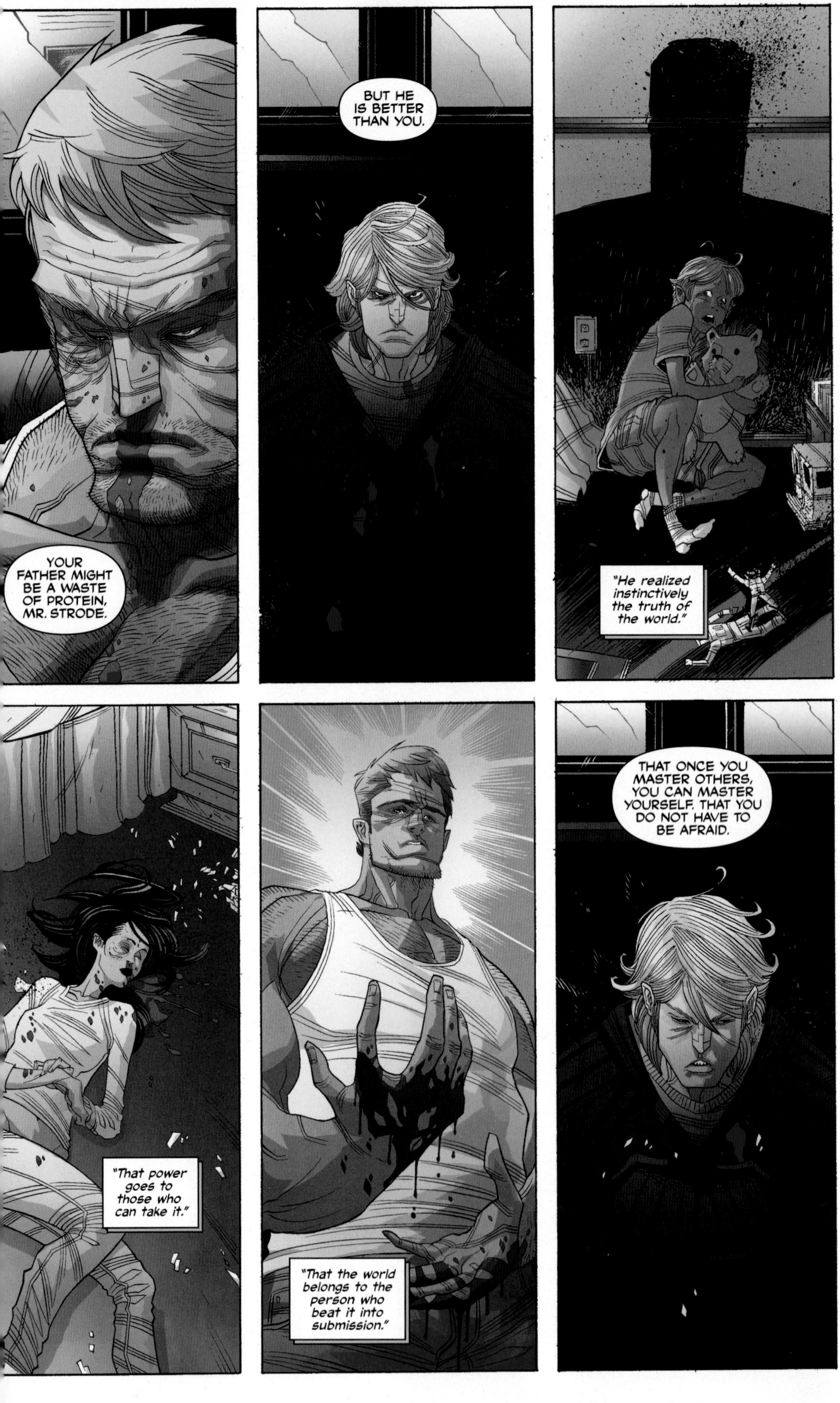
YOUR FATHER MIGHT BE A WASTE OF PROTEIN, MR. STRODE.
BUT HE IS BETTER THAN YOU.
"He realized instinctively the truth of the world."
"That power goes to those who can take it."
"That the world belongs to the person who beat it into submission."
THAT ONCE YOU MASTER OTHERS, YOU CAN MASTER YOURSELF. THAT YOU DO NOT HAVE TO BE AFRAID.

"...talents."

YOUR FATHER HERE WASTED HIS TALENTS. HE COULD HAVE BEEN SOMETHING SPECIAL. HE COULD HAVE BEEN GREAT.

INSTEAD HE'S JUST AN ORDINARY ASS, OF WHICH THERE IS NO SHORTAGE IN THE WORLD.

FFFF.

WHAT DO YOU WANT?

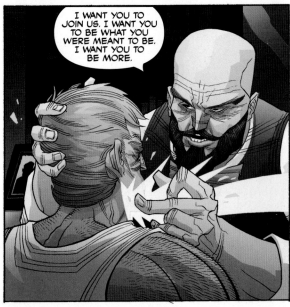

I WANT YOU TO JOIN US. I WANT YOU TO BE WHAT YOU WERE MEANT TO BE. I WANT YOU TO BE MORE.

BUT RIGHT NOW, I WANT YOU TO KILL YOUR FATHER.

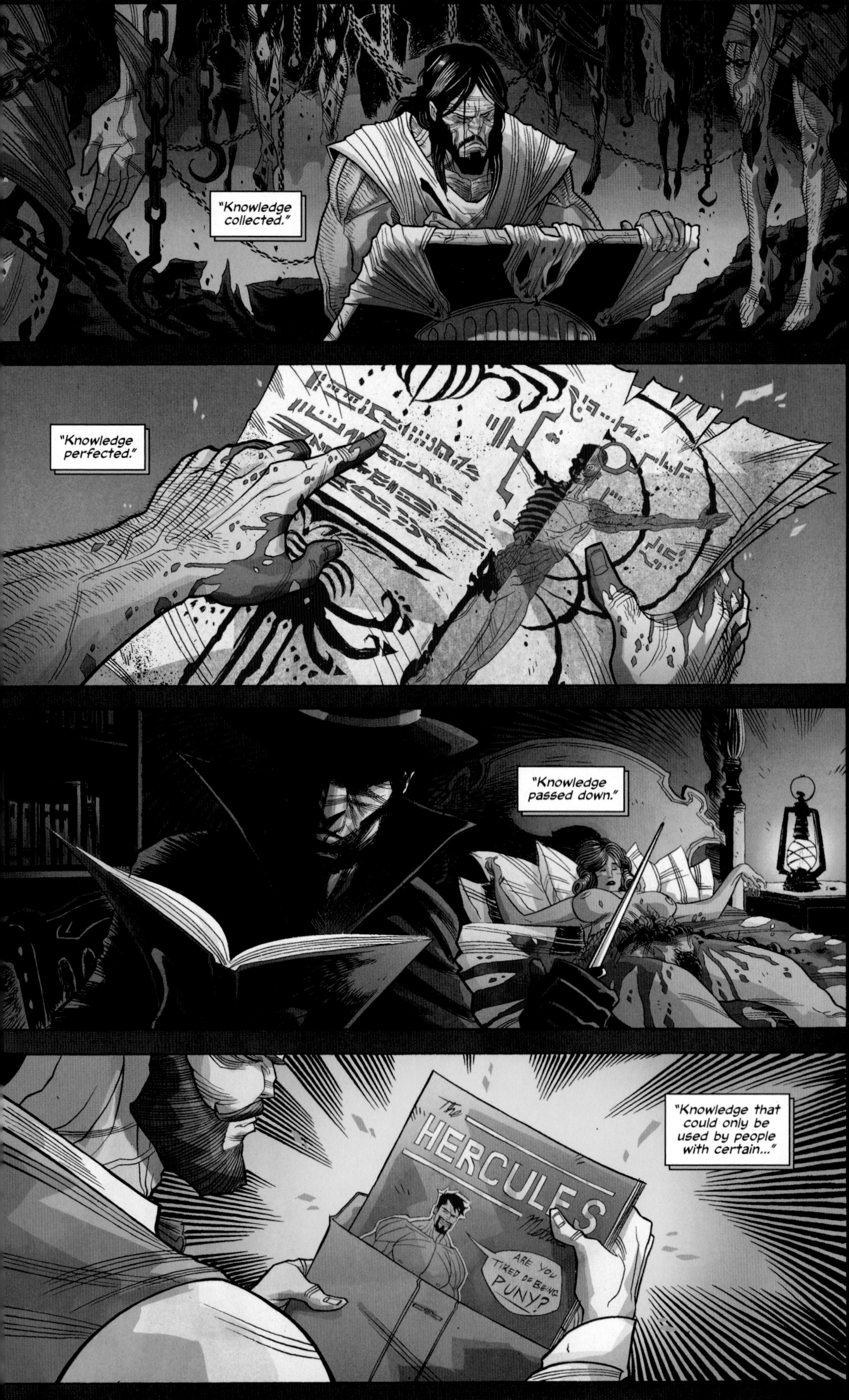
"Knowledge collected."
"Knowledge perfected."
"Knowledge passed down."
"Knowledge that could only be used by people with certain..."
The HERCULES
ARE YOU TIRED OF BEING PUNY?

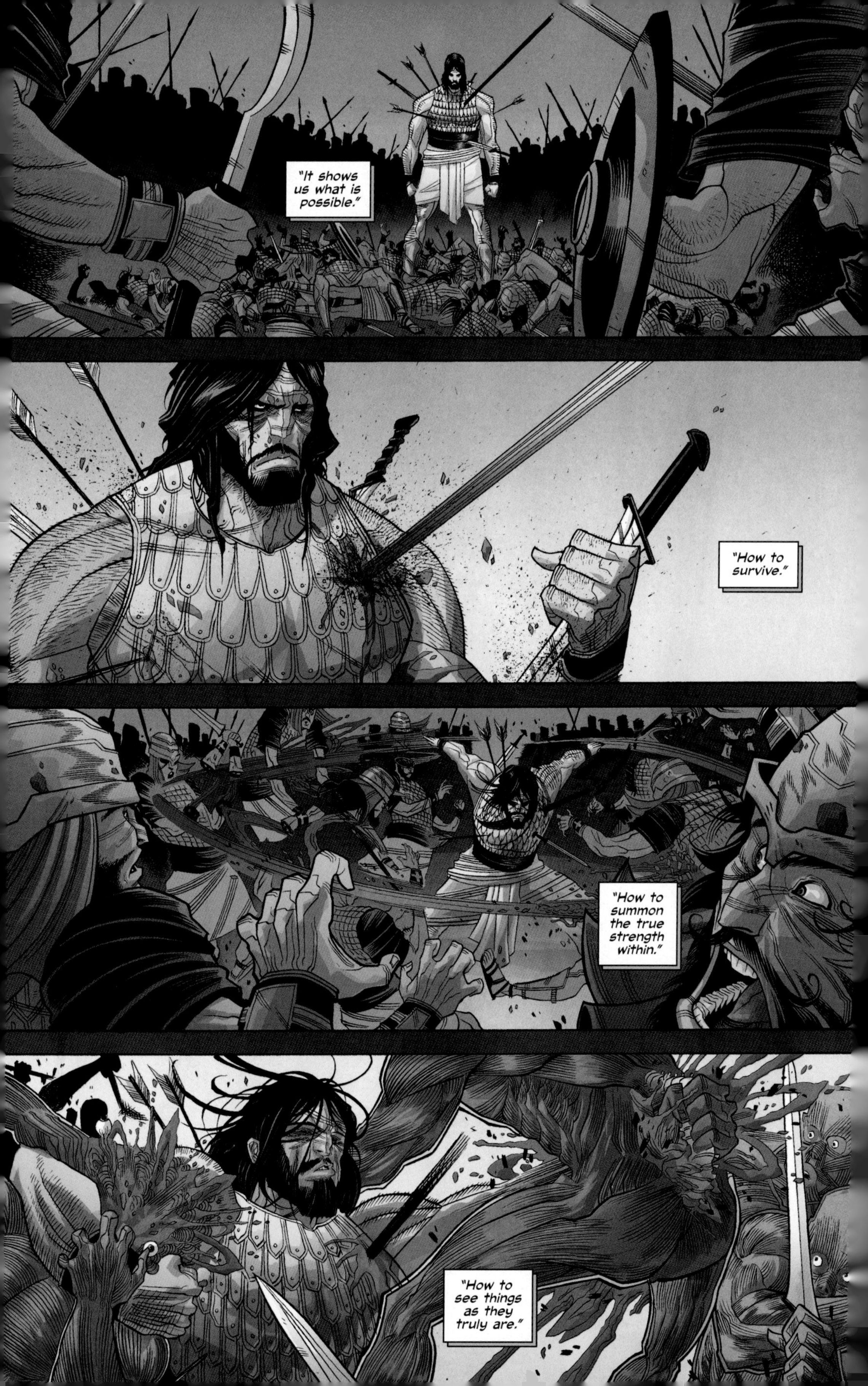
"It shows us what is possible."
"How to survive."
"How to summon the true strength within."
"How to see things as they truly are."

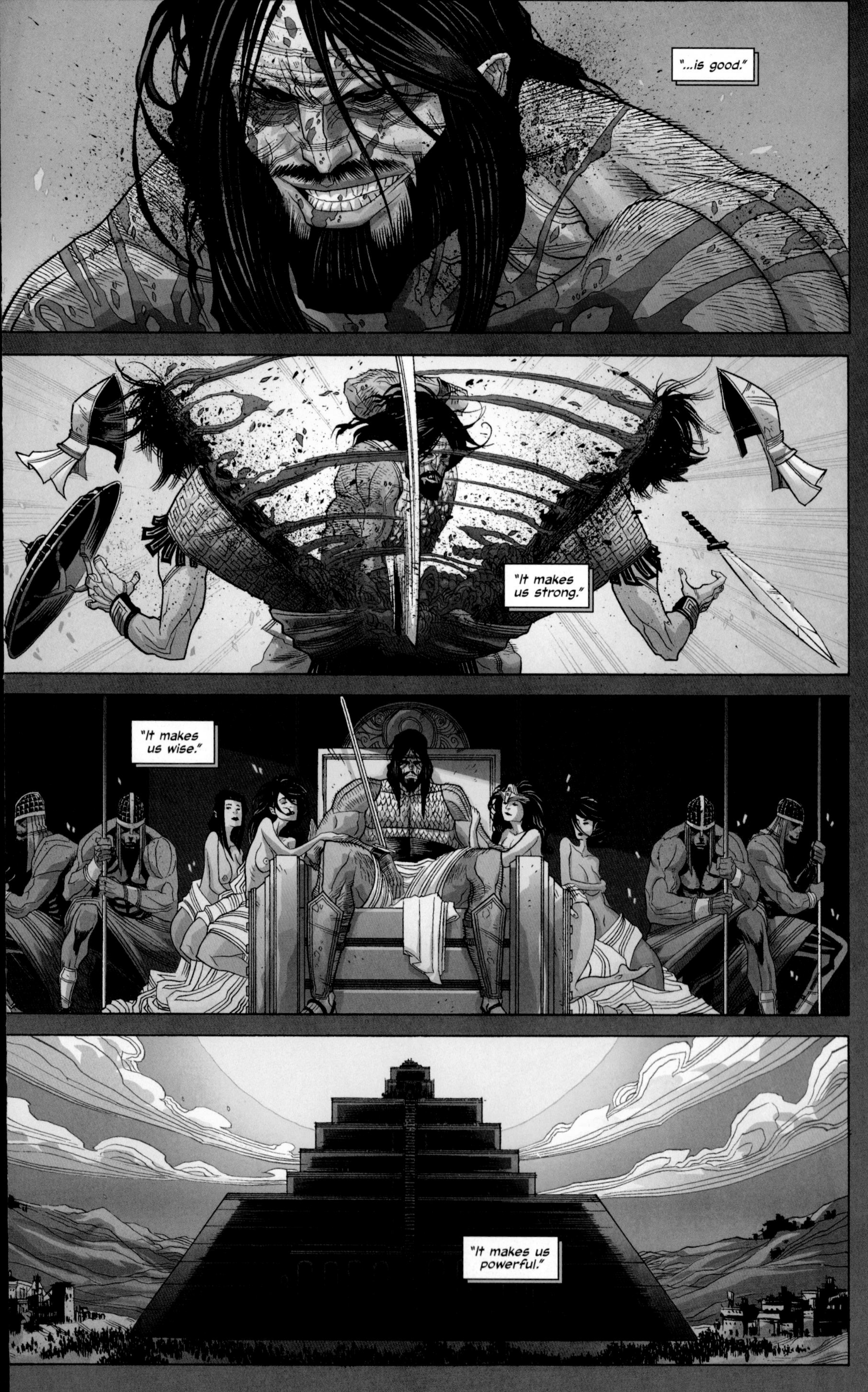
"...is good."
"It makes us strong."
"It makes us wise."
"It makes us powerful."

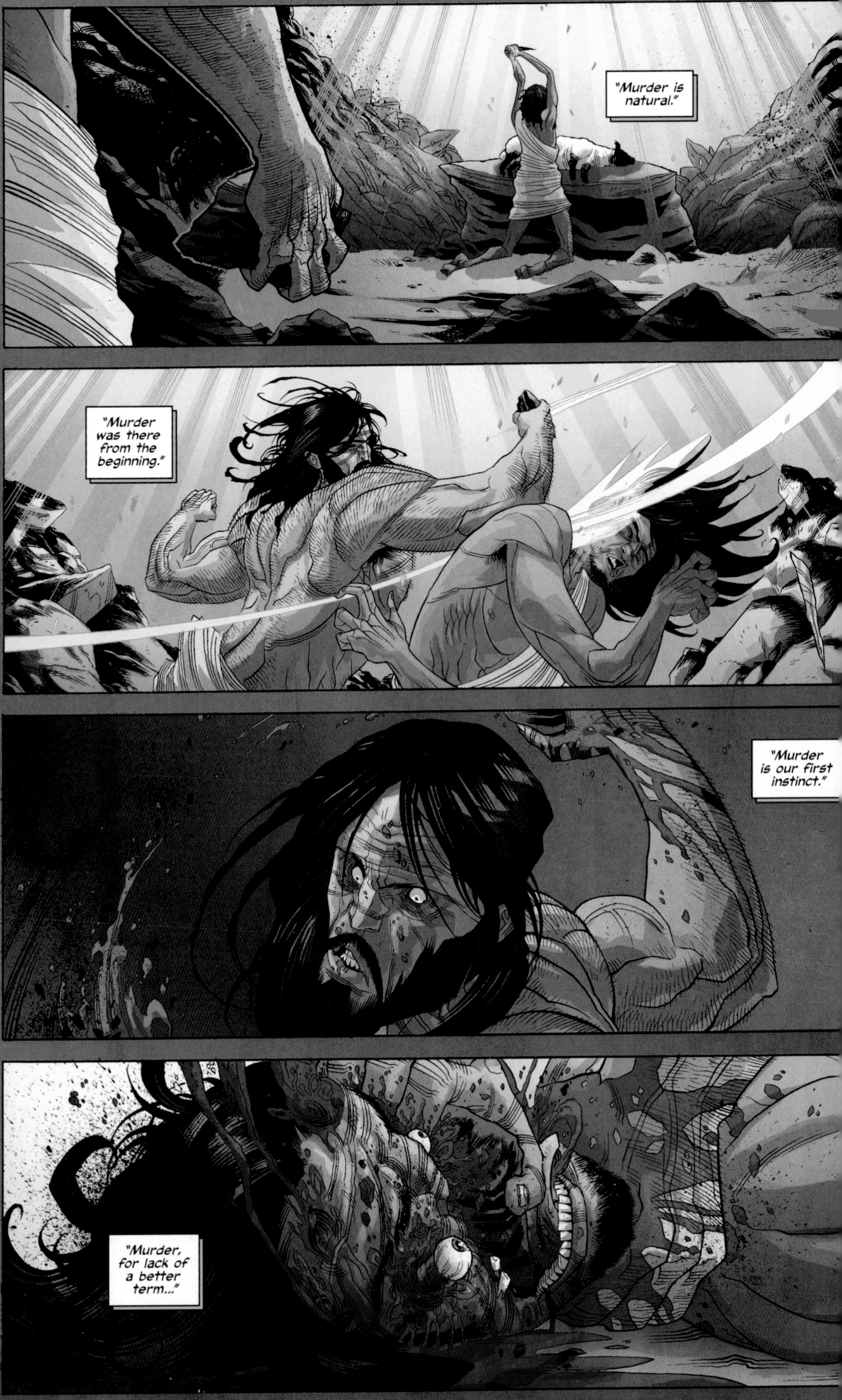
"Murder is natural."
"Murder was there from the beginning."
"Murder is our first instinct."
"Murder, for lack of a better term..."

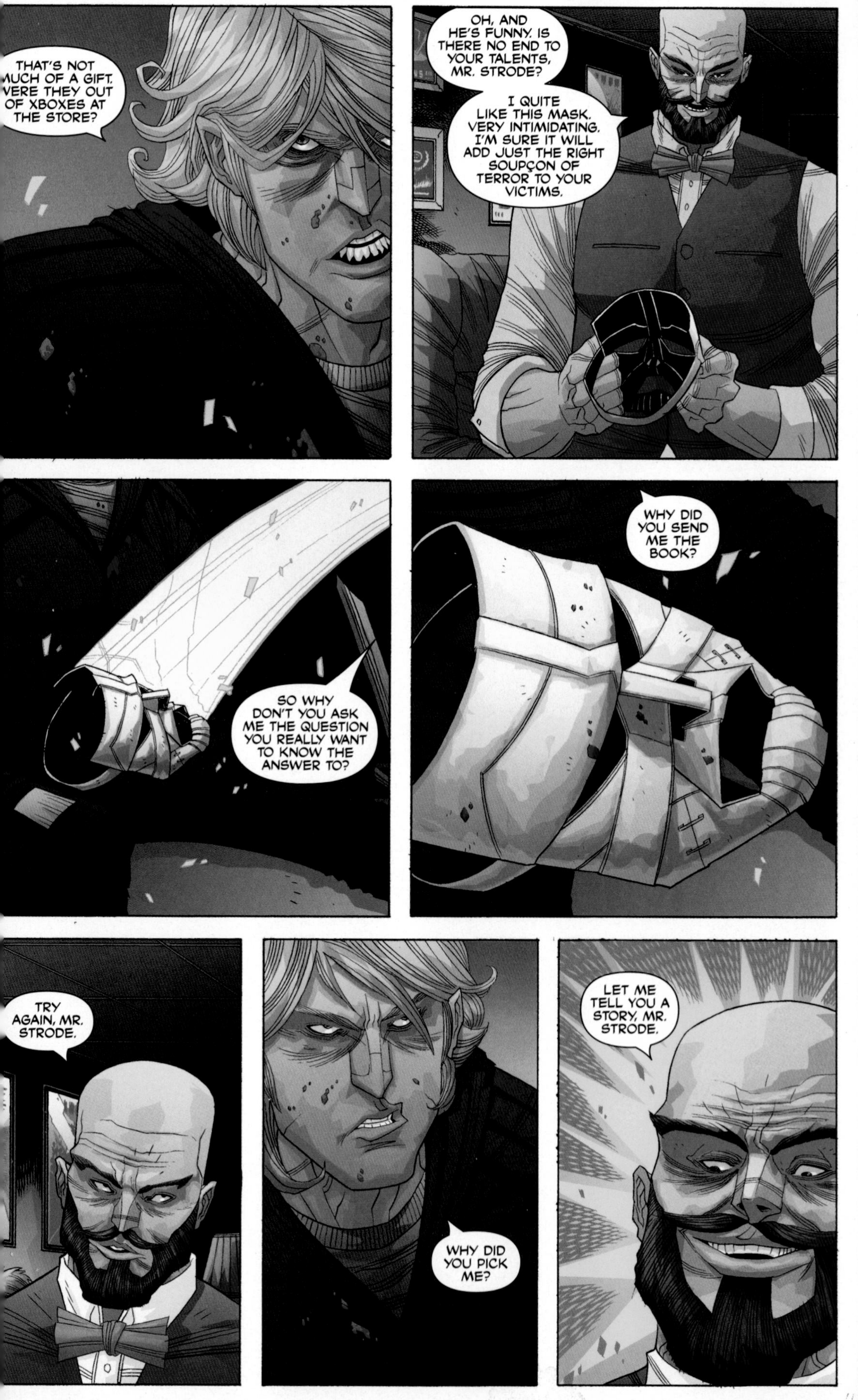
THAT'S NOT MUCH OF A GIFT. WERE THEY OUT OF XBOXES AT THE STORE?
OH, AND HE'S FUNNY. IS THERE NO END TO YOUR TALENTS, MR. STRODE?
I QUITE LIKE THIS MASK. VERY INTIMIDATING. I'M SURE IT WILL ADD JUST THE RIGHT SOUPÇON OF TERROR TO YOUR VICTIMS.
SO WHY DON'T YOU ASK ME THE QUESTION YOU REALLY WANT TO KNOW THE ANSWER TO?
WHY DID YOU SEND ME THE BOOK?
TRY AGAIN, MR. STRODE.
WHY DID YOU PICK ME?
LET ME TELL YOU A STORY, MR. STRODE.

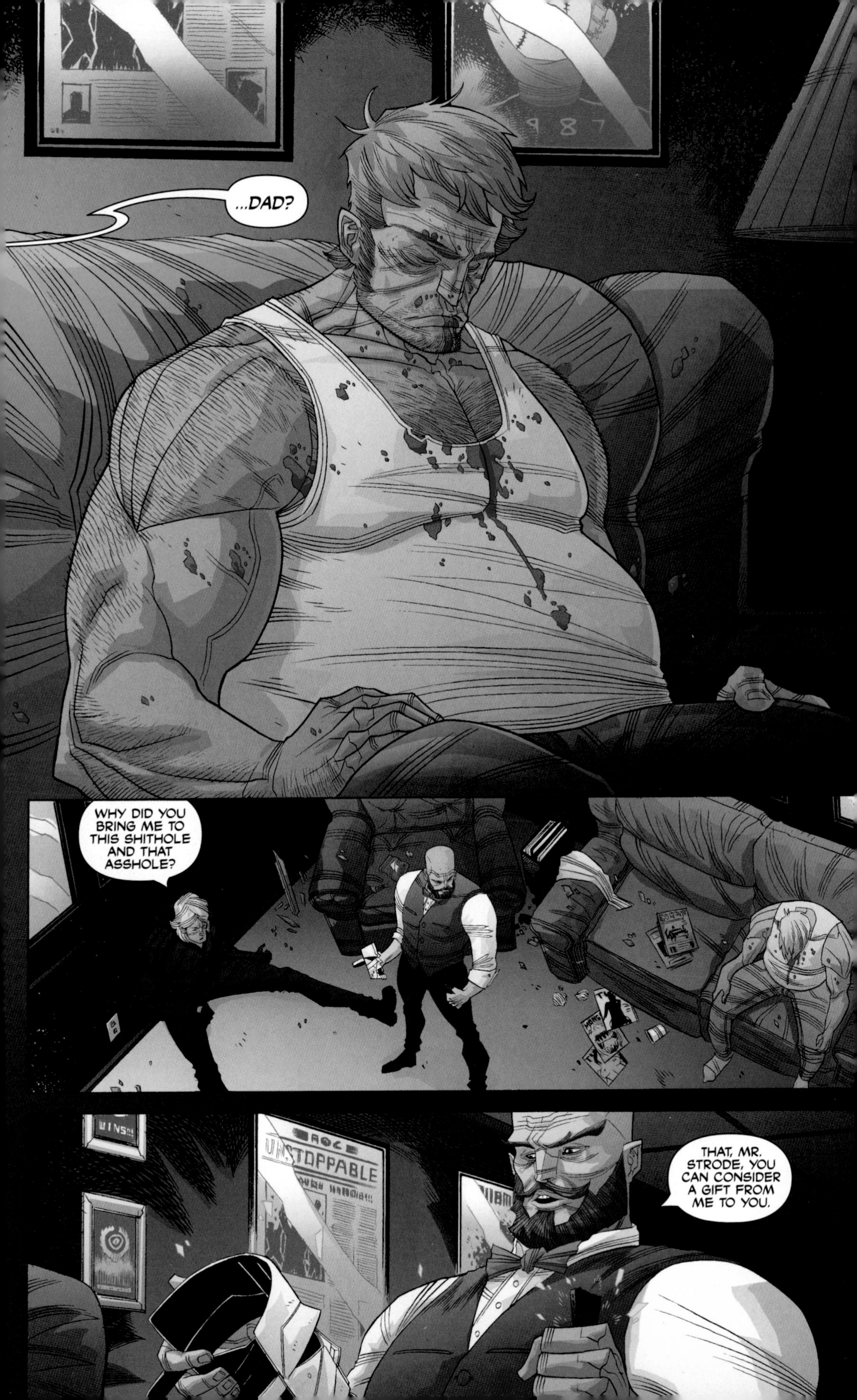
...DAD?
WHY DID YOU BRING ME TO THIS SHITHOLE AND THAT ASSHOLE?
THAT, MR. STRODE, YOU CAN CONSIDER A GIFT FROM ME TO YOU.

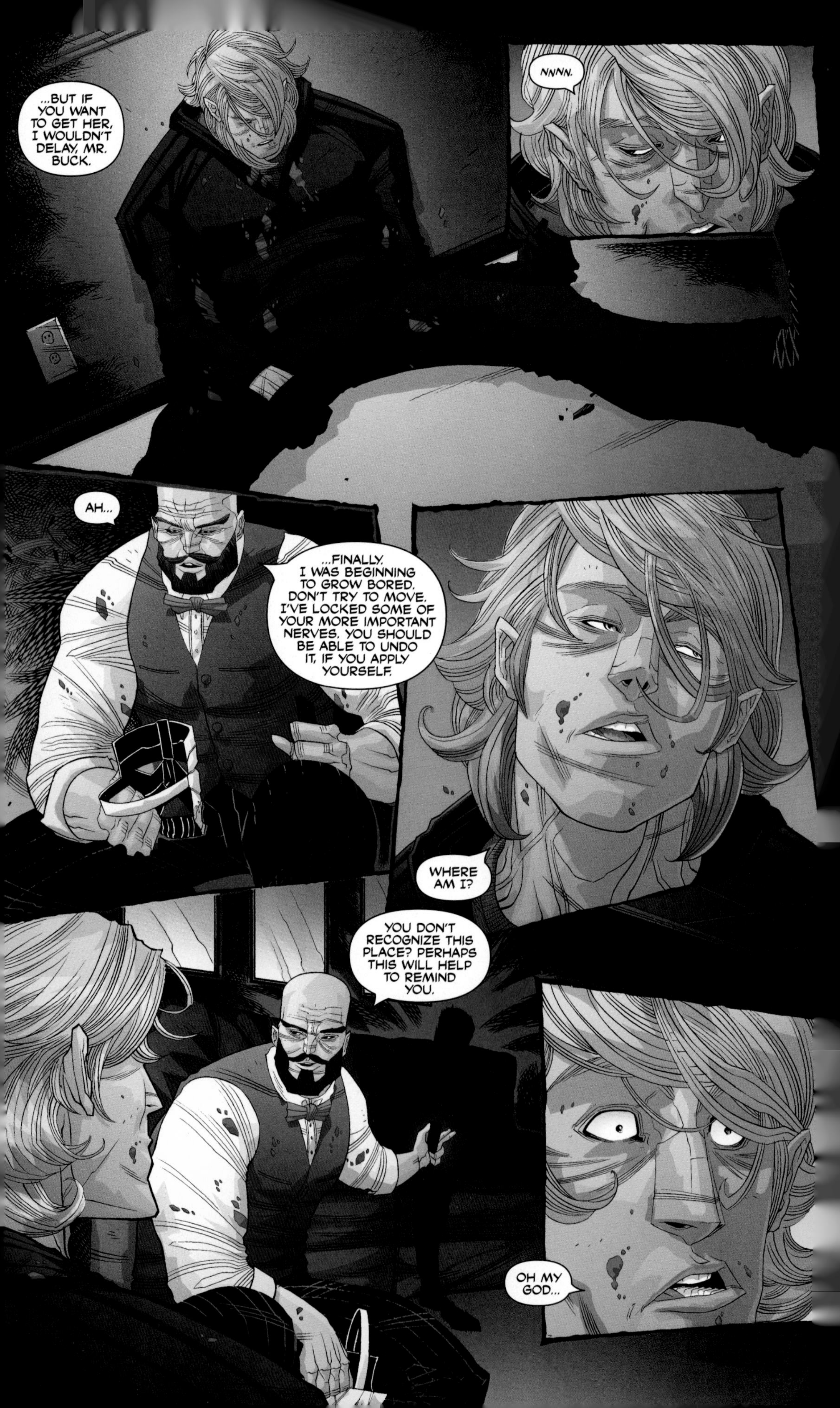

...BUT IF YOU WANT TO GET HER, I WOULDN'T DELAY, MR. BUCK.
NNNN.
AH...
...FINALLY. I WAS BEGINNING TO GROW BORED. DON'T TRY TO MOVE. I'VE LOCKED SOME OF YOUR MORE IMPORTANT NERVES. YOU SHOULD BE ABLE TO UNDO IT, IF YOU APPLY YOURSELF.
WHERE AM I?
YOU DON'T RECOGNIZE THIS PLACE? PERHAPS THIS WILL HELP TO REMIND YOU.
OH MY GOD...

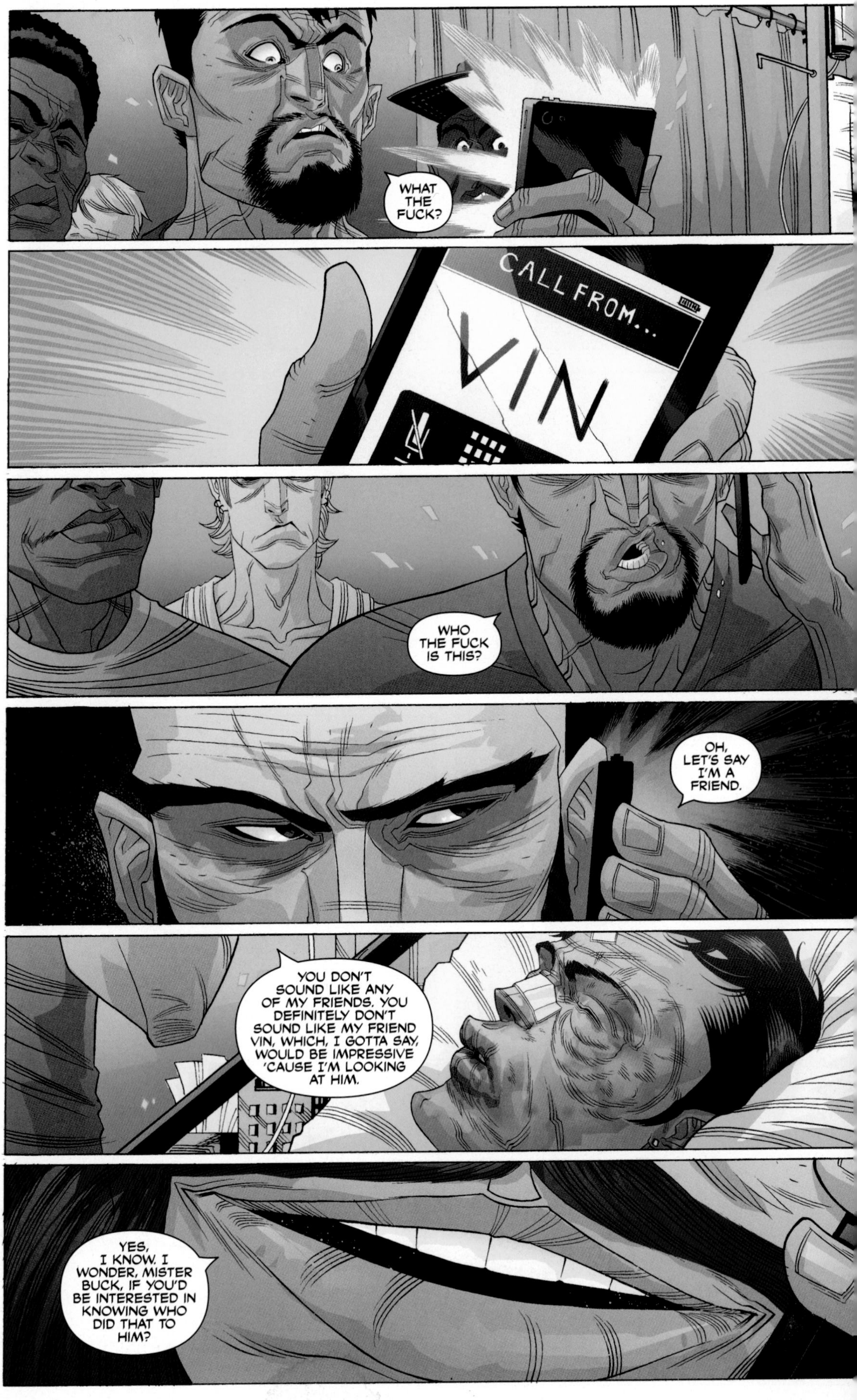
WHAT THE FUCK?
CALL FROM...
VIN
WHO THE FUCK IS THIS?
OH, LET'S SAY I'M A FRIEND.
YOU DON'T SOUND LIKE ANY OF MY FRIENDS. YOU DEFINITELY DON'T SOUND LIKE MY FRIEND VIN, WHICH, I GOTTA SAY, WOULD BE IMPRESSIVE 'CAUSE I'M LOOKING AT HIM.
YES, I KNOW. I WONDER, MISTER BUCK, IF YOU'D BE INTERESTED IN KNOWING WHO DID THAT TO HIM?

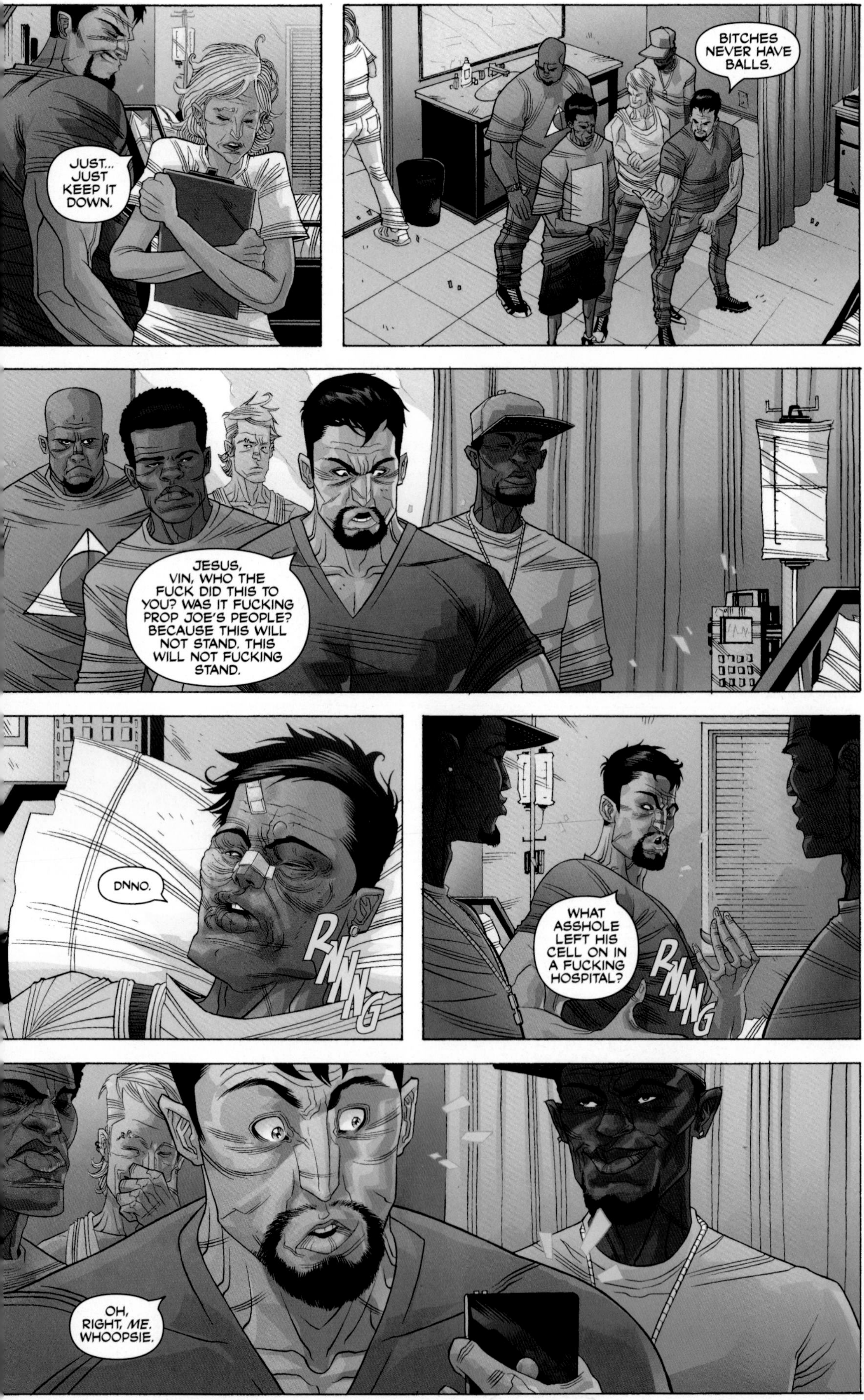
JUST... JUST KEEP IT DOWN.
BITCHES NEVER HAVE BALLS.
JESUS, VIN, WHO THE FUCK DID THIS TO YOU? WAS IT FUCKING PROP JOE'S PEOPLE? BECAUSE THIS WILL NOT STAND. THIS WILL NOT FUCKING STAND.
DNNO.
RNNNG
WHAT ASSHOLE LEFT HIS CELL ON IN A FUCKING HOSPITAL?
RNNNG
OH, RIGHT, *ME*. WHOOPSIE.

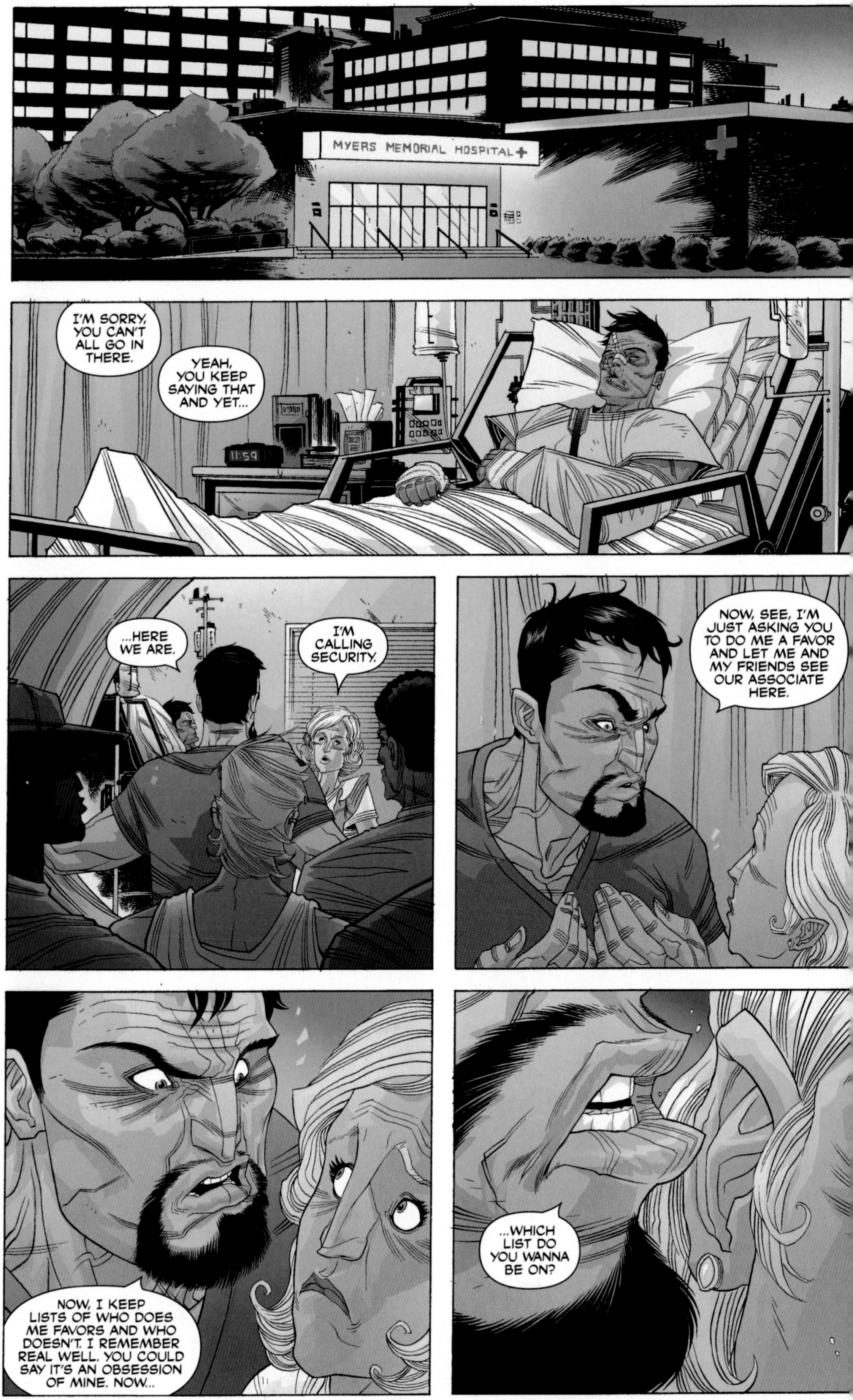
MYERS MEMORIAL HOSPITAL
I'M SORRY, YOU CAN'T ALL GO IN THERE.
YEAH, YOU KEEP SAYING THAT AND YET...
11:59
...HERE WE ARE.
I'M CALLING SECURITY.
NOW, SEE, I'M JUST ASKING YOU TO DO ME A FAVOR AND LET ME AND MY FRIENDS SEE OUR ASSOCIATE HERE.
NOW, I KEEP LISTS OF WHO DOES ME FAVORS AND WHO DOESN'T. I REMEMBER REAL WELL. YOU COULD SAY IT'S AN OBSESSION OF MINE. NOW...
...WHICH LIST DO YOU WANNA BE ON?

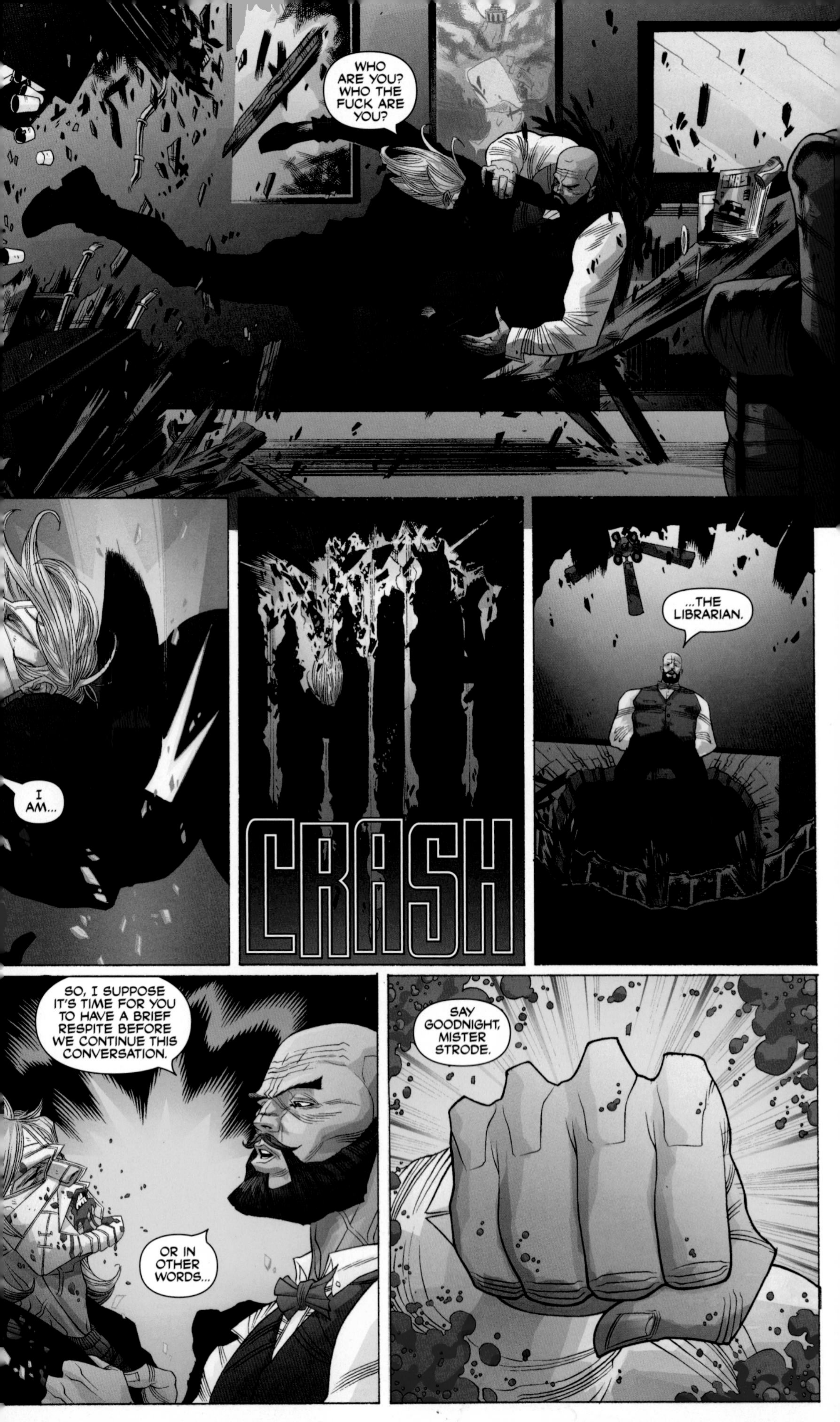

WHO ARE YOU? WHO THE FUCK ARE YOU?
I AM...
CRASH
...THE LIBRARIAN.
SO, I SUPPOSE IT'S TIME FOR YOU TO HAVE A BRIEF RESPITE BEFORE WE CONTINUE THIS CONVERSATION.
OR IN OTHER WORDS...
SAY GOODNIGHT, MISTER STRODE.

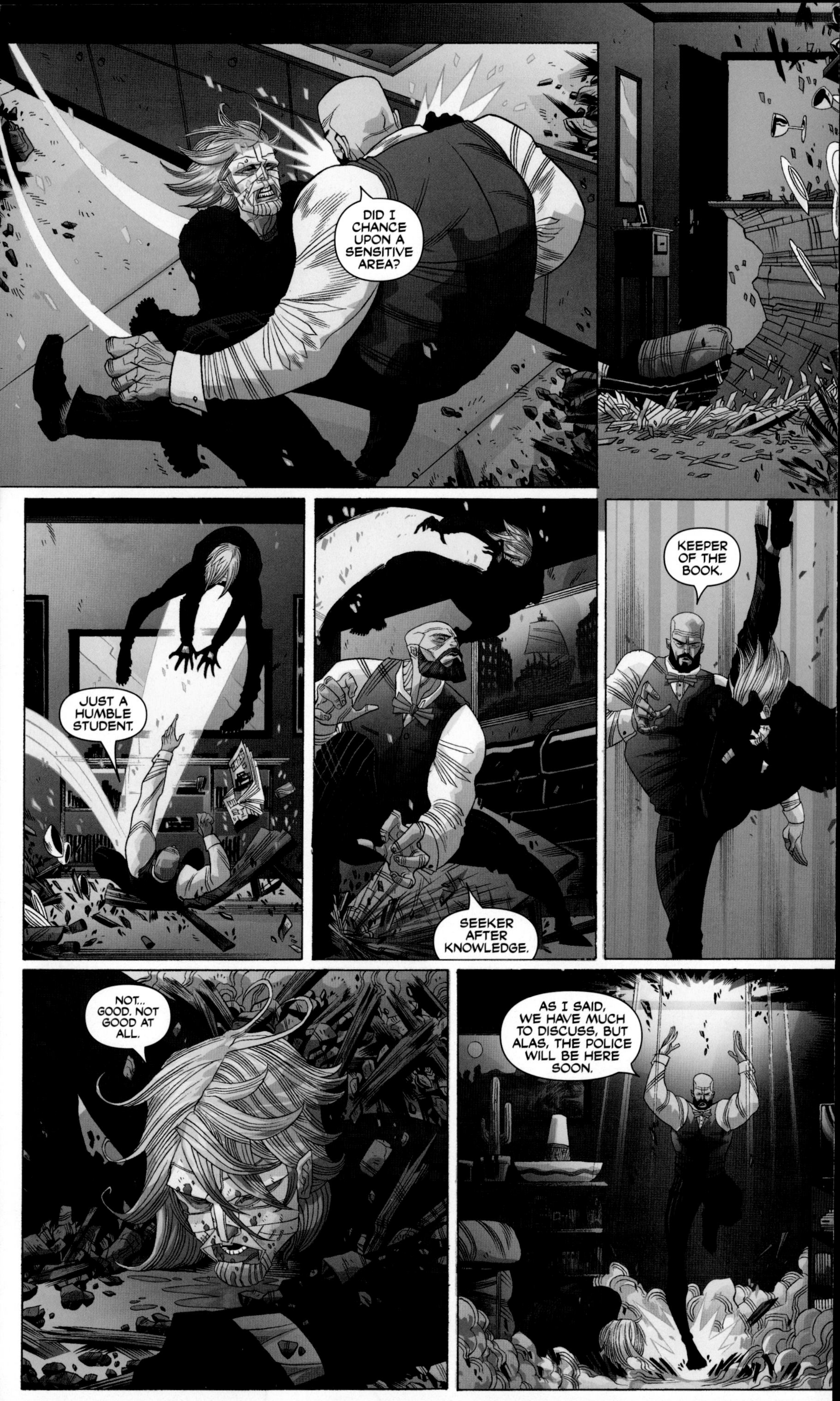
DID I CHANCE UPON A SENSITIVE AREA?
JUST A HUMBLE STUDENT.
SEEKER AFTER KNOWLEDGE.
KEEPER OF THE BOOK.
NOT... GOOD. NOT GOOD AT ALL.
AS I SAID, WE HAVE MUCH TO DISCUSS, BUT ALAS, THE POLICE WILL BE HERE SOON.

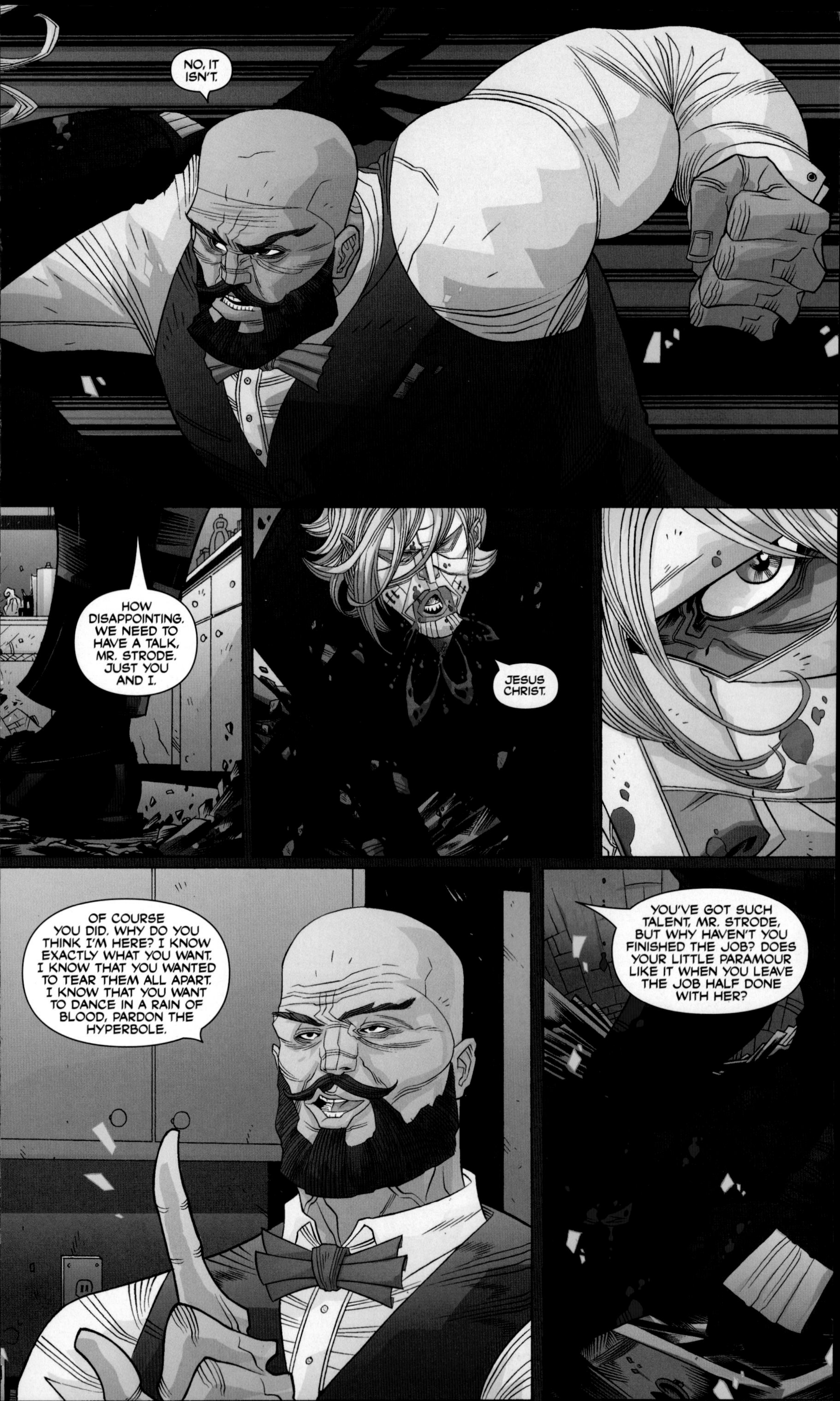
NO, IT ISN'T.
HOW DISAPPOINTING. WE NEED TO HAVE A TALK, MR. STRODE. JUST YOU AND I.
JESUS CHRIST.
OF COURSE YOU DID. WHY DO YOU THINK I'M HERE? I KNOW EXACTLY WHAT YOU WANT. I KNOW THAT YOU WANTED TO TEAR THEM ALL APART. I KNOW THAT YOU WANT TO DANCE IN A RAIN OF BLOOD, PARDON THE HYPERBOLE.
YOU'VE GOT SUCH TALENT, MR. STRODE, BUT WHY HAVEN'T YOU FINISHED THE JOB? DOES YOUR LITTLE PARAMOUR LIKE IT WHEN YOU LEAVE THE JOB HALF DONE WITH HER?

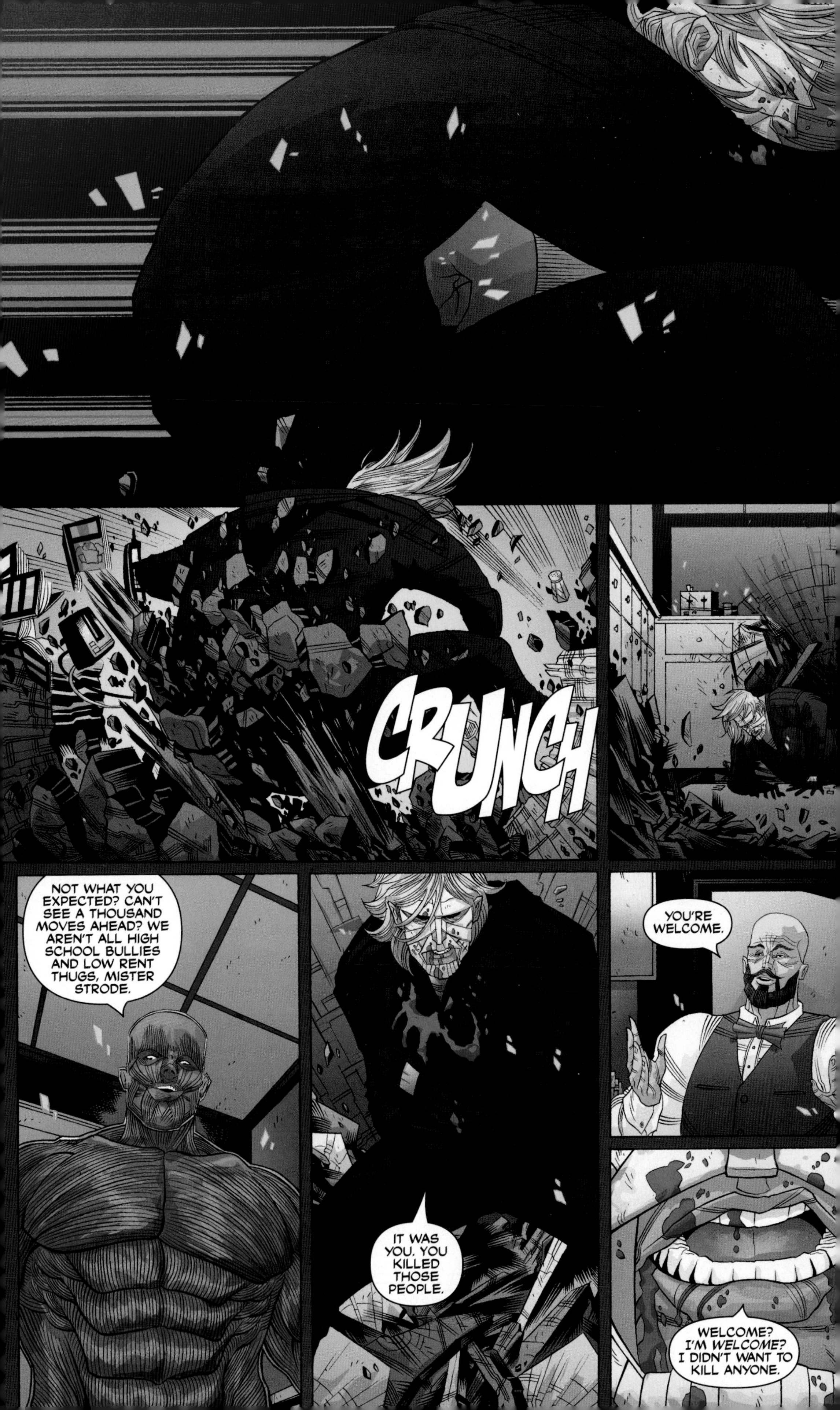
CRUNCH
NOT WHAT YOU EXPECTED? CAN'T SEE A THOUSAND MOVES AHEAD? WE AREN'T ALL HIGH SCHOOL BULLIES AND LOW RENT THUGS, MISTER STRODE.
IT WAS YOU. YOU KILLED THOSE PEOPLE.
YOU'RE WELCOME.
WELCOME? I'M *WELCOME*? I DIDN'T WANT TO KILL ANYONE.

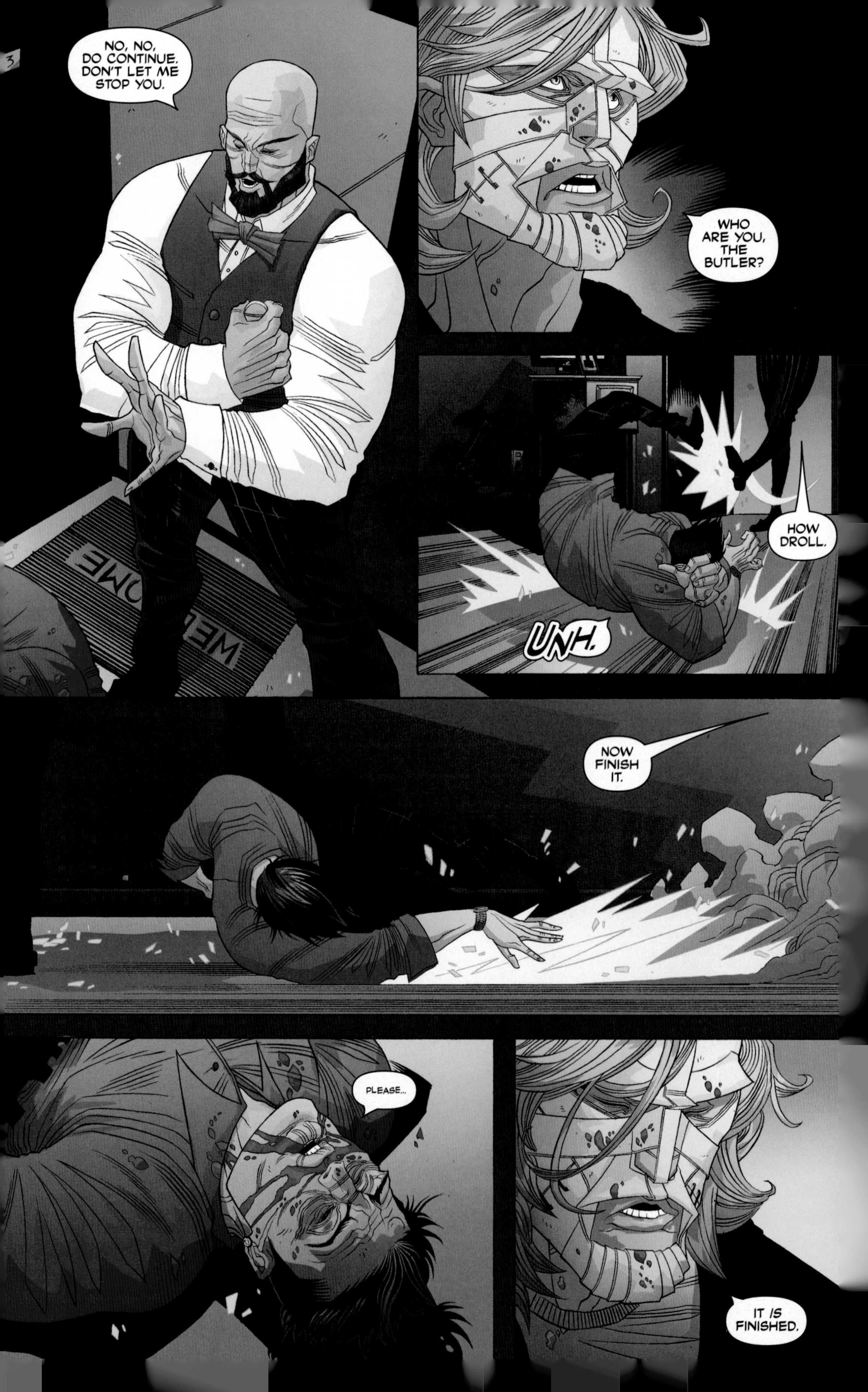
NO, NO, DO CONTINUE. DON'T LET ME STOP YOU.
WHO ARE YOU, THE BUTLER?
HOW DROLL.
UNH.
NOW FINISH IT.
PLEASE...
IT IS FINISHED.

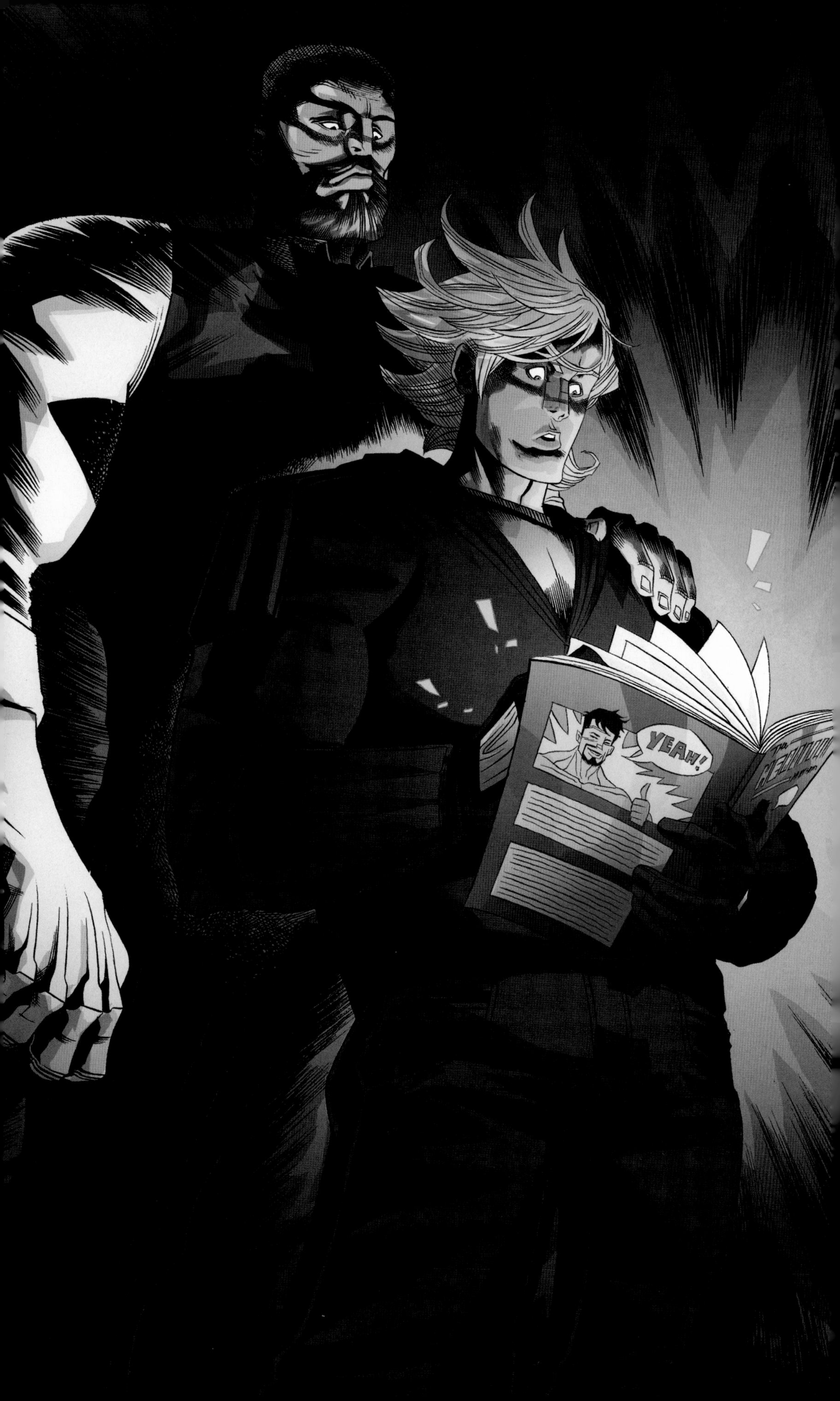
YEAH!

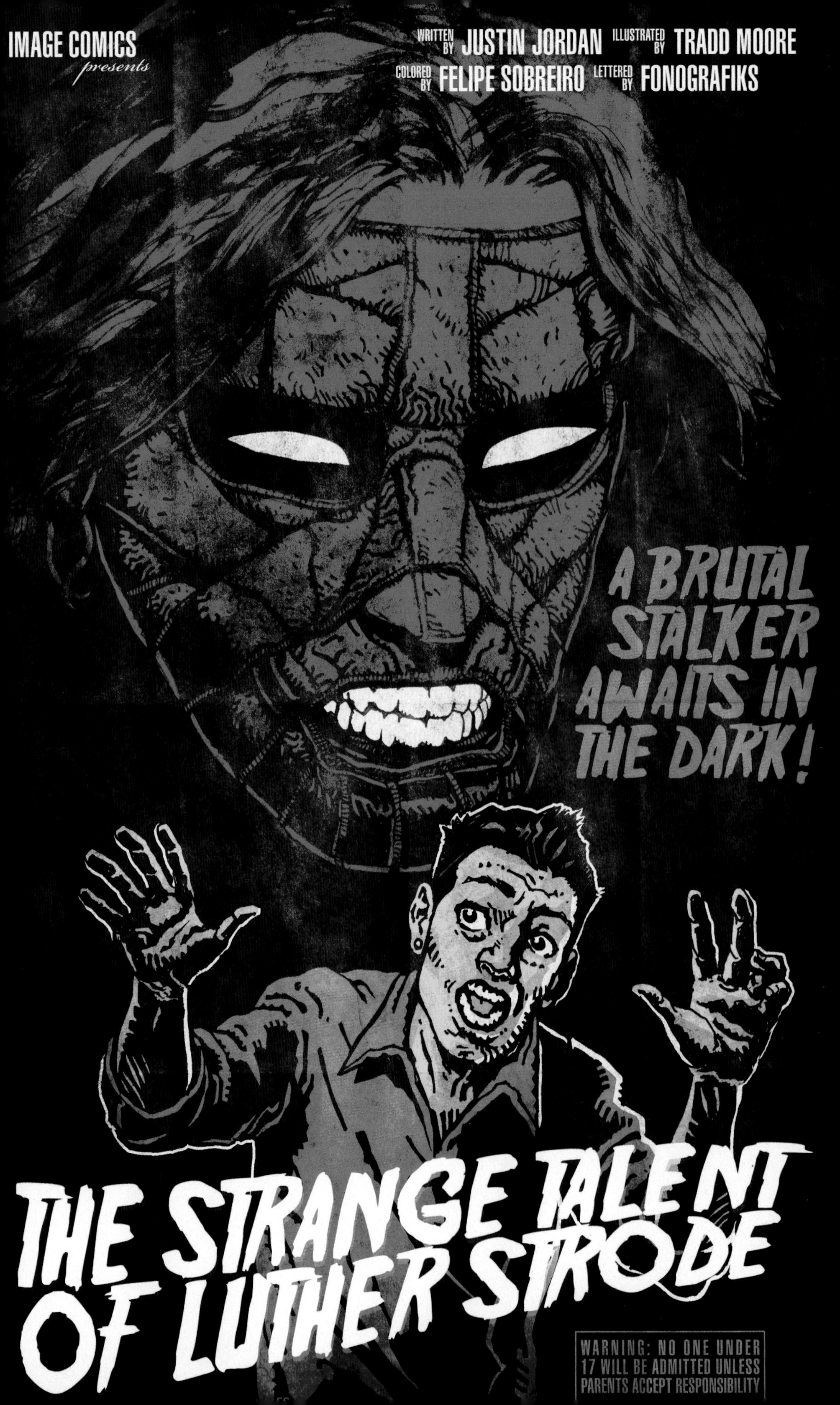
IMAGE COMICS presents
WRITTEN BY JUSTIN JORDAN ILLUSTRATED BY TRADD MOORE
COLORED BY FELIPE SOBREIRO LETTERED BY FONOGRAFIKS
A BRUTAL STALKER AWAITS IN THE DARK!
THE STRANGE TALENT OF LUTHER STRODE
WARNING: NO ONE UNDER 17 WILL BE ADMITTED UNLESS PARENTS ACCEPT RESPONSIBILITY

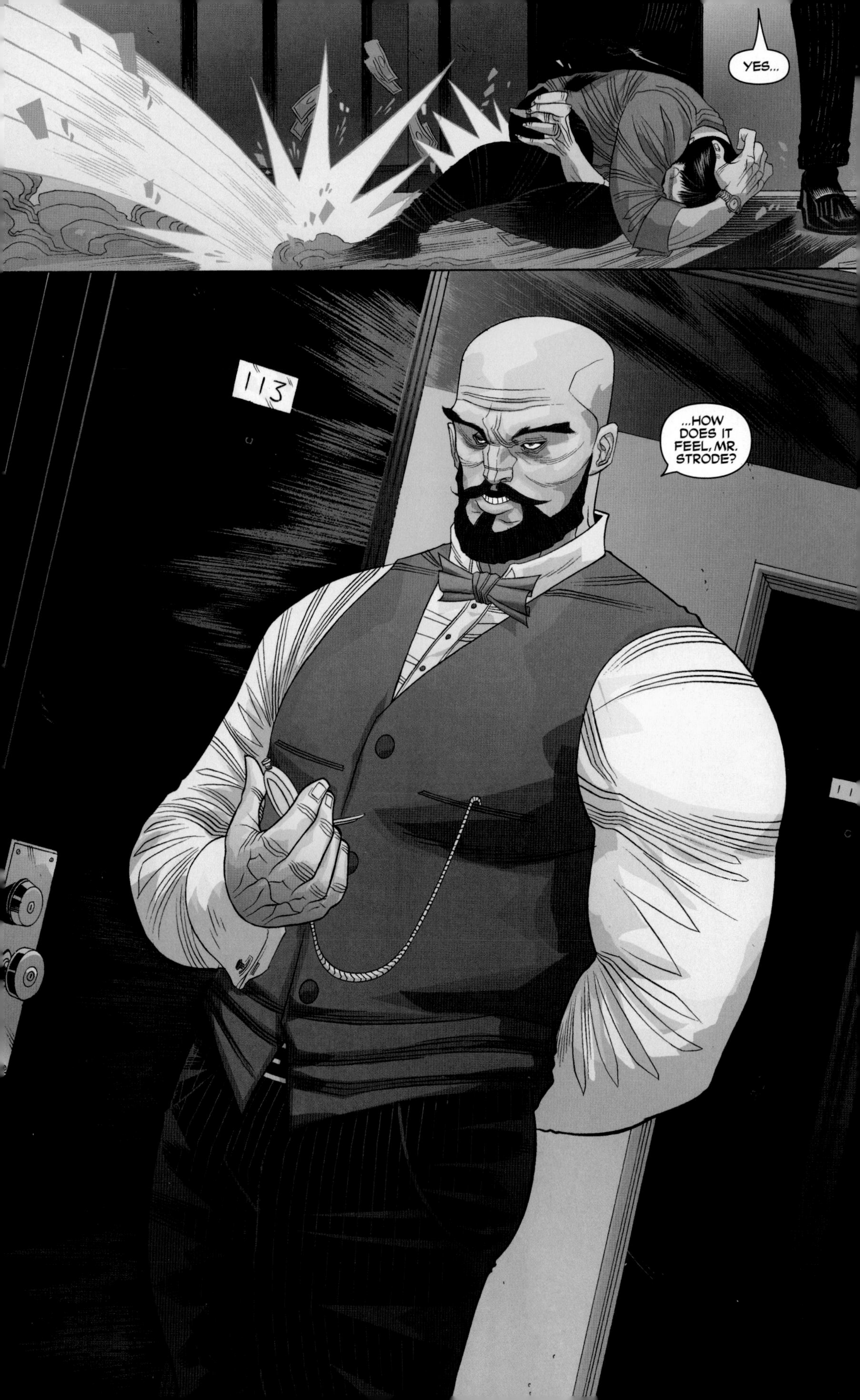
YES...
...HOW DOES IT FEEL, MR. STRODE?
113

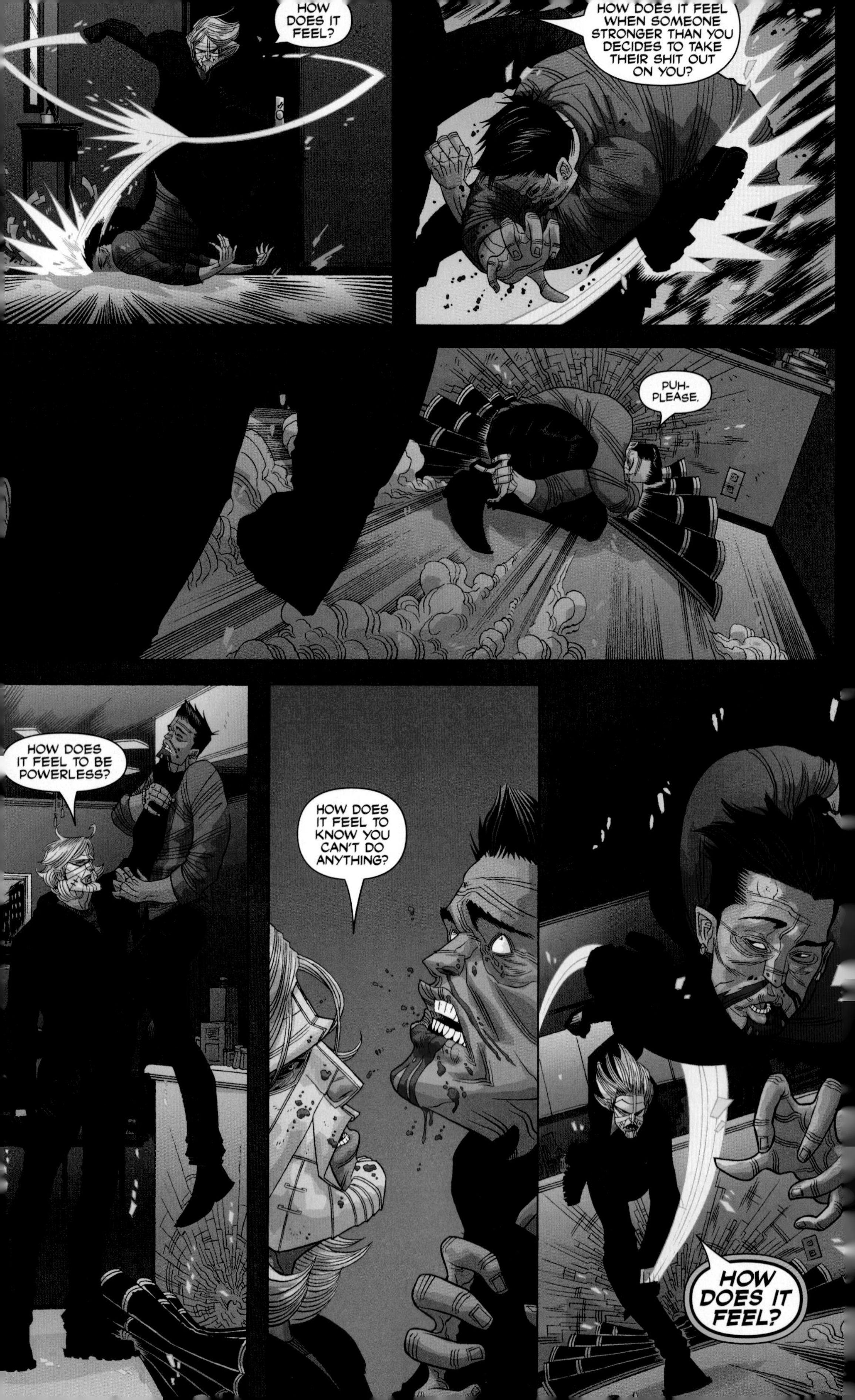
HOW DOES IT FEEL?
HOW DOES IT FEEL WHEN SOMEONE STRONGER THAN YOU DECIDES TO TAKE THEIR SHIT OUT ON YOU?
PUH- PLEASE.
HOW DOES IT FEEL TO BE POWERLESS?
HOW DOES IT FEEL TO KNOW YOU CAN'T DO ANYTHING?
HOW DOES IT FEEL?

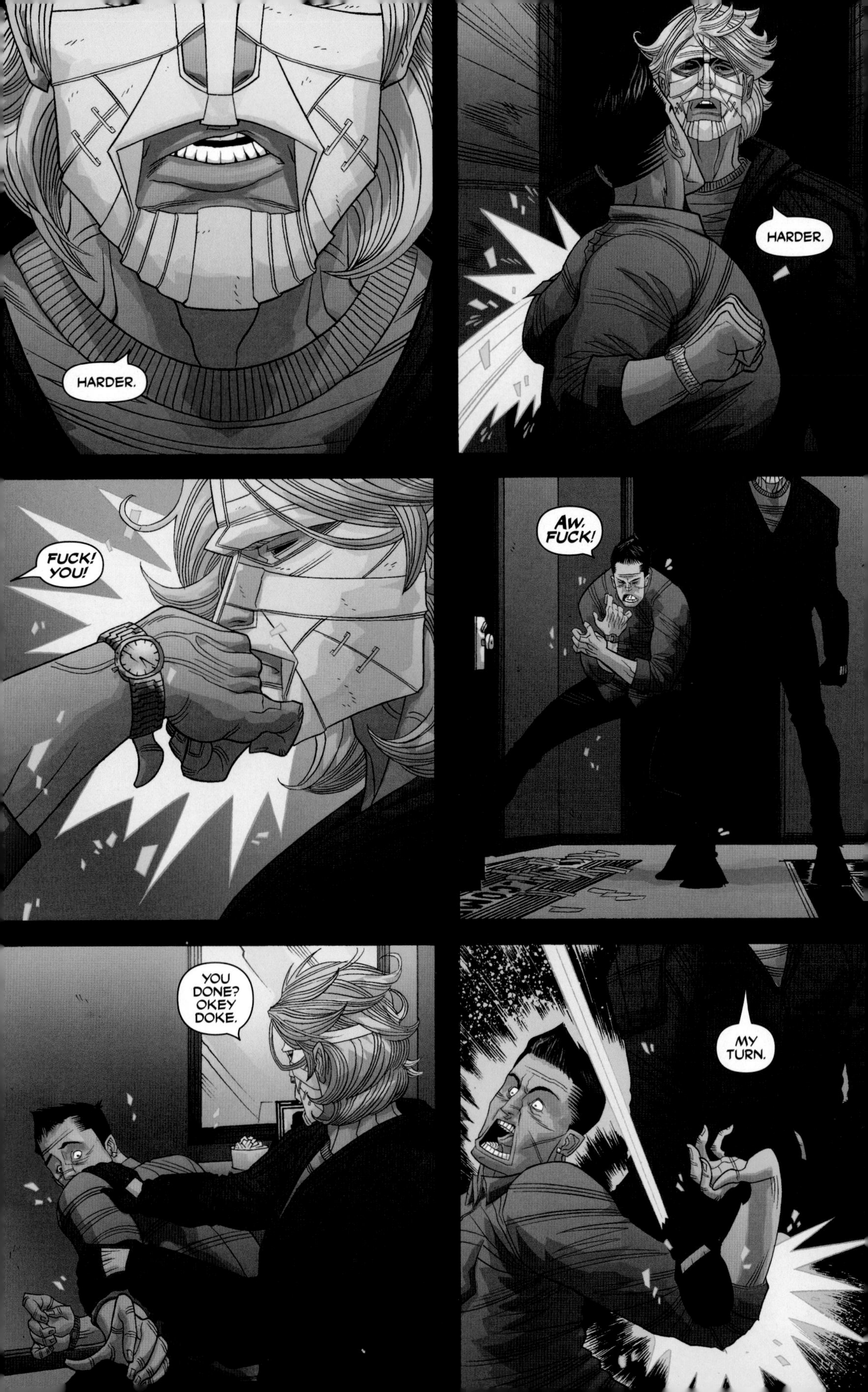
HARDER.
HARDER.
FUCK! YOU!
AW, FUCK!
YOU DONE? OKEY DOKE.
MY TURN.

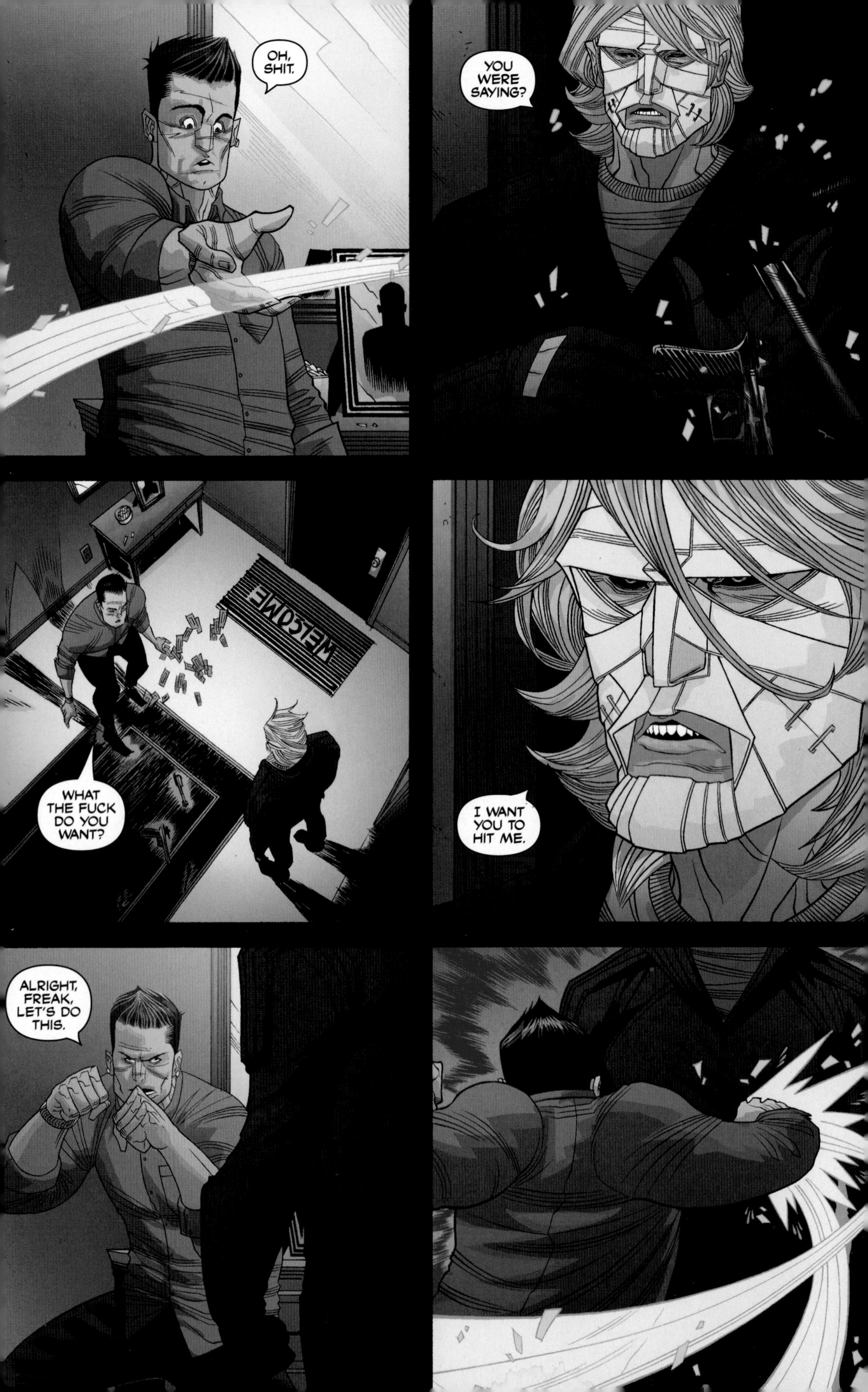
OH, SHIT.
YOU WERE SAYING?
WELCOME
WHAT THE FUCK DO YOU WANT?
I WANT YOU TO HIT ME.
ALRIGHT, FREAK, LET'S DO THIS.

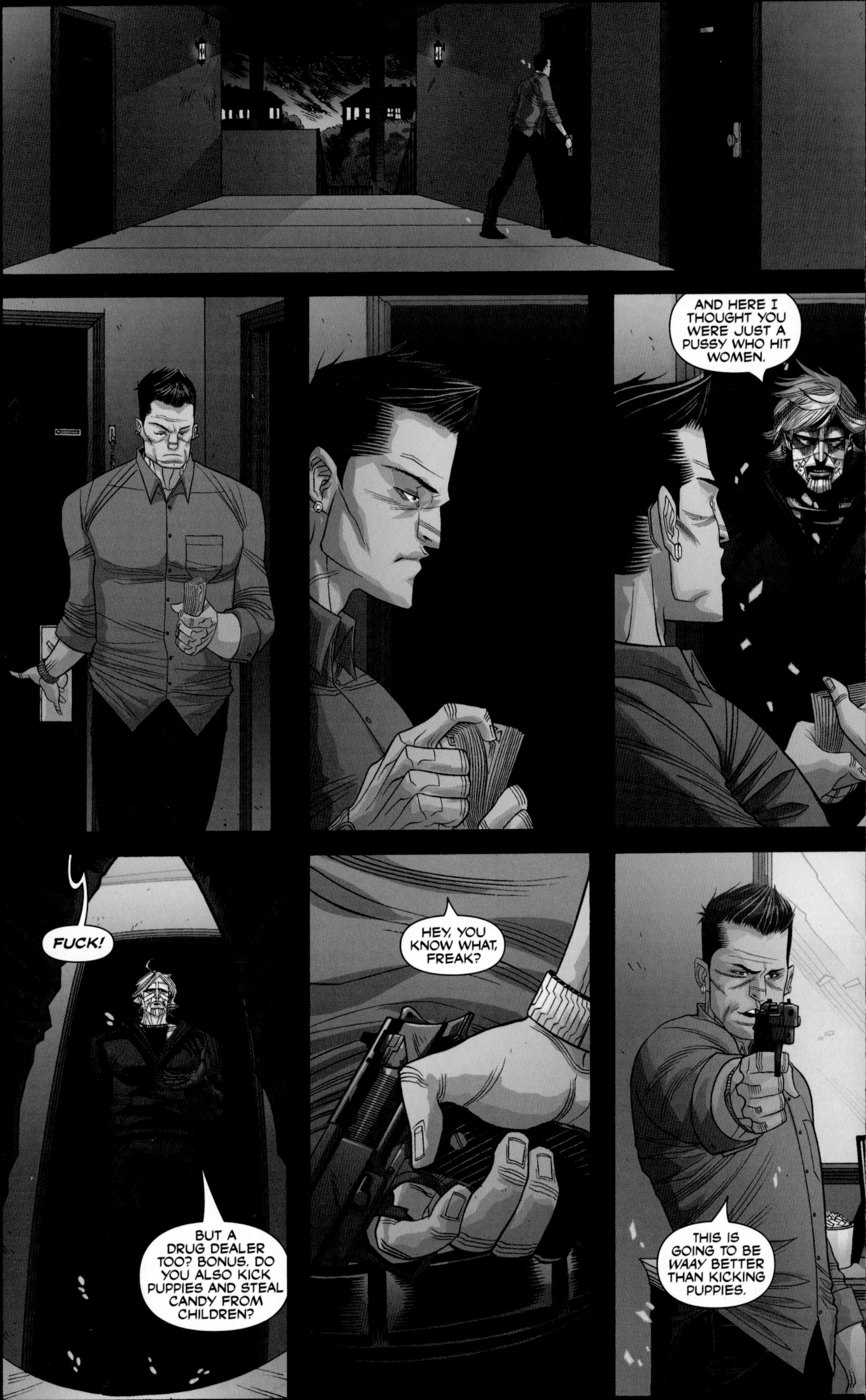
AND HERE I THOUGHT YOU WERE JUST A PUSSY WHO HIT WOMEN.
FUCK!
BUT A DRUG DEALER TOO? BONUS. DO YOU ALSO KICK PUPPIES AND STEAL CANDY FROM CHILDREN?
HEY, YOU KNOW WHAT, FREAK?
THIS IS GOING TO BE *WAAY* BETTER THAN KICKING PUPPIES.

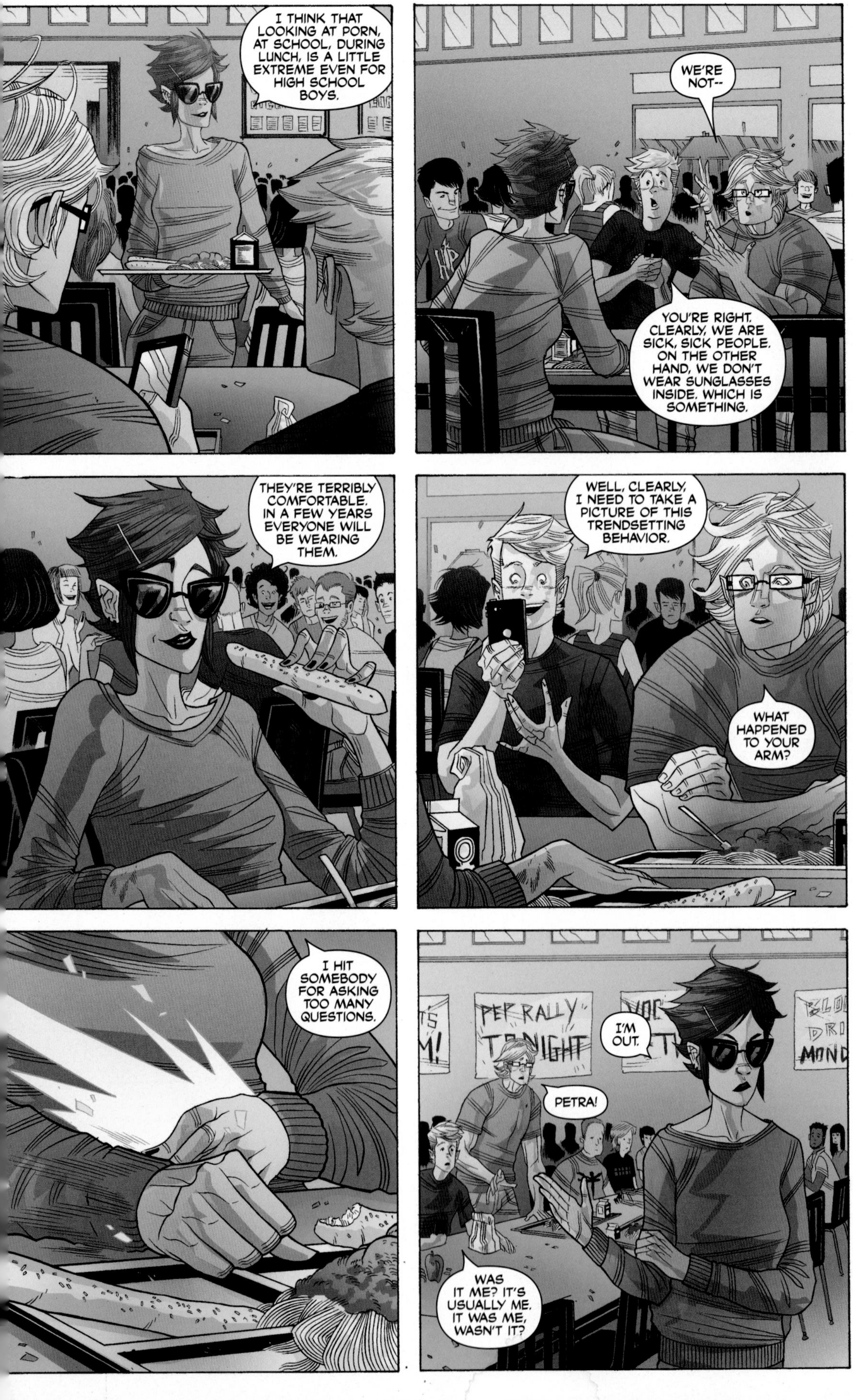
I THINK THAT LOOKING AT PORN, AT SCHOOL, DURING LUNCH, IS A LITTLE EXTREME EVEN FOR HIGH SCHOOL BOYS.
WE'RE NOT--
YOU'RE RIGHT. CLEARLY, WE ARE SICK, SICK PEOPLE. ON THE OTHER HAND, WE DON'T WEAR SUNGLASSES INSIDE. WHICH IS SOMETHING.
THEY'RE TERRIBLY COMFORTABLE. IN A FEW YEARS EVERYONE WILL BE WEARING THEM.
WELL, CLEARLY, I NEED TO TAKE A PICTURE OF THIS TRENDSETTING BEHAVIOR.
WHAT HAPPENED TO YOUR ARM?
I HIT SOMEBODY FOR ASKING TOO MANY QUESTIONS.
PEP RALLY TONIGHT
I'M OUT.
PETRA!
WAS IT ME? IT'S USUALLY ME. IT WAS ME, WASN'T IT?

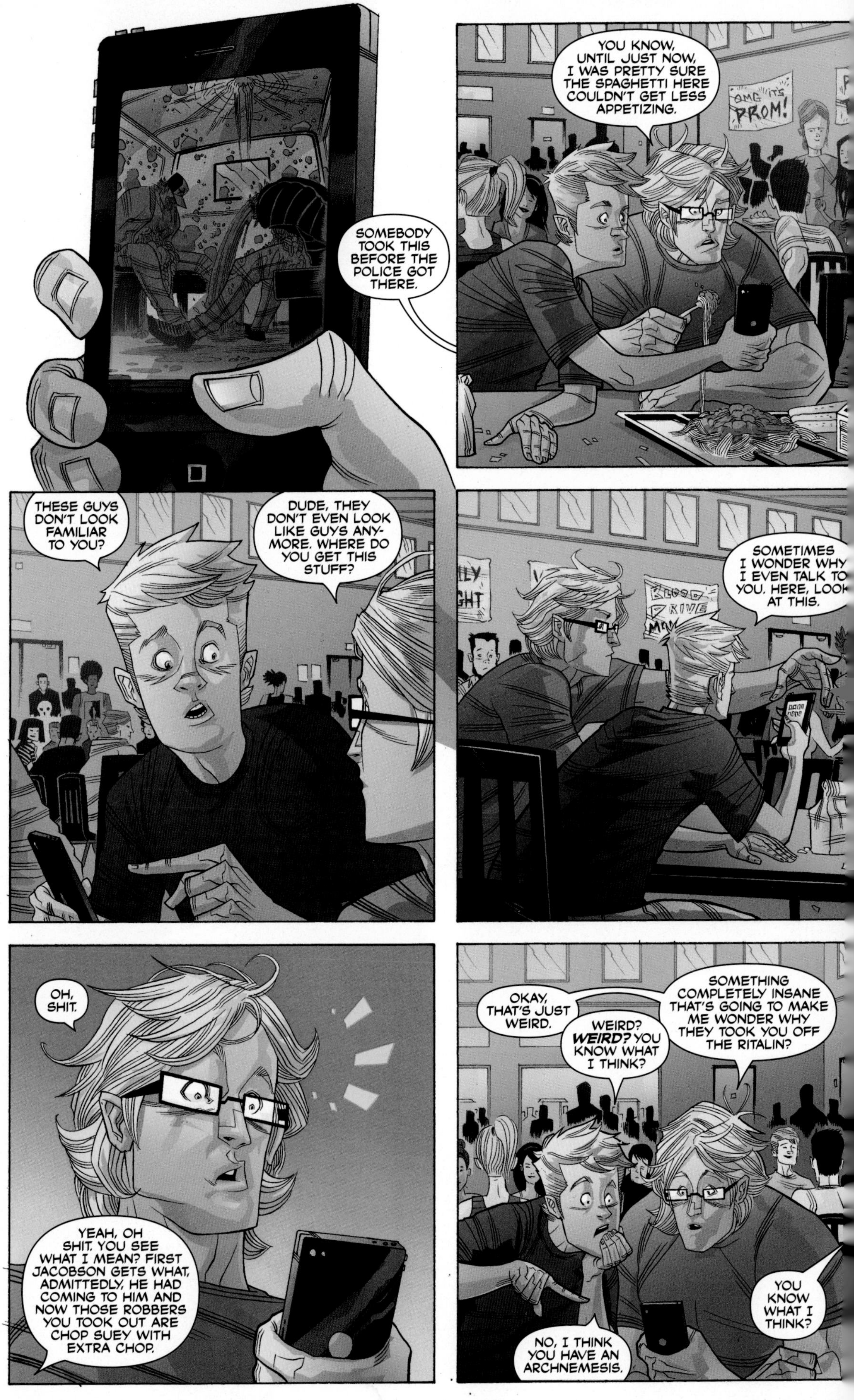

SOMEBODY TOOK THIS BEFORE THE POLICE GOT THERE.
YOU KNOW, UNTIL JUST NOW, I WAS PRETTY SURE THE SPAGHETTI HERE COULDN'T GET LESS APPETIZING.
OMG IT'S PROM!
THESE GUYS DON'T LOOK FAMILIAR TO YOU?
DUDE, THEY DON'T EVEN LOOK LIKE GUYS ANY-MORE. WHERE DO YOU GET THIS STUFF?
SOMETIMES I WONDER WHY I EVEN TALK TO YOU. HERE, LOOK AT THIS.
BLOOD DRIVE
OH, SHIT.
YEAH, OH SHIT. YOU SEE WHAT I MEAN? FIRST JACOBSON GETS WHAT, ADMITTEDLY, HE HAD COMING TO HIM AND NOW THOSE ROBBERS YOU TOOK OUT ARE CHOP SUEY WITH EXTRA CHOP.
OKAY, THAT'S JUST WEIRD.
WEIRD? ***WEIRD?*** YOU KNOW WHAT I THINK?
SOMETHING COMPLETELY INSANE THAT'S GOING TO MAKE ME WONDER WHY THEY TOOK YOU OFF THE RITALIN?
YOU KNOW WHAT I THINK?
NO, I THINK YOU HAVE AN ARCHNEMESIS.

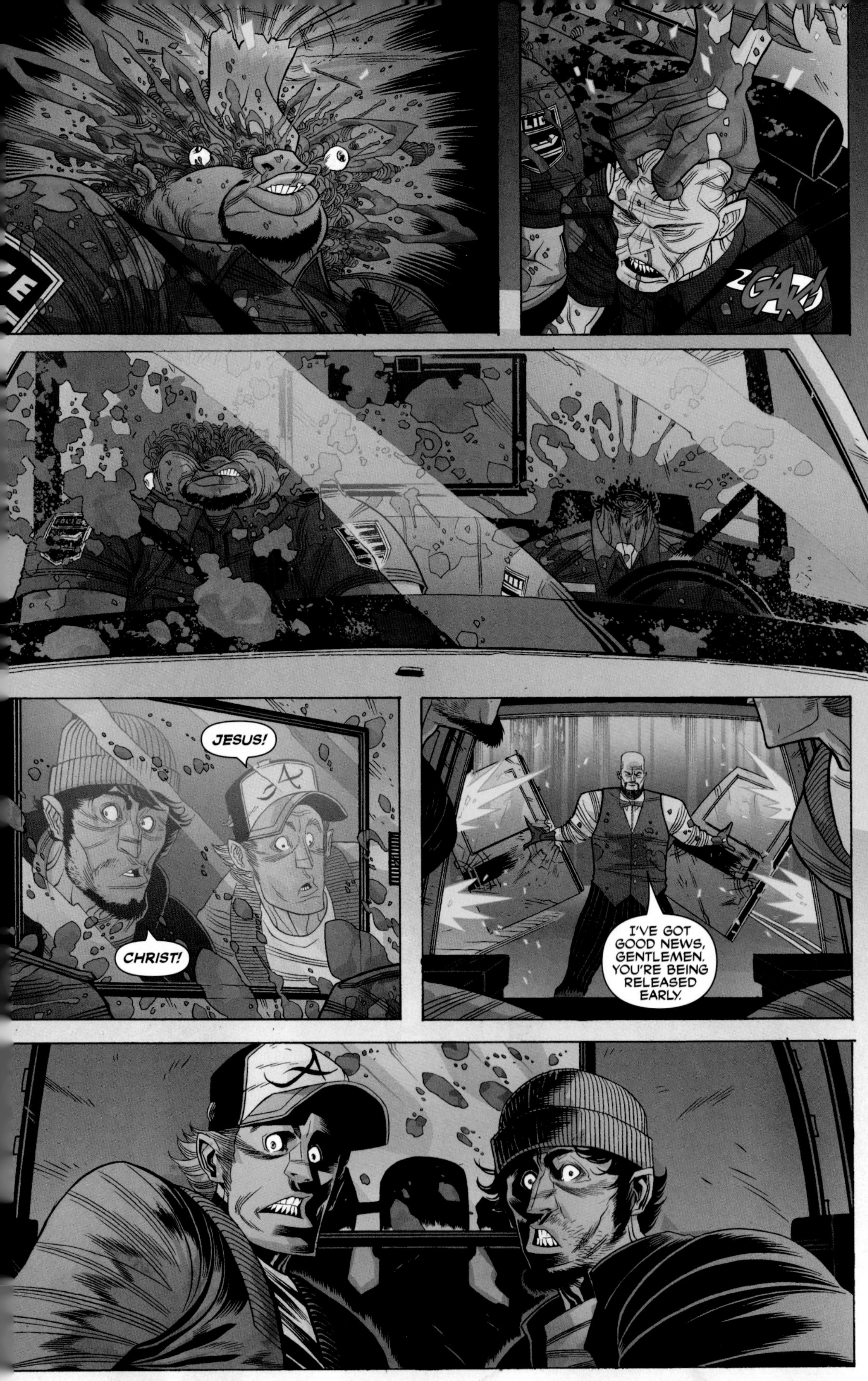
GAK!
JESUS!
CHRIST!
I'VE GOT GOOD NEWS, GENTLEMEN. YOU'RE BEING RELEASED EARLY.

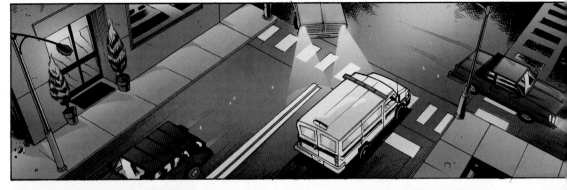

MAN, I'M GOING TO FIND THAT GUY AND I AM GOING TO PUT A BULLET IN HIS HEAD.

FUCK THAT, I AM GOING TO PUT THOSE BULLETS UP HIS *ASS*.

HEY, DO YOU TWO REALIZE WE CAN HEAR YOU UP HERE? ANYTHING YOU SAY CAN AND WILL, ET CETERA?

FUCK YOU, PIG!

WELL, THANK GOD WE GOT THOSE TWO CRIMINAL MASTERMINDS OFF THE STREET.

HRN.

THUNK

WHAT THE HELL WAS THAT?

HRN.

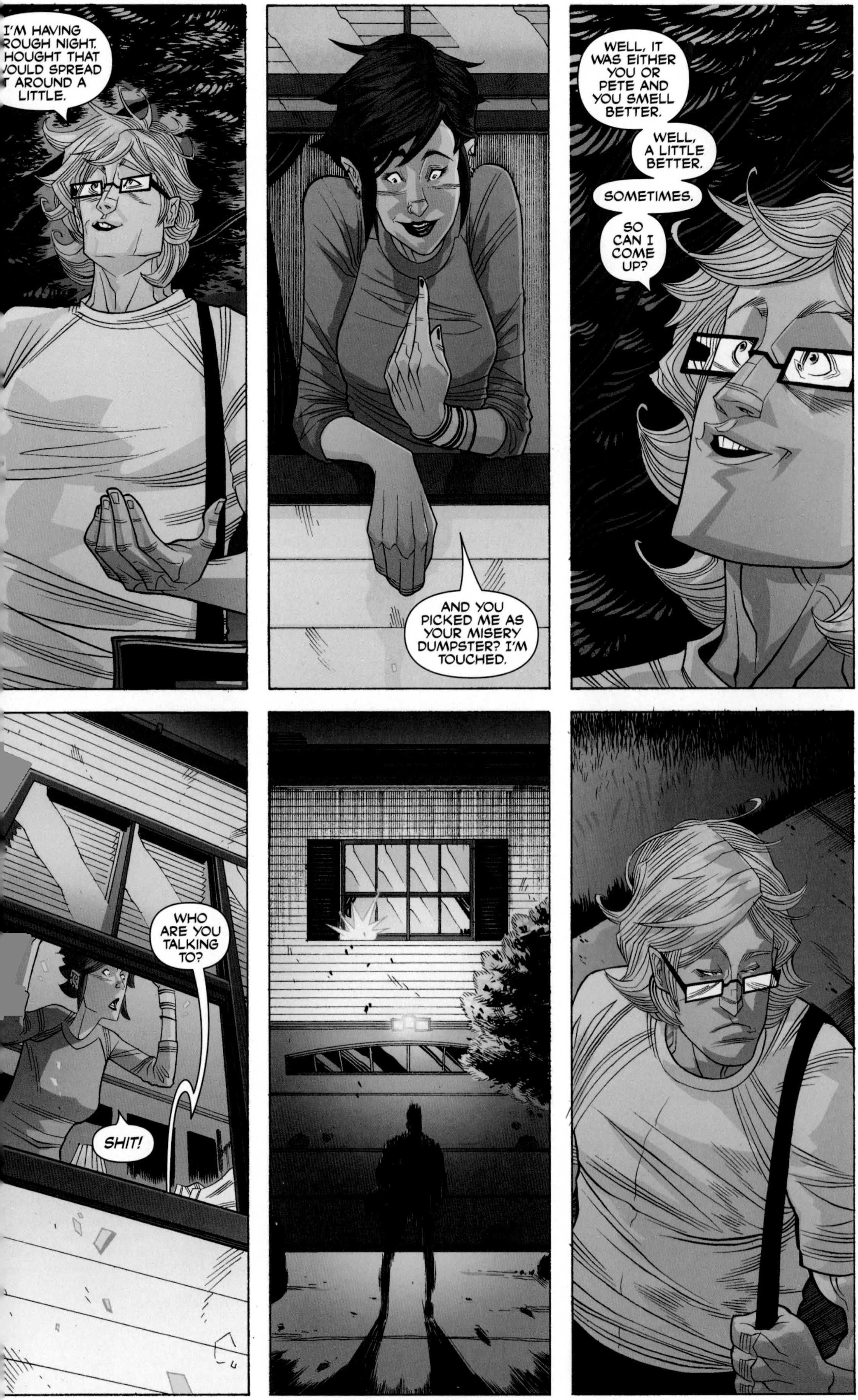
I'M HAVING ROUGH NIGHT. HOUGHT THAT OULD SPREAD T AROUND A LITTLE.
AND YOU PICKED ME AS YOUR MISERY DUMPSTER? I'M TOUCHED.
WELL, IT WAS EITHER YOU OR PETE AND YOU SMELL BETTER.
WELL, A LITTLE BETTER.
SOMETIMES.
SO CAN I COME UP?
WHO ARE YOU TALKING TO?
SHIT!

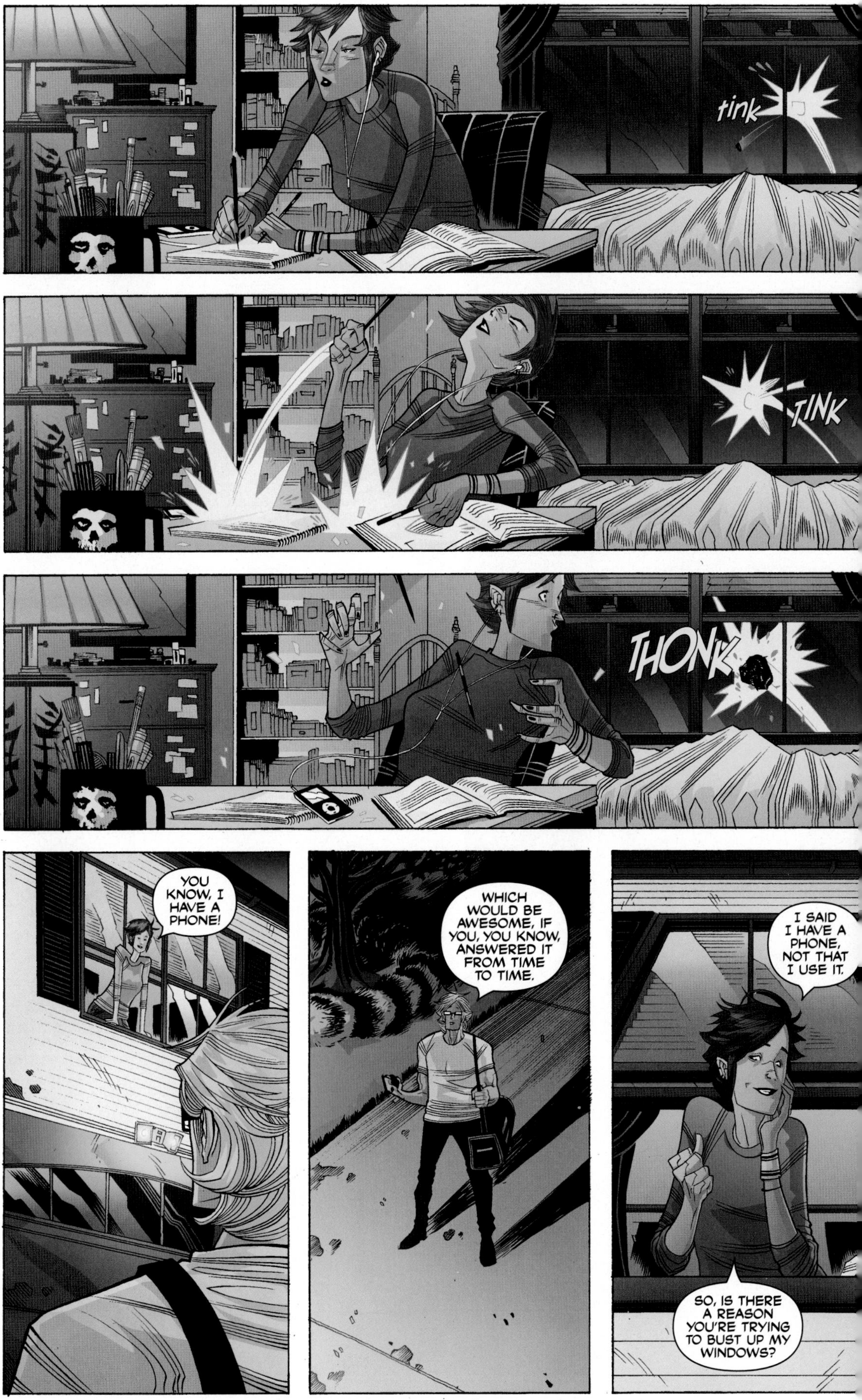
tink
TINK
THONK
YOU KNOW, I HAVE A PHONE!
WHICH WOULD BE AWESOME, IF YOU, YOU KNOW, ANSWERED IT FROM TIME TO TIME.
I SAID I HAVE A PHONE, NOT THAT I USE IT.
SO, IS THERE A REASON YOU'RE TRYING TO BUST UP MY WINDOWS?

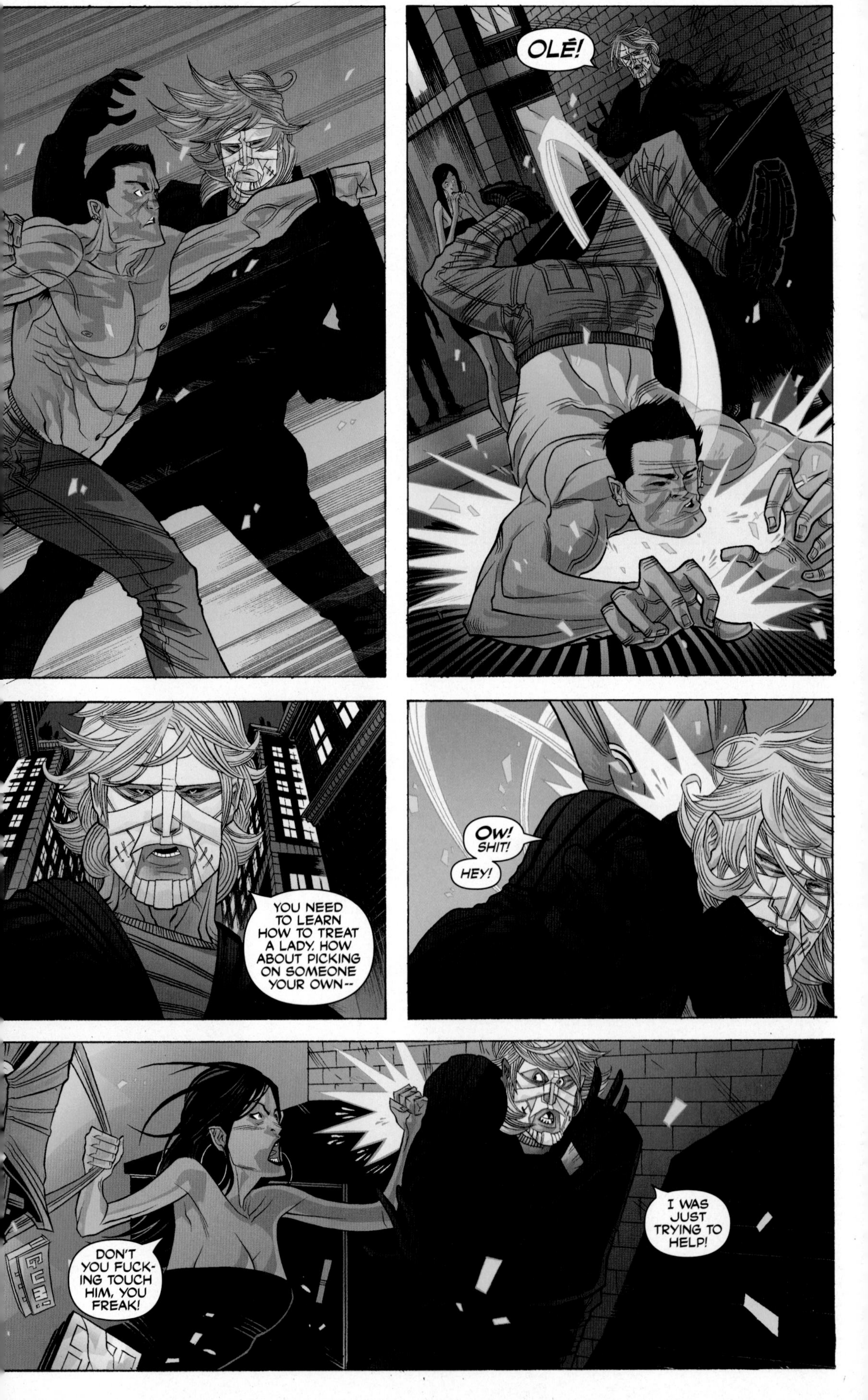
OLÉ!
YOU NEED TO LEARN HOW TO TREAT A LADY. HOW ABOUT PICKING ON SOMEONE YOUR OWN--
OW! SHIT!
HEY!
DON'T YOU FUCK-ING TOUCH HIM, YOU FREAK!
I WAS JUST TRYING TO HELP!

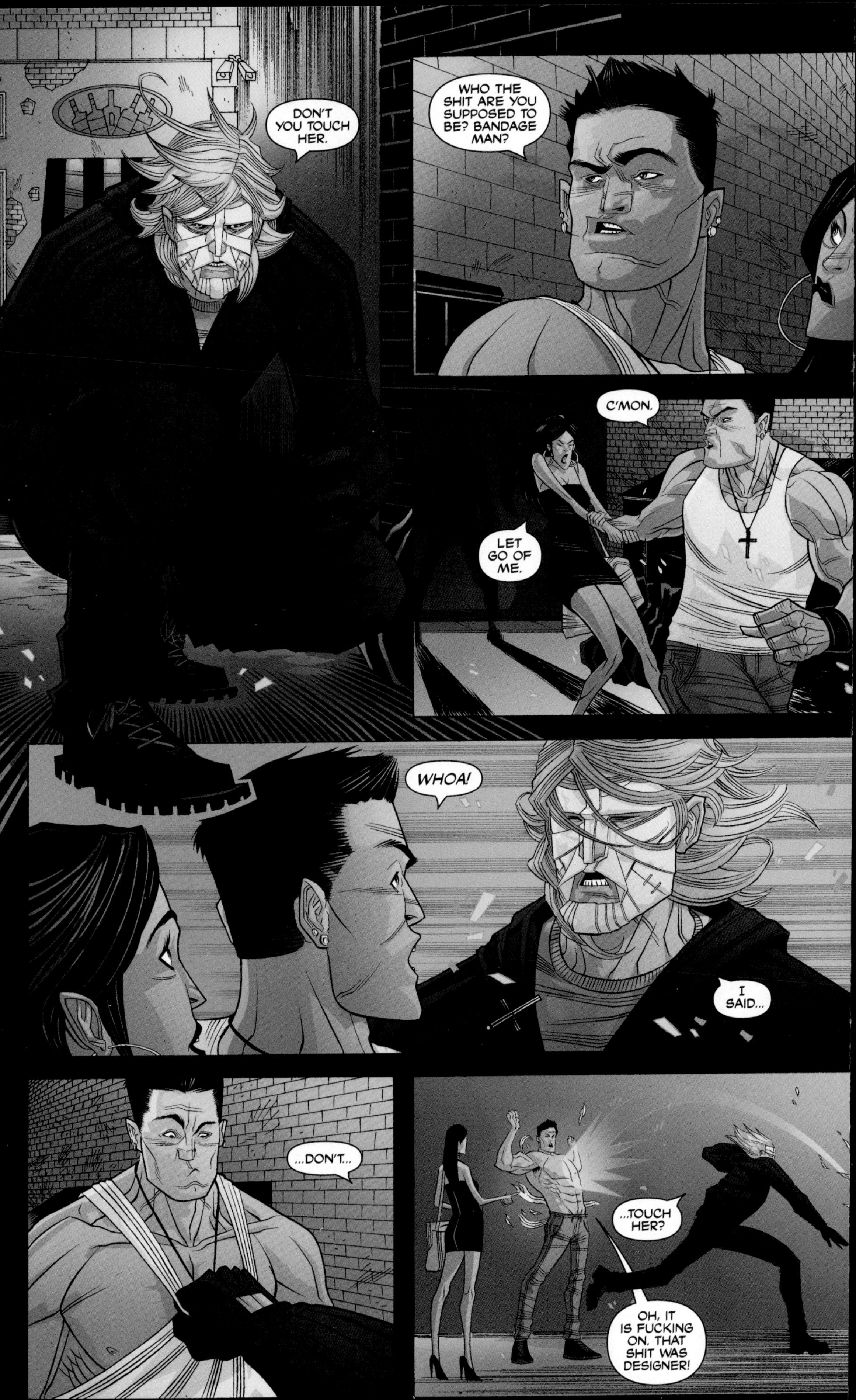
DON'T YOU TOUCH HER.
WHO THE SHIT ARE YOU SUPPOSED TO BE? BANDAGE MAN?
C'MON.
LET GO OF ME.
WHOA!
I SAID...
...DON'T...
...TOUCH HER?
OH, IT IS FUCKING ON. THAT SHIT WAS DESIGNER!

ALL NIGHT OUT HERE, AND THE NUMBER OF COWARDLY AND SUPERSTITIOUS CRIMINALS? ZERO.

I THOUGHT THIS CITY WAS SUPPOSED TO HAVE A CRIME PROBLEM?

AND WHY DON'T YOU JUST SHUT THE FUCK UP FOR A CHANGE?

WHY DON'T YOU GO FUCK YOUR-SELF?

ALWAYS FUCKING EMBARRASS-ING ME.

LET GO OF ME!

I AM FUCKING SICK OF YOU.

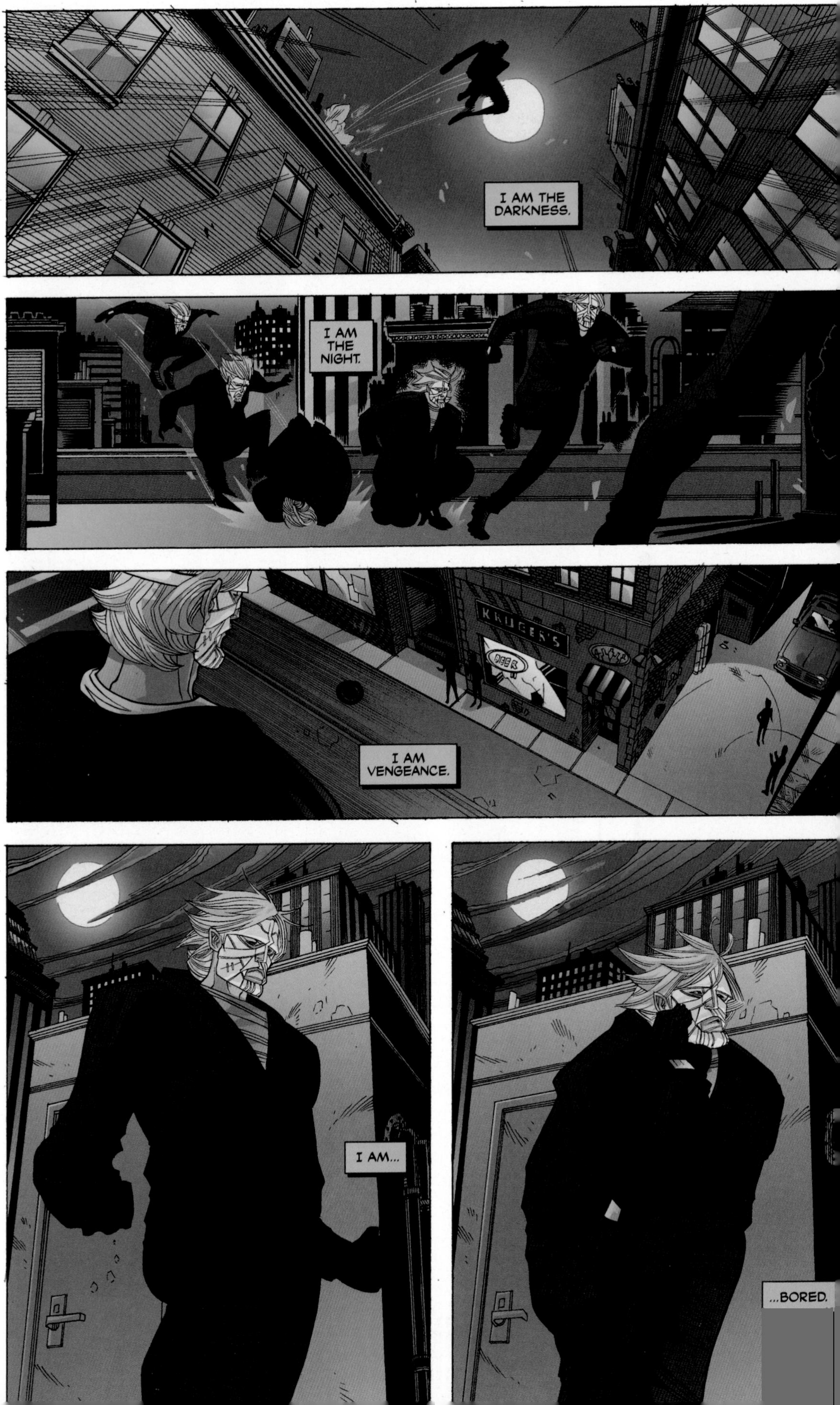

I AM THE DARKNESS.
I AM THE NIGHT.
KRUGER'S
I AM VENGEANCE.
I AM...
...BORED.

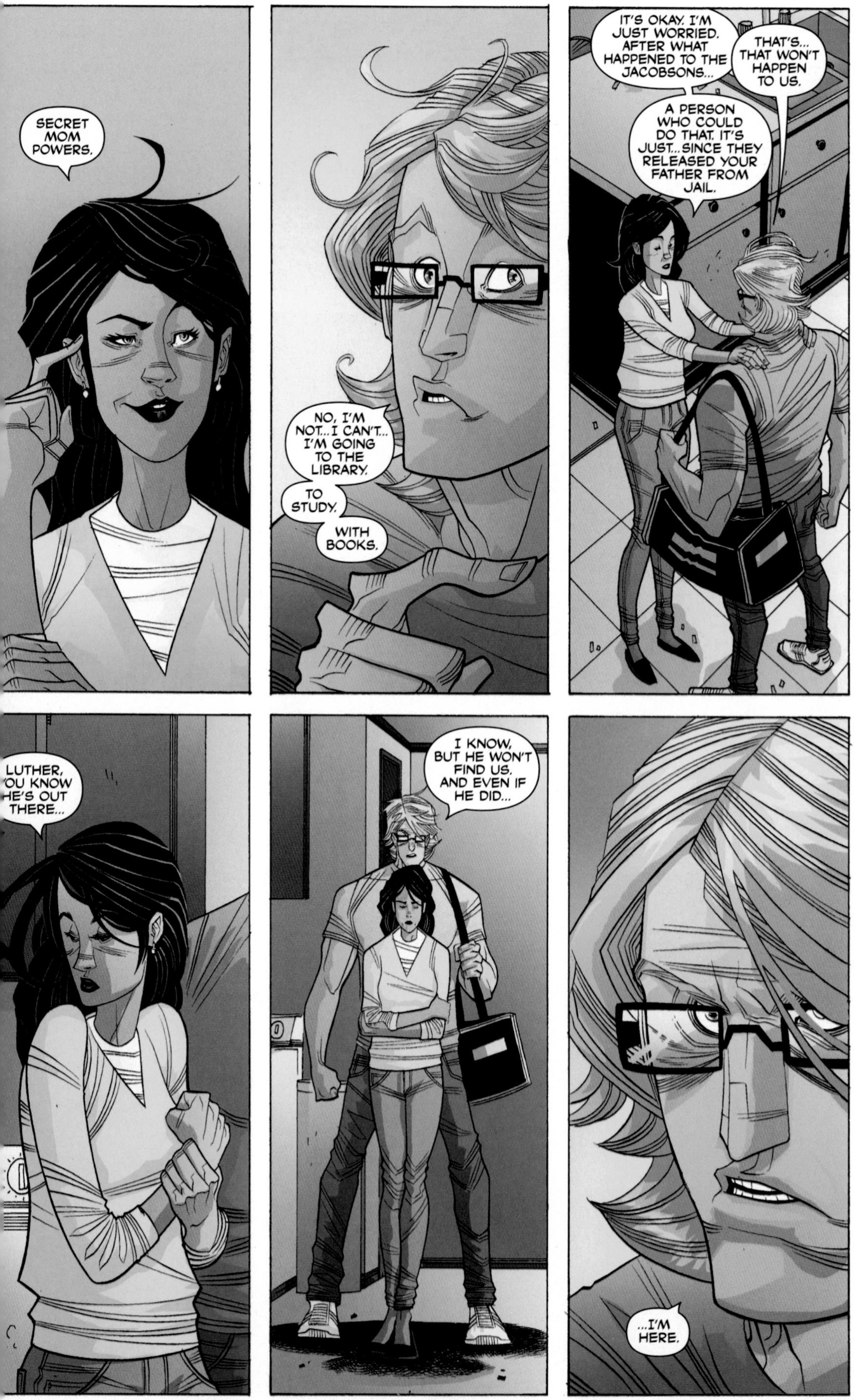

SECRET MOM POWERS.
NO, I'M NOT... I CAN'T... I'M GOING TO THE LIBRARY.
TO STUDY.
WITH BOOKS.
IT'S OKAY. I'M JUST WORRIED. AFTER WHAT HAPPENED TO THE JACOBSONS...
THAT'S... THAT WON'T HAPPEN TO US.
A PERSON WHO COULD DO THAT. IT'S JUST... SINCE THEY RELEASED YOUR FATHER FROM JAIL.
LUTHER, YOU KNOW HE'S OUT THERE...
I KNOW, BUT HE WON'T FIND US. AND EVEN IF HE DID...
...I'M HERE.

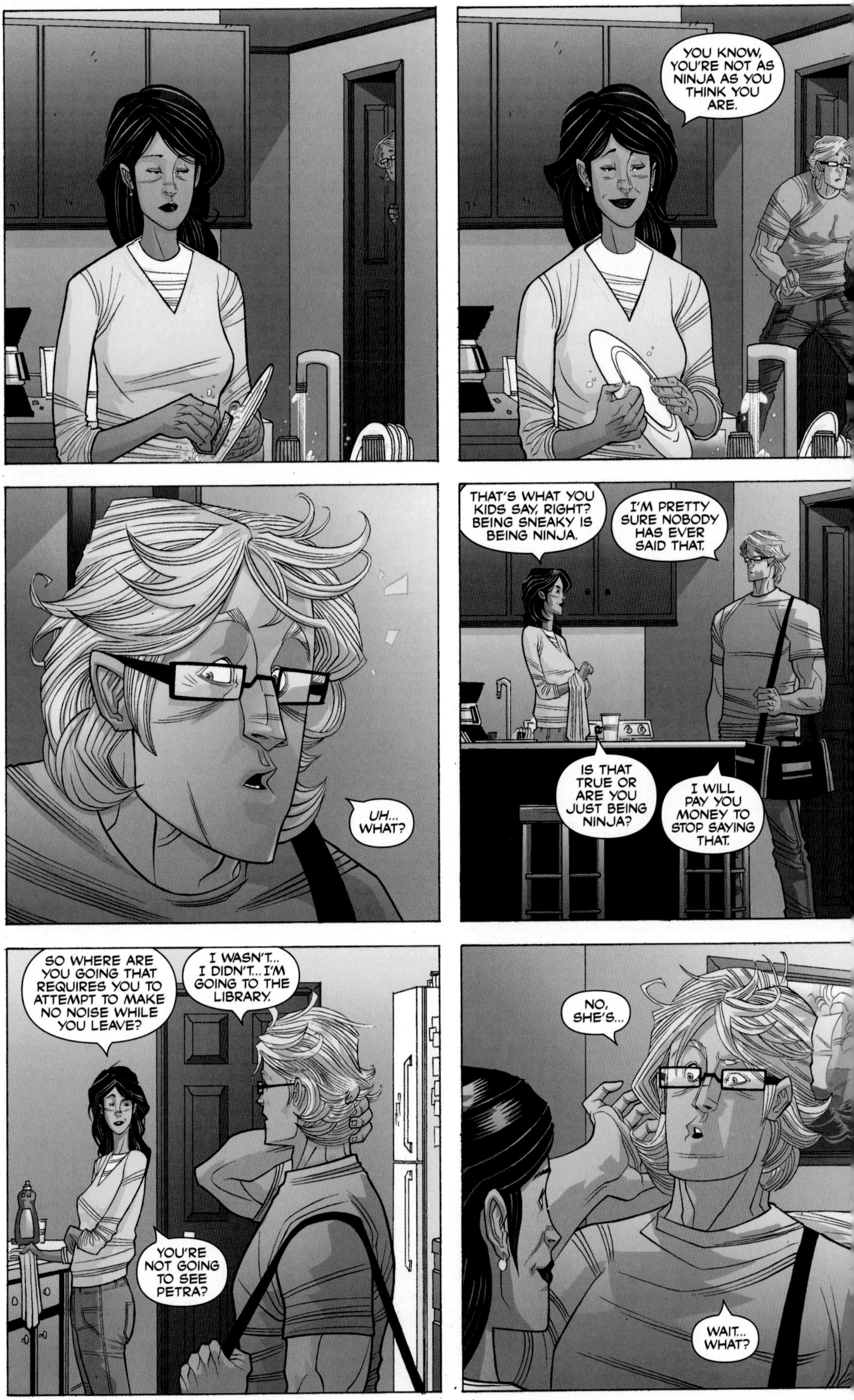
YOU KNOW, YOU'RE NOT AS NINJA AS YOU THINK YOU ARE.
UH... WHAT?
THAT'S WHAT YOU KIDS SAY, RIGHT? BEING SNEAKY IS BEING NINJA.
I'M PRETTY SURE NOBODY HAS EVER SAID THAT.
IS THAT TRUE OR ARE YOU JUST BEING NINJA?
I WILL PAY YOU MONEY TO STOP SAYING THAT.
SO WHERE ARE YOU GOING THAT REQUIRES YOU TO ATTEMPT TO MAKE NO NOISE WHILE YOU LEAVE?
I WASN'T... I DIDN'T... I'M GOING TO THE LIBRARY.
YOU'RE NOT GOING TO SEE PETRA?
NO, SHE'S...
WAIT... WHAT?

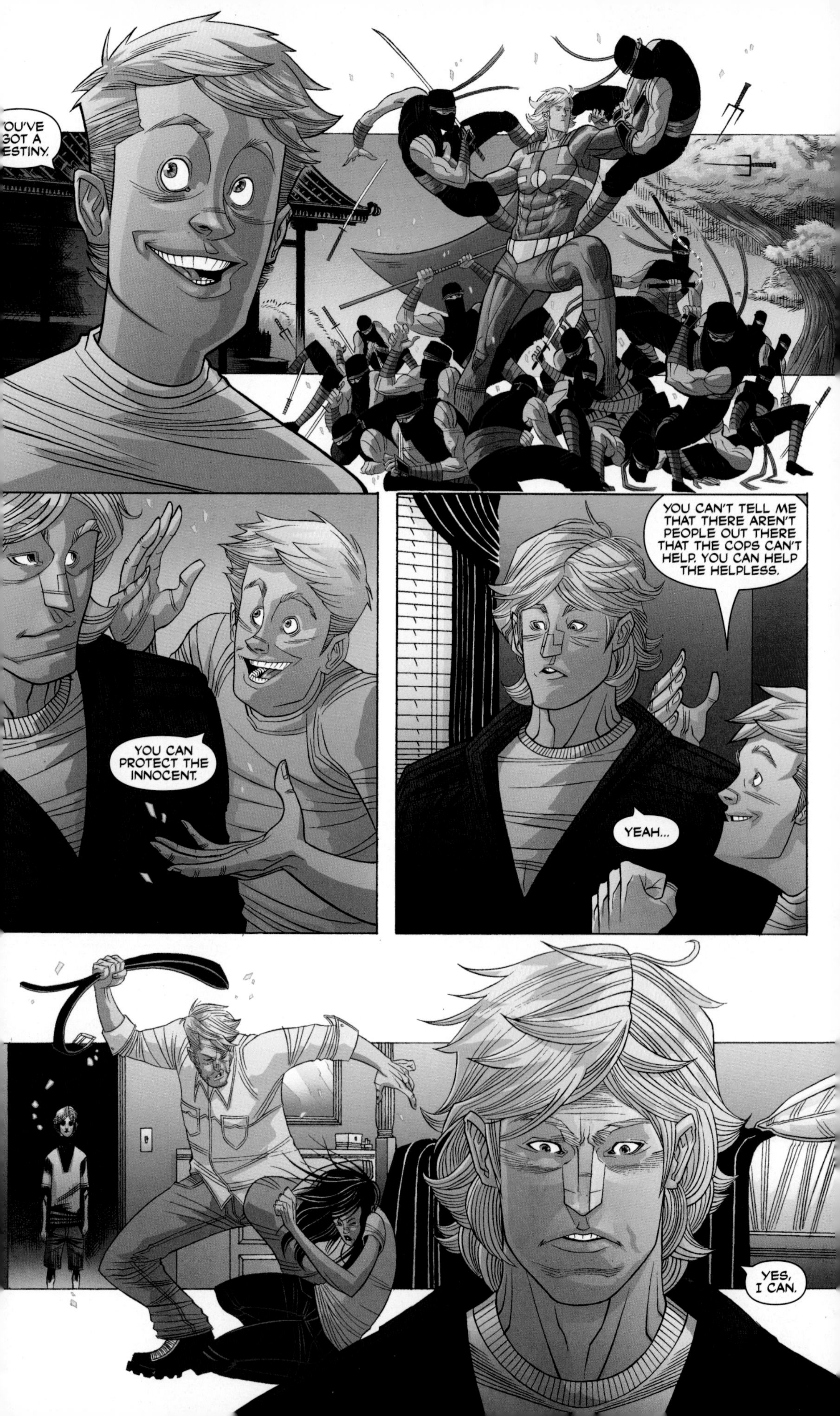

YOU'VE GOT A ESTINY.
YOU CAN PROTECT THE INNOCENT.
YOU CAN'T TELL ME THAT THERE AREN'T PEOPLE OUT THERE THAT THE COPS CAN'T HELP. YOU CAN HELP THE HELPLESS.
YEAH...
YES, I CAN.

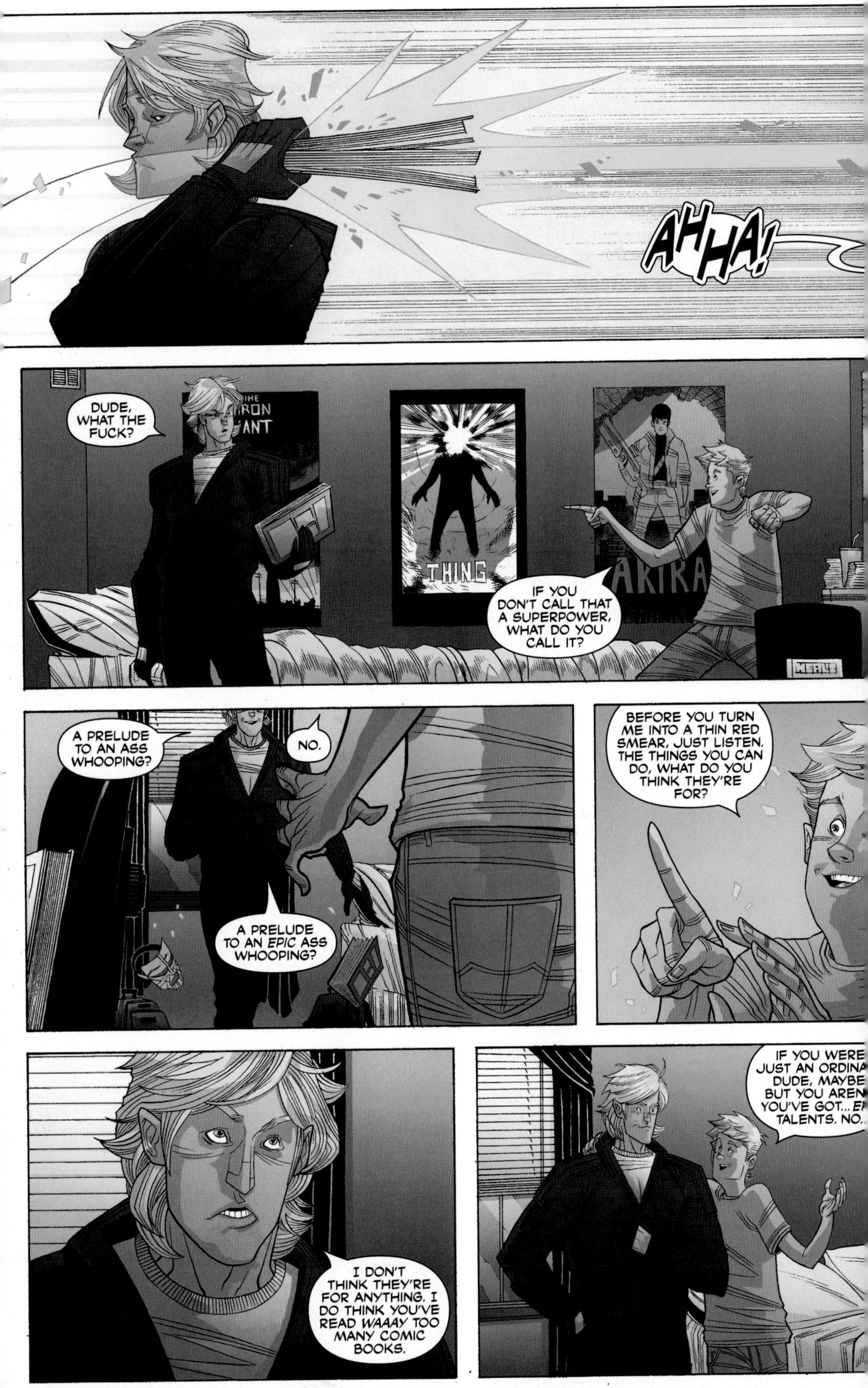
AHHA!
DUDE, WHAT THE FUCK?
THE IRON GIANT
THING
AKIRA
IF YOU DON'T CALL THAT A SUPERPOWER, WHAT DO YOU CALL IT?
A PRELUDE TO AN ASS WHOOPING?
NO.
A PRELUDE TO AN *EPIC* ASS WHOOPING?
BEFORE YOU TURN ME INTO A THIN RED SMEAR, JUST LISTEN. THE THINGS YOU CAN DO, WHAT DO YOU THINK THEY'RE FOR?
I DON'T THINK THEY'RE FOR ANYTHING. I DO THINK YOU'VE READ *WAAAY* TOO MANY COMIC BOOKS.
IF YOU WERE JUST AN ORDINA DUDE, MAYBE BUT YOU AREN YOU'VE GOT... *E* TALENTS. NO.

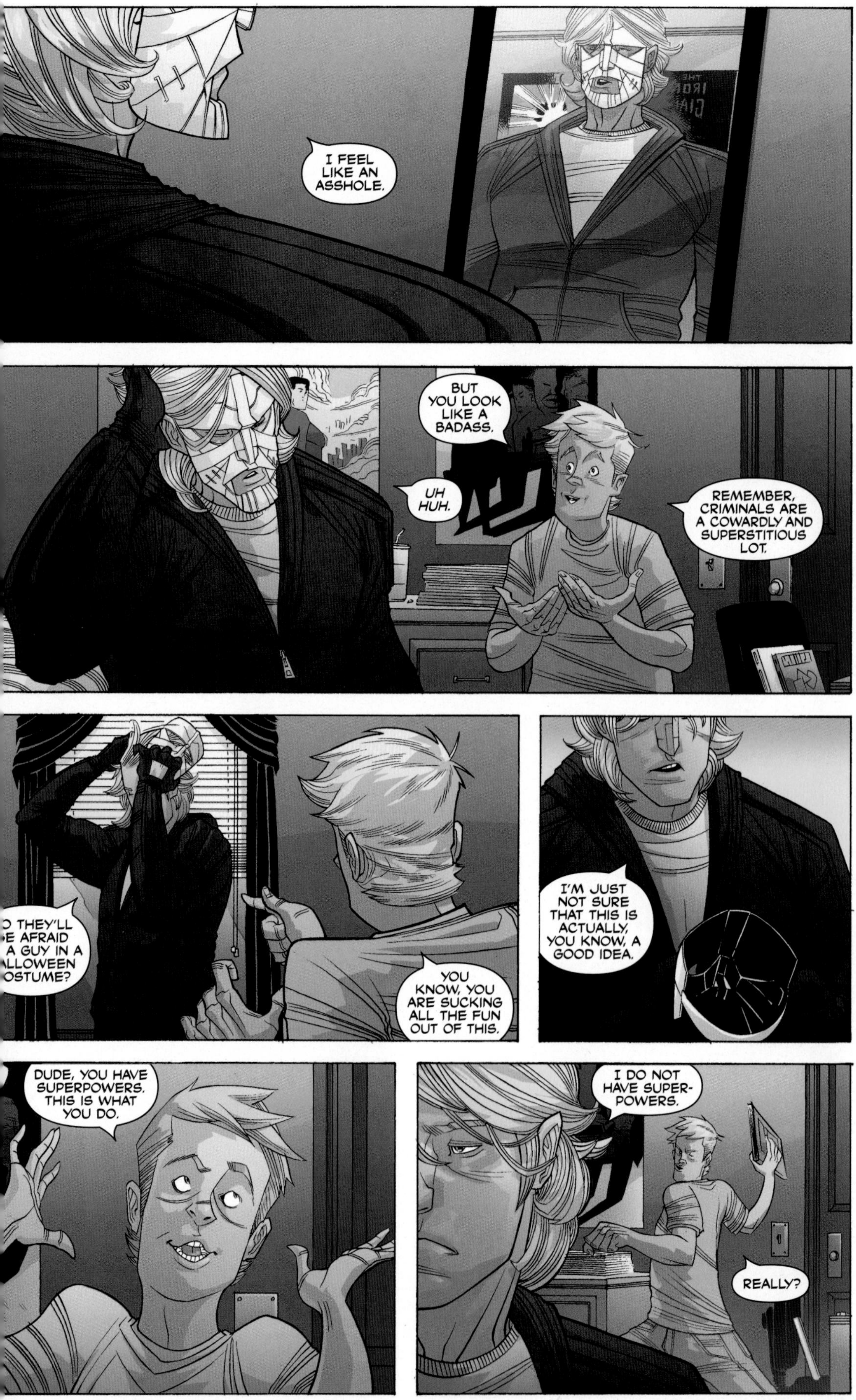

I FEEL LIKE AN ASSHOLE.
BUT YOU LOOK LIKE A BADASS.
UH HUH.
REMEMBER, CRIMINALS ARE A COWARDLY AND SUPERSTITIOUS LOT.
O THEY'LL E AFRAID A GUY IN A ALLOWEEN OSTUME?
YOU KNOW, YOU ARE SUCKING ALL THE FUN OUT OF THIS.
I'M JUST NOT SURE THAT THIS IS ACTUALLY, YOU KNOW, A GOOD IDEA.
DUDE, YOU HAVE SUPERPOWERS. THIS IS WHAT YOU DO.
I DO NOT HAVE SUPER-POWERS.
REALLY?

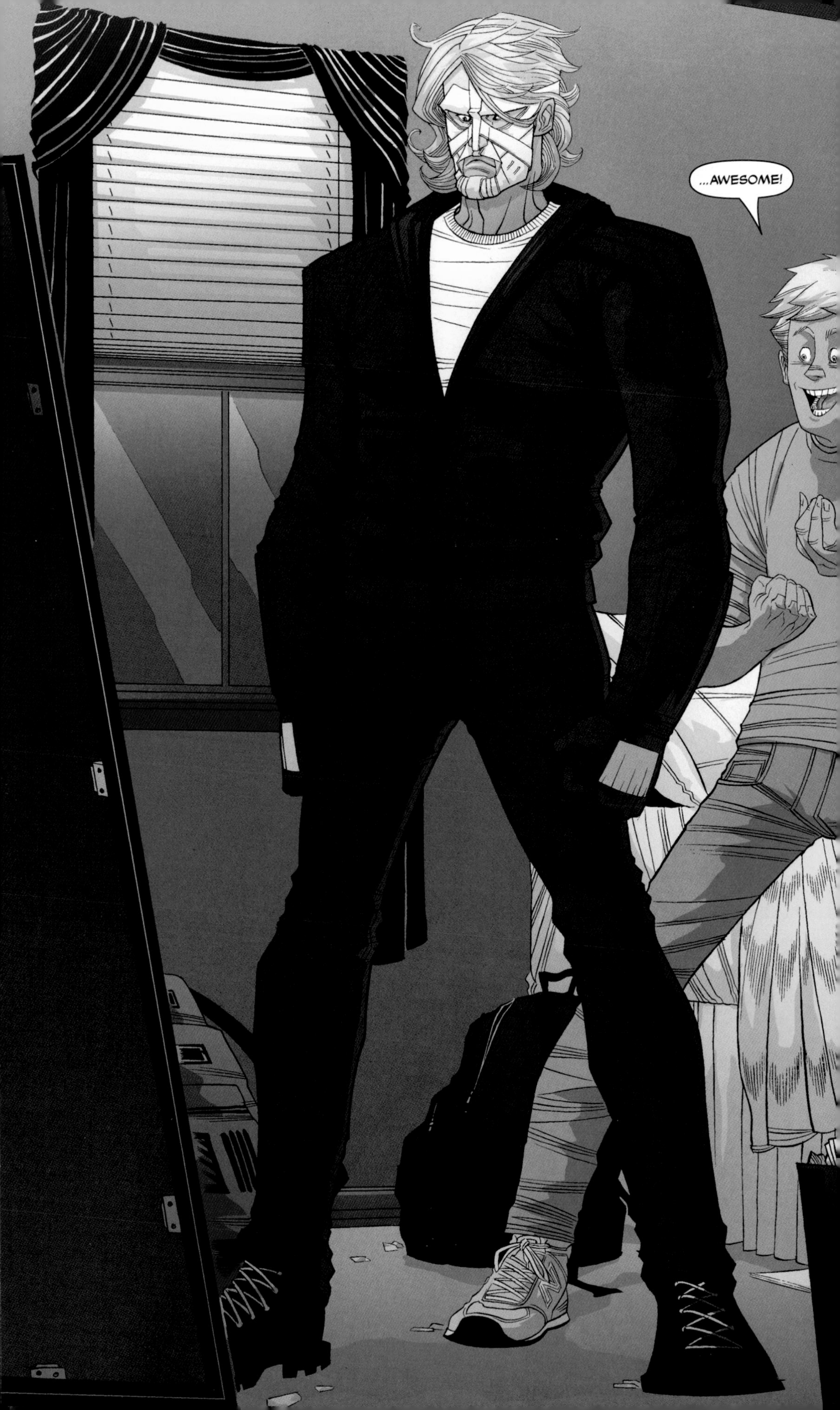
...AWESOME!

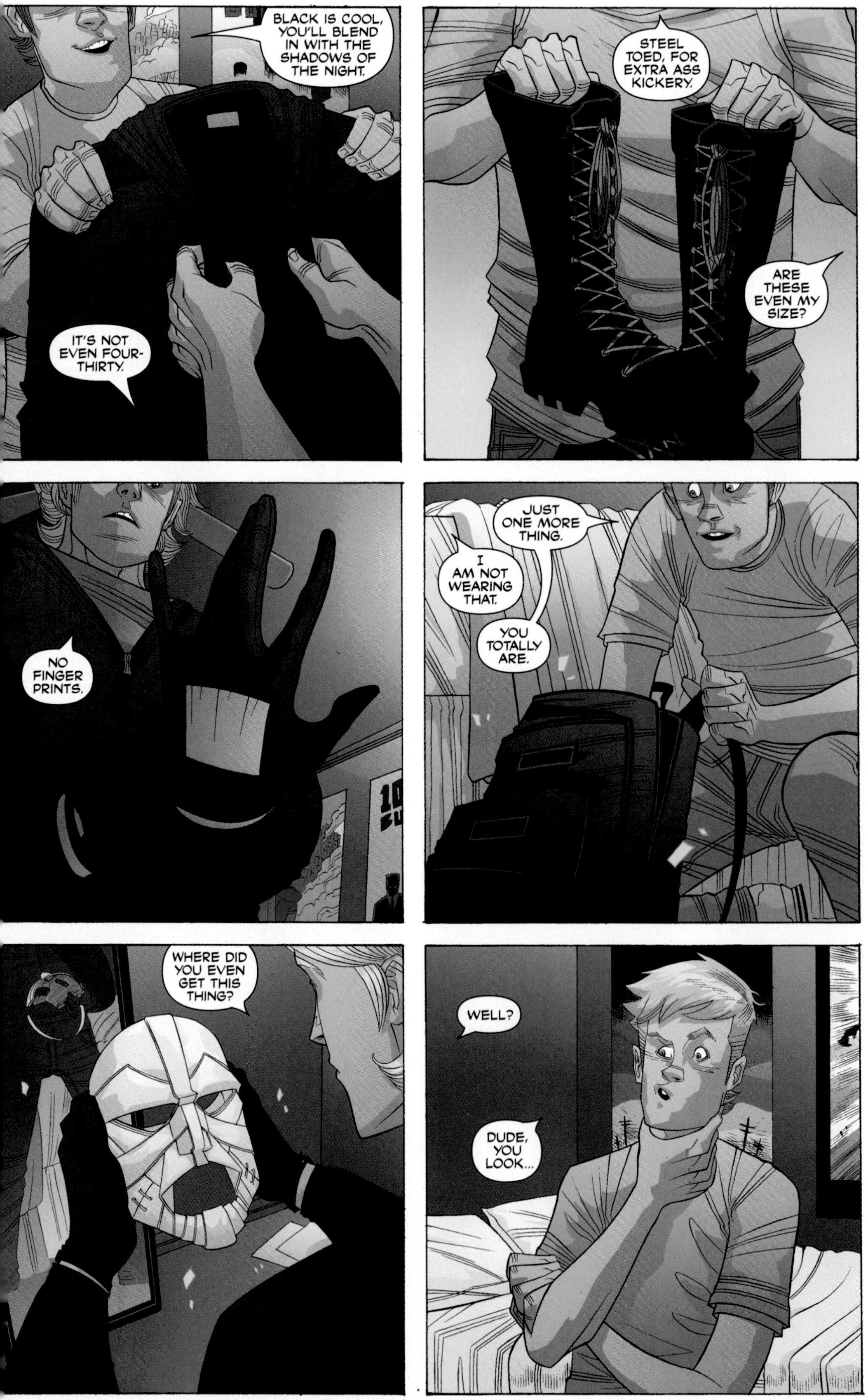
BLACK IS COOL, YOU'LL BLEND IN WITH THE SHADOWS OF THE NIGHT.
IT'S NOT EVEN FOUR-THIRTY.
STEEL TOED, FOR EXTRA ASS KICKERY.
ARE THESE EVEN MY SIZE?
NO FINGER PRINTS.
JUST ONE MORE THING.
I AM NOT WEARING THAT.
YOU TOTALLY ARE.
WHERE DID YOU EVEN GET THIS THING?
WELL?
DUDE, YOU LOOK...

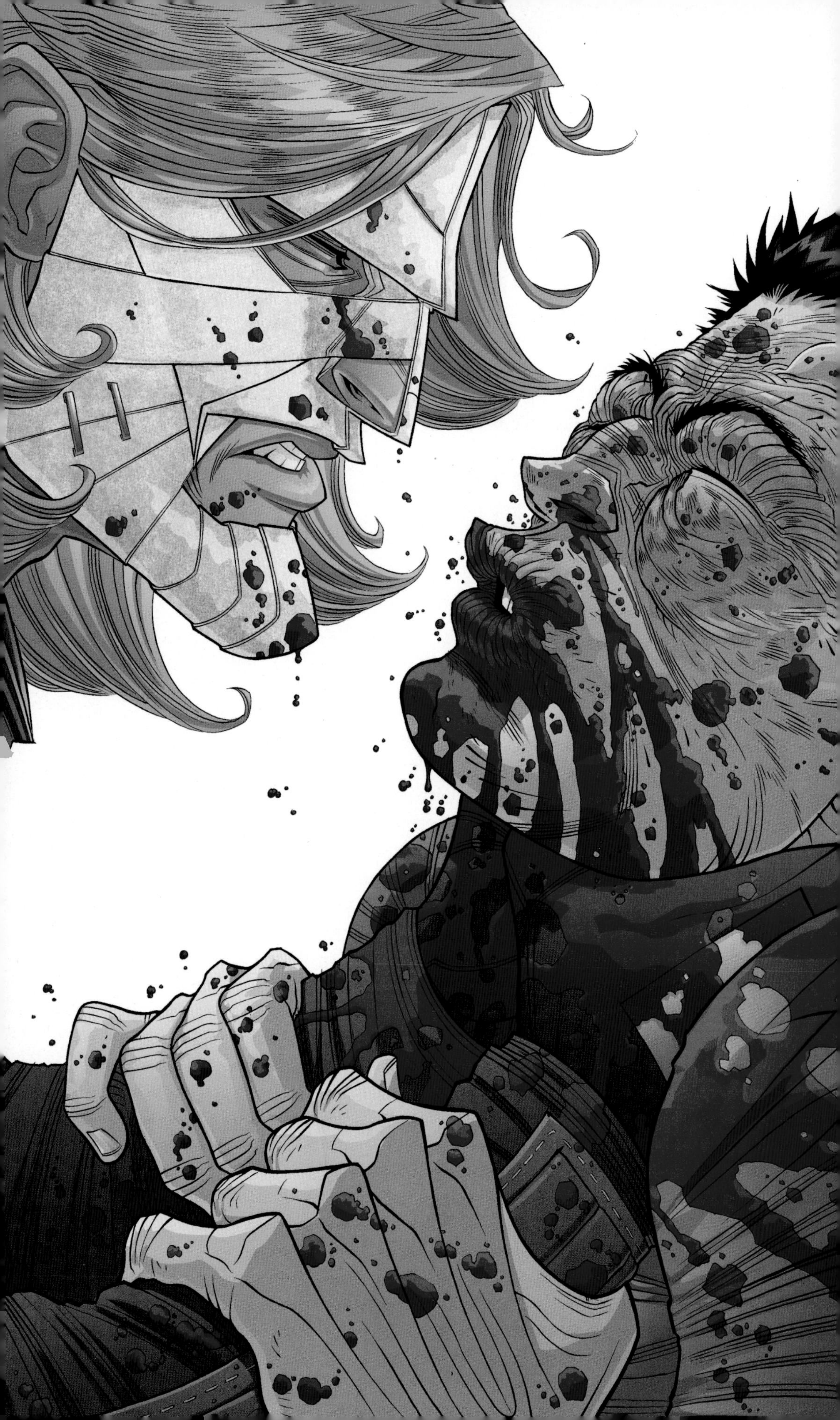

MYSTERIOUS HERO FOILS ROBBERY

by GEORGE A. CUNNINGHAM

Local shoppers are breathing a little easier after an armed robbery was stopped by an unknown man last Friday.

At approximately 5 PM on Friday, two assailants entered the Curious Duck convenience store on West Elm armed with handguns. The would be robbers demanded the contents of the cash register and threatened Mr. Glarin, the Curious Duck's owner as well as the shop's customers.

The attempted robbery was foiled by an as yet unknown third party, who distracted the robbers by throwing store items at them and then knocking them unconscious by using some unknown form of martial arts.

"It was amazing" said one of the customers, "I've never seen any move that fast. Or use beef jerky as a weapon."

This unknown hero, accompanied by a sidekick described as loud, blonde and kind of fat, fled the scene before police arrived, and his identity has yet to be determined. If any readers know who the hero of the Curious Duck is, they urged to contact the local police.

"I wish he would have stayed after stopping the robbers," Glarin said, " He didn't pay for the jerky or the milk."

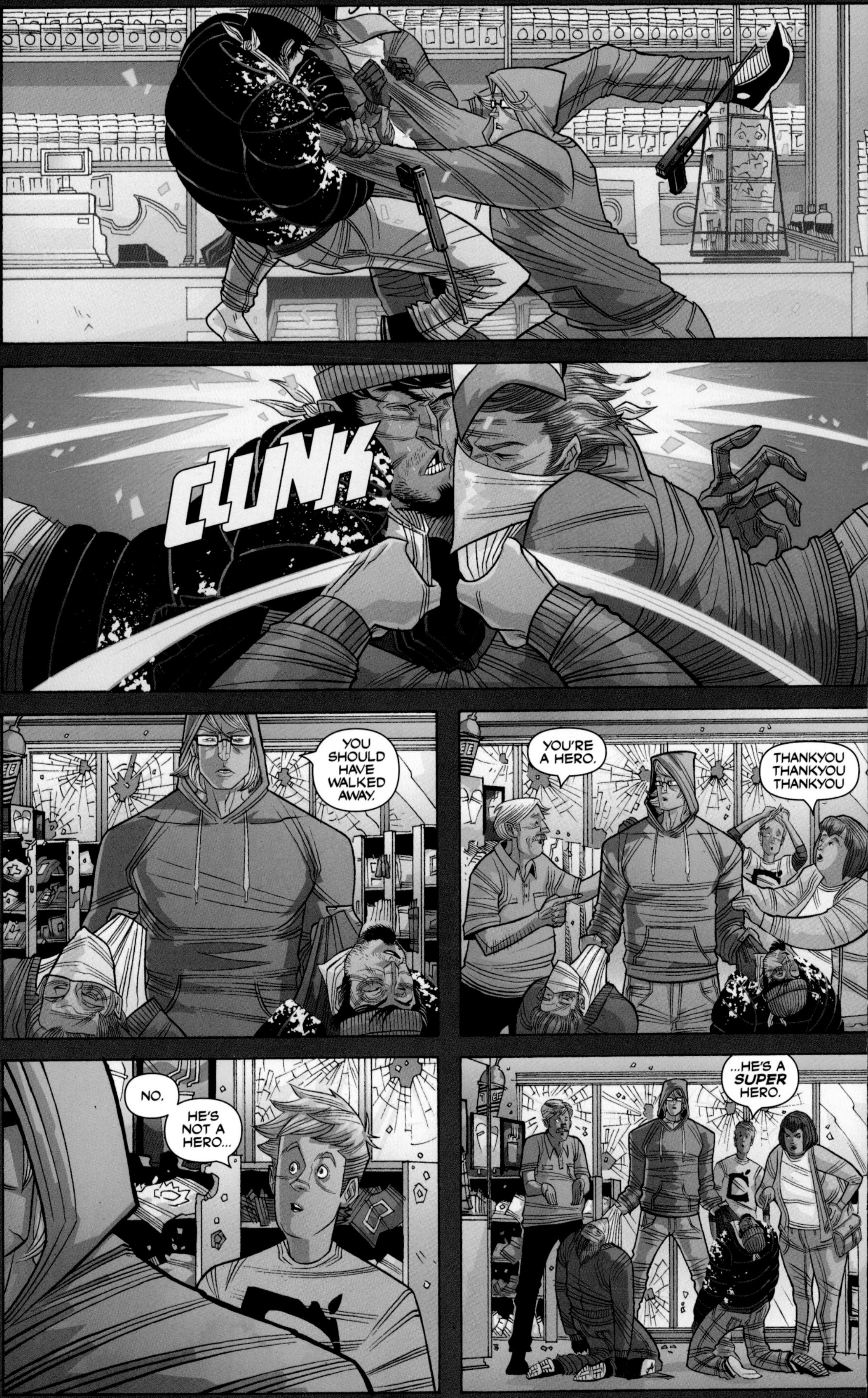
CLUNK
YOU SHOULD HAVE WALKED AWAY.
YOU'RE A HERO.
THANKYOU THANKYOU THANKYOU
NO.
HE'S NOT A HERO...
...HE'S A SUPER HERO.

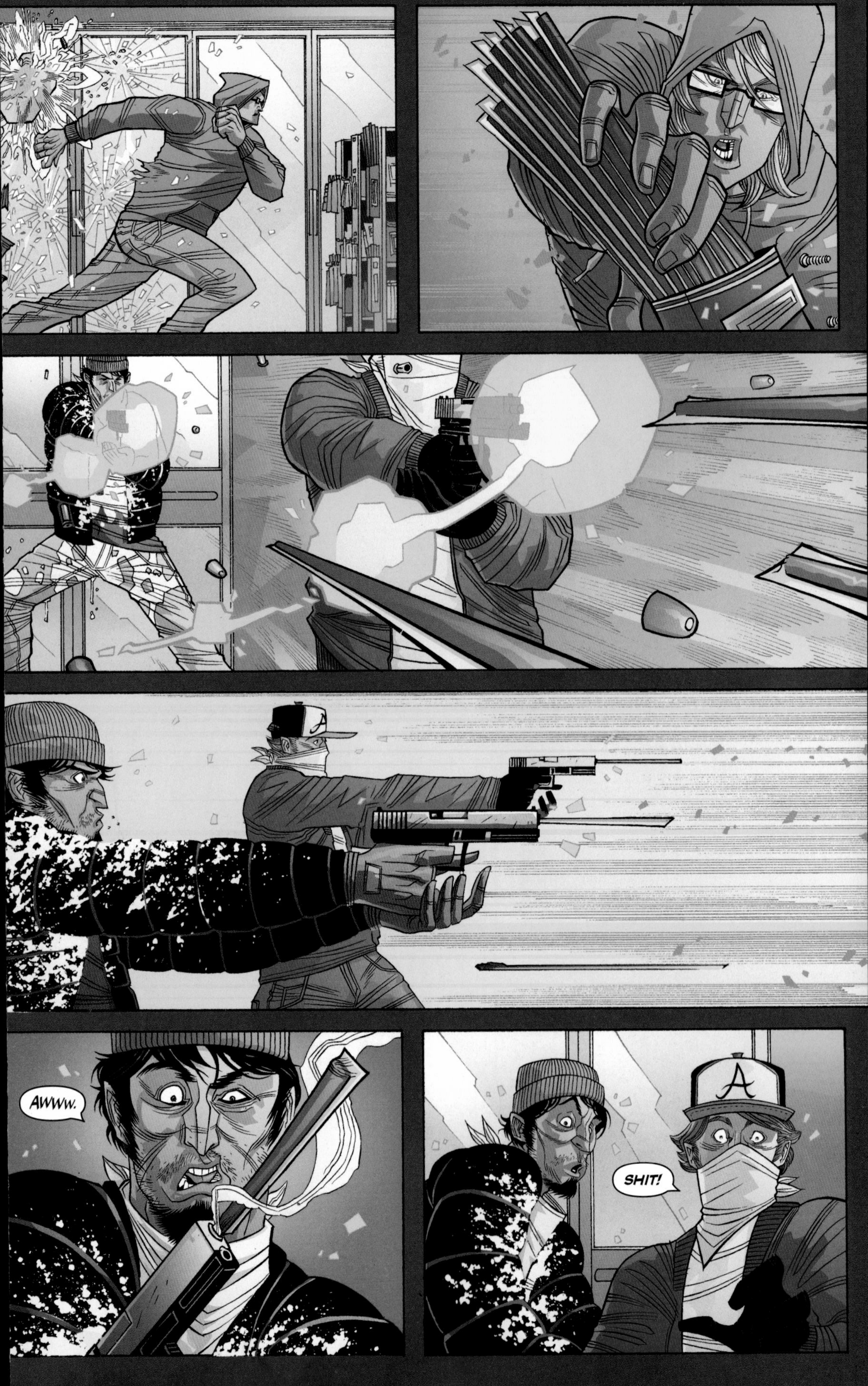
AWWW.
SHIT!

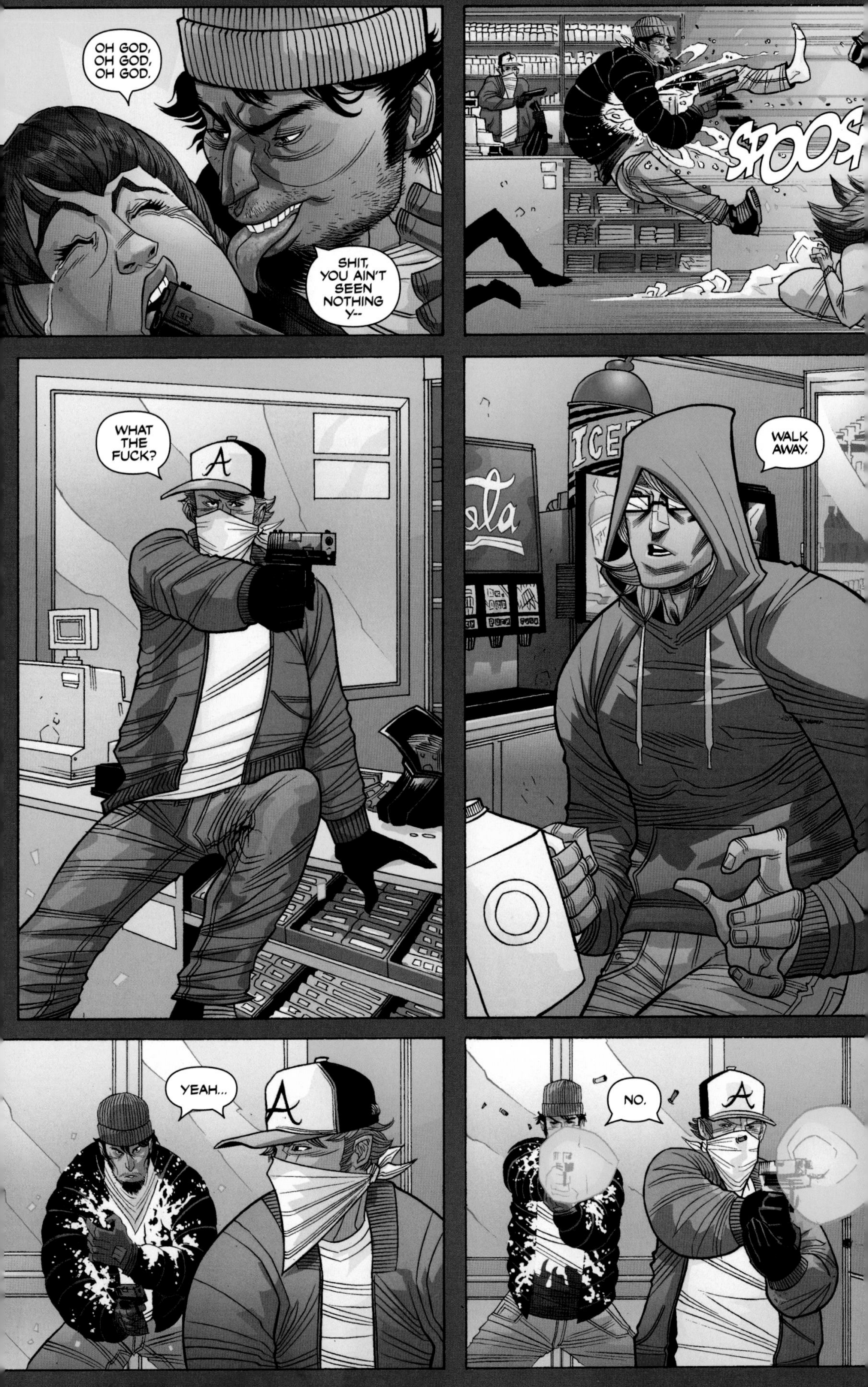
OH GOD, OH GOD, OH GOD.
SHIT, YOU AIN'T SEEN NOTHING Y--
SPOOS
WHAT THE FUCK?
WALK AWAY.
YEAH...
NO.

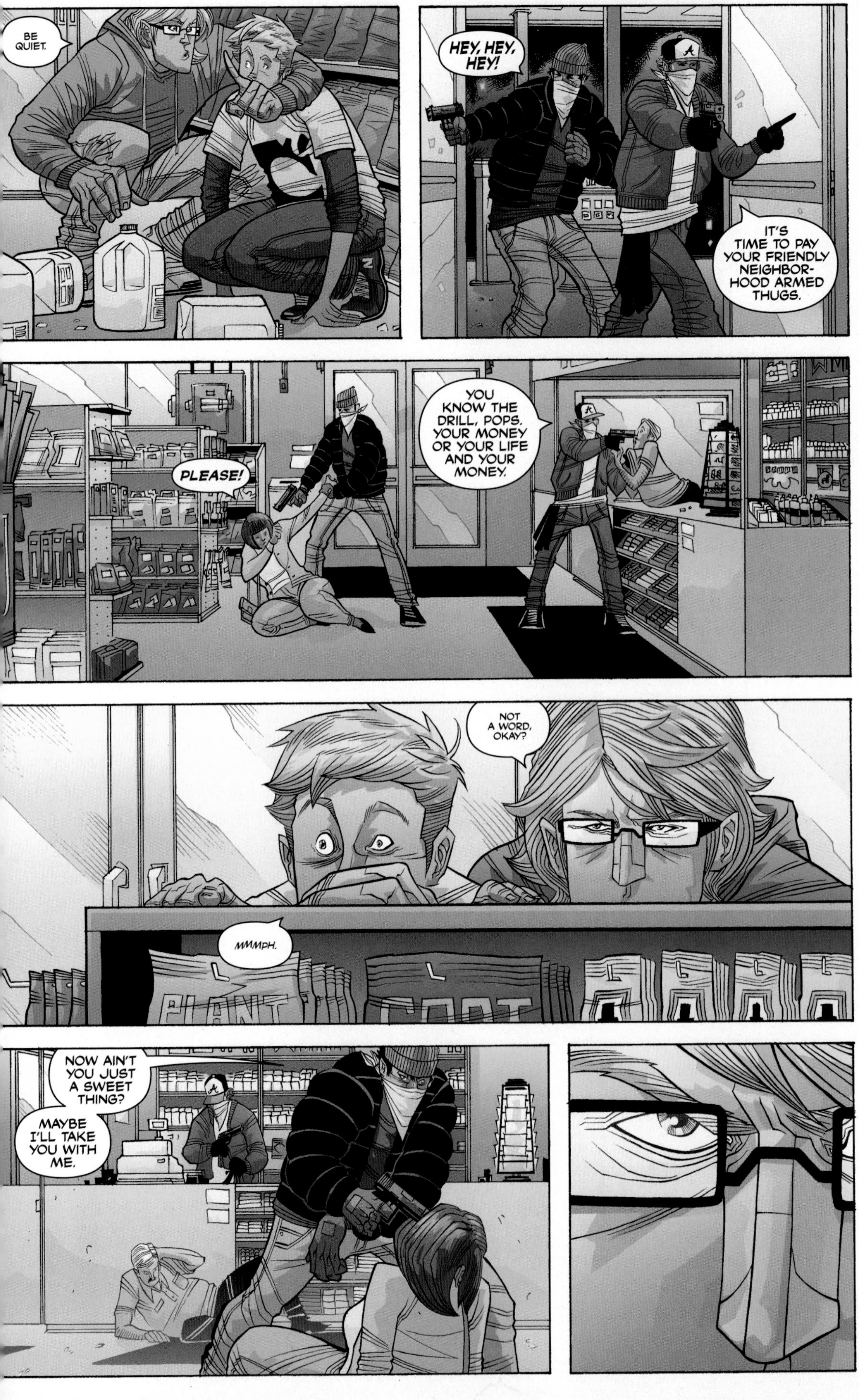
BE QUIET.
HEY, HEY, HEY!
IT'S TIME TO PAY YOUR FRIENDLY NEIGHBOR-HOOD ARMED THUGS.
PLEASE!
YOU KNOW THE DRILL, POPS. YOUR MONEY OR YOUR LIFE AND YOUR MONEY.
NOT A WORD, OKAY?
MMMPH.
NOW AIN'T YOU JUST A SWEET THING?
MAYBE I'LL TAKE YOU WITH ME.

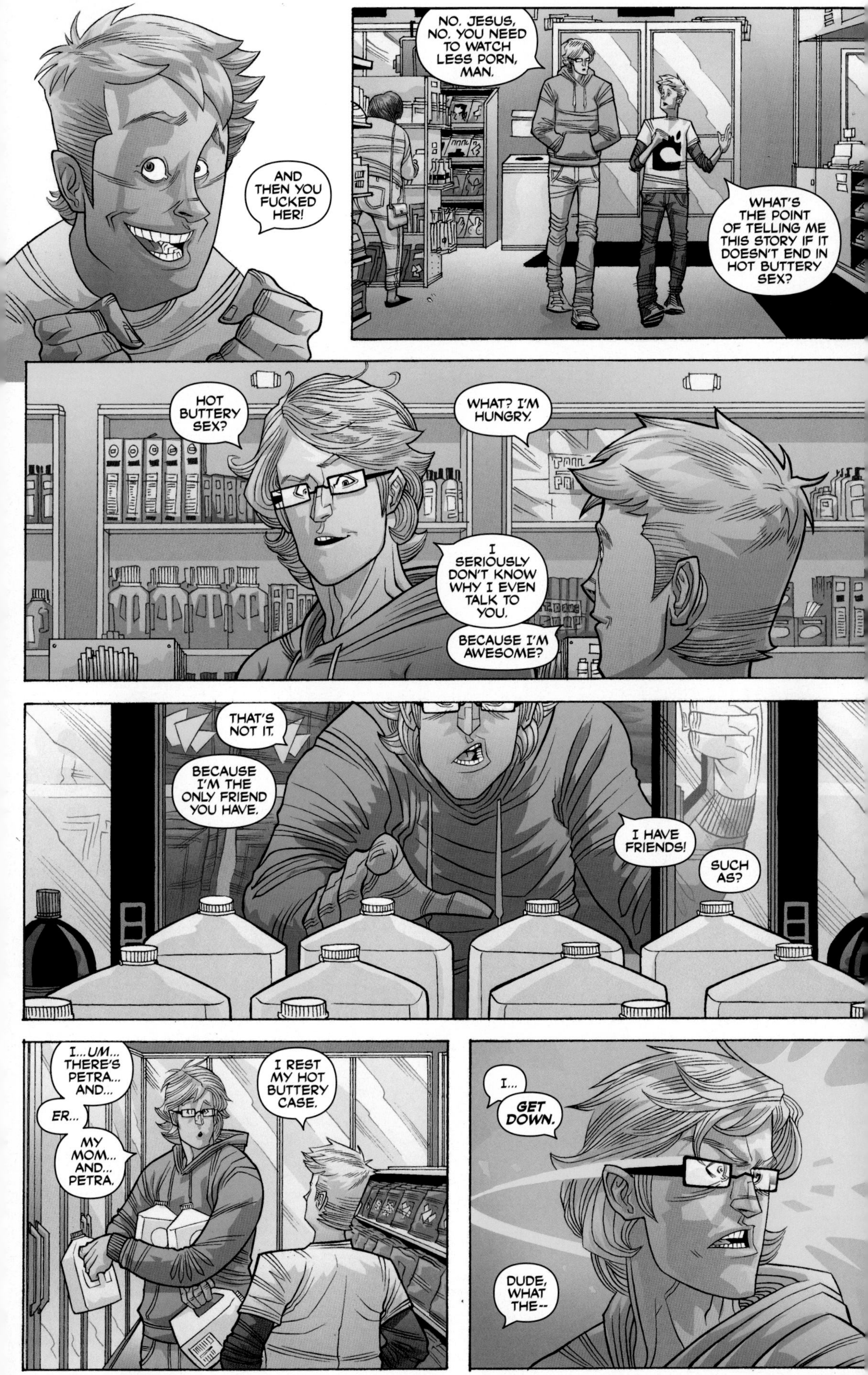
AND THEN YOU FUCKED HER!
NO. JESUS, NO. YOU NEED TO WATCH LESS PORN, MAN.
WHAT'S THE POINT OF TELLING ME THIS STORY IF IT DOESN'T END IN HOT BUTTERY SEX?
HOT BUTTERY SEX?
WHAT? I'M HUNGRY.
I SERIOUSLY DON'T KNOW WHY I EVEN TALK TO YOU.
BECAUSE I'M AWESOME?
THAT'S NOT IT.
BECAUSE I'M THE ONLY FRIEND YOU HAVE.
I HAVE FRIENDS!
SUCH AS?
I...UM... THERE'S PETRA... AND...
ER...
MY MOM... AND... PETRA.
I REST MY HOT BUTTERY CASE.
I...
GET DOWN.
DUDE, WHAT THE--

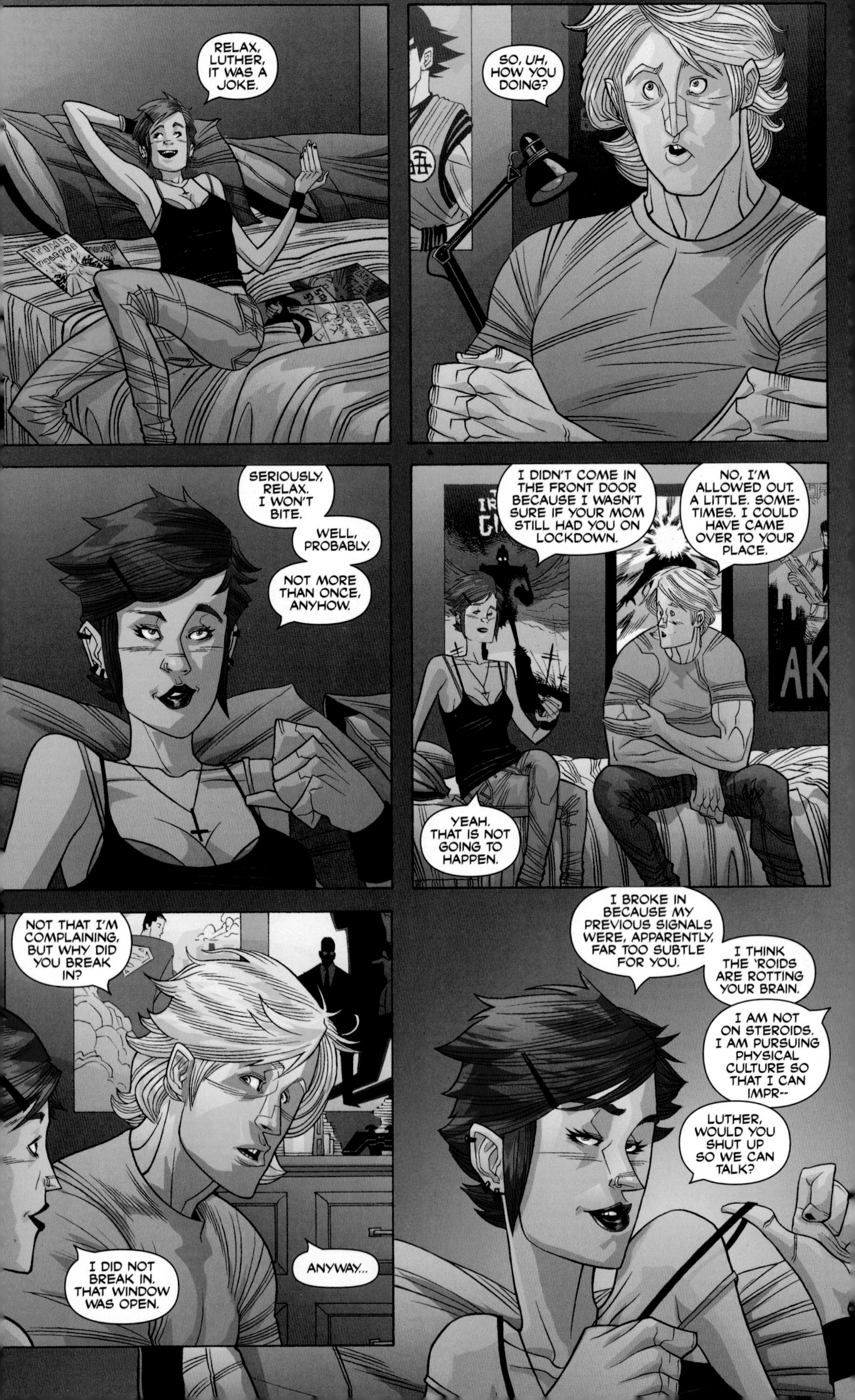
RELAX, LUTHER, IT WAS A JOKE.
SO, *UH*, HOW YOU DOING?
SERIOUSLY, RELAX. I WON'T BITE.
WELL, PROBABLY.
NOT MORE THAN ONCE, ANYHOW.
I DIDN'T COME IN THE FRONT DOOR BECAUSE I WASN'T SURE IF YOUR MOM STILL HAD YOU ON LOCKDOWN.
NO, I'M ALLOWED OUT. A LITTLE. SOME-TIMES. I COULD HAVE CAME OVER TO YOUR PLACE.
YEAH. THAT IS NOT GOING TO HAPPEN.
NOT THAT I'M COMPLAINING, BUT WHY DID YOU BREAK IN?
I DID NOT BREAK IN. THAT WINDOW WAS OPEN.
ANYWAY...
I BROKE IN BECAUSE MY PREVIOUS SIGNALS WERE, APPARENTLY, FAR TOO SUBTLE FOR YOU.
I THINK THE 'ROIDS ARE ROTTING YOUR BRAIN.
I AM NOT ON STEROIDS. I AM PURSUING PHYSICAL CULTURE SO THAT I CAN IMPR--
LUTHER, WOULD YOU SHUT UP SO WE CAN TALK?

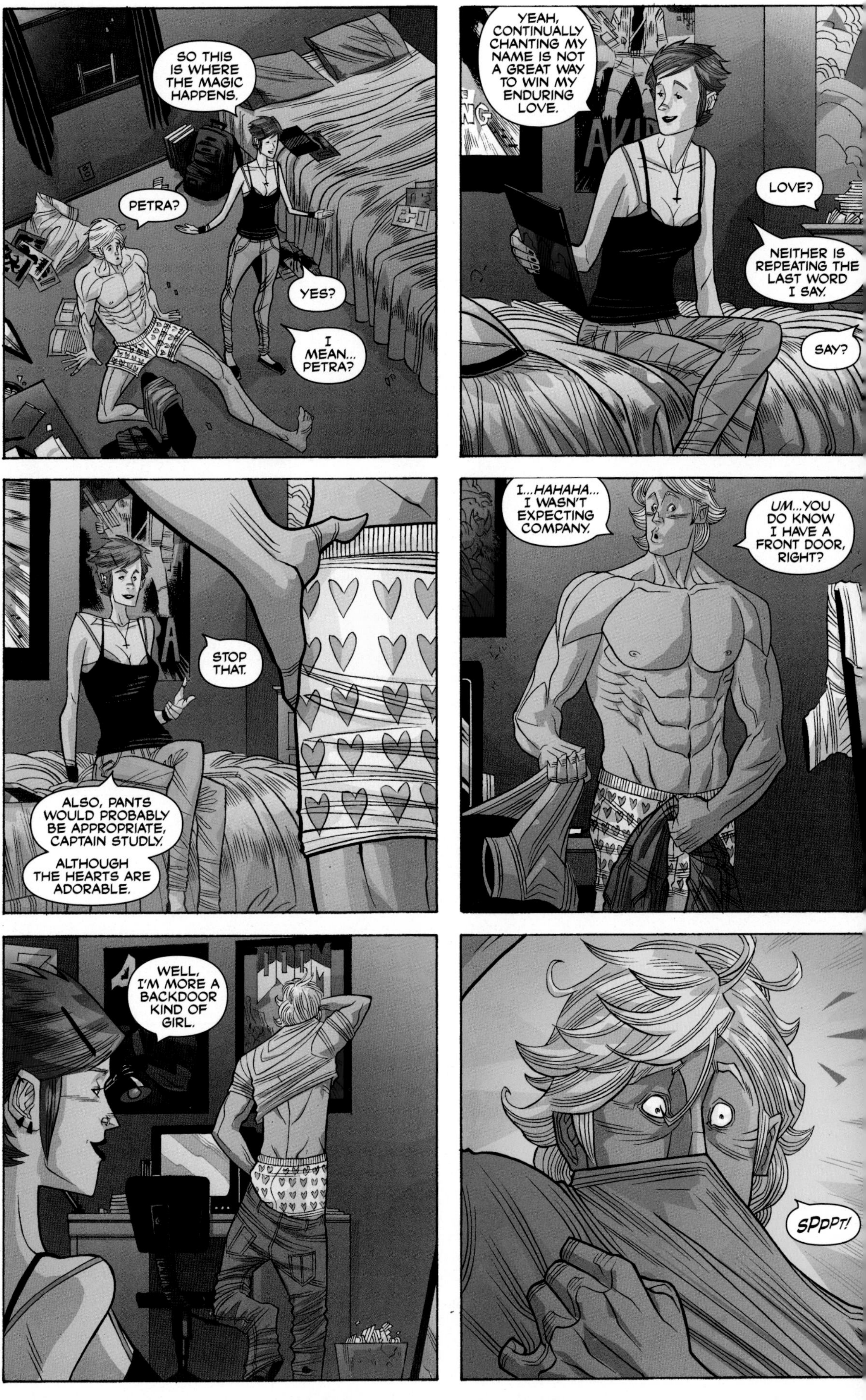

SO THIS IS WHERE THE MAGIC HAPPENS.
PETRA?
YES?
I MEAN... PETRA?
YEAH, CONTINUALLY CHANTING MY NAME IS NOT A GREAT WAY TO WIN MY ENDURING LOVE.
LOVE?
NEITHER IS REPEATING THE LAST WORD I SAY.
SAY?
STOP THAT.
ALSO, PANTS WOULD PROBABLY BE APPROPRIATE, CAPTAIN STUDLY.
ALTHOUGH THE HEARTS ARE ADORABLE.
I...HAHAHA... I WASN'T EXPECTING COMPANY.
UM...YOU DO KNOW I HAVE A FRONT DOOR, RIGHT?
WELL, I'M MORE A BACKDOOR KIND OF GIRL.
DOOM
SPPPT!

WHUMP

SO, OW.

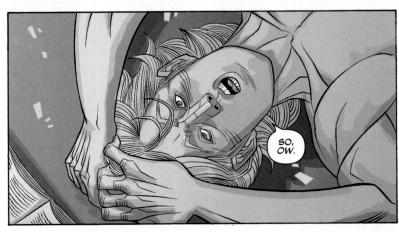

DON'T WORRY, I HAVE THAT EFFECT ON ALL THE GUYS.

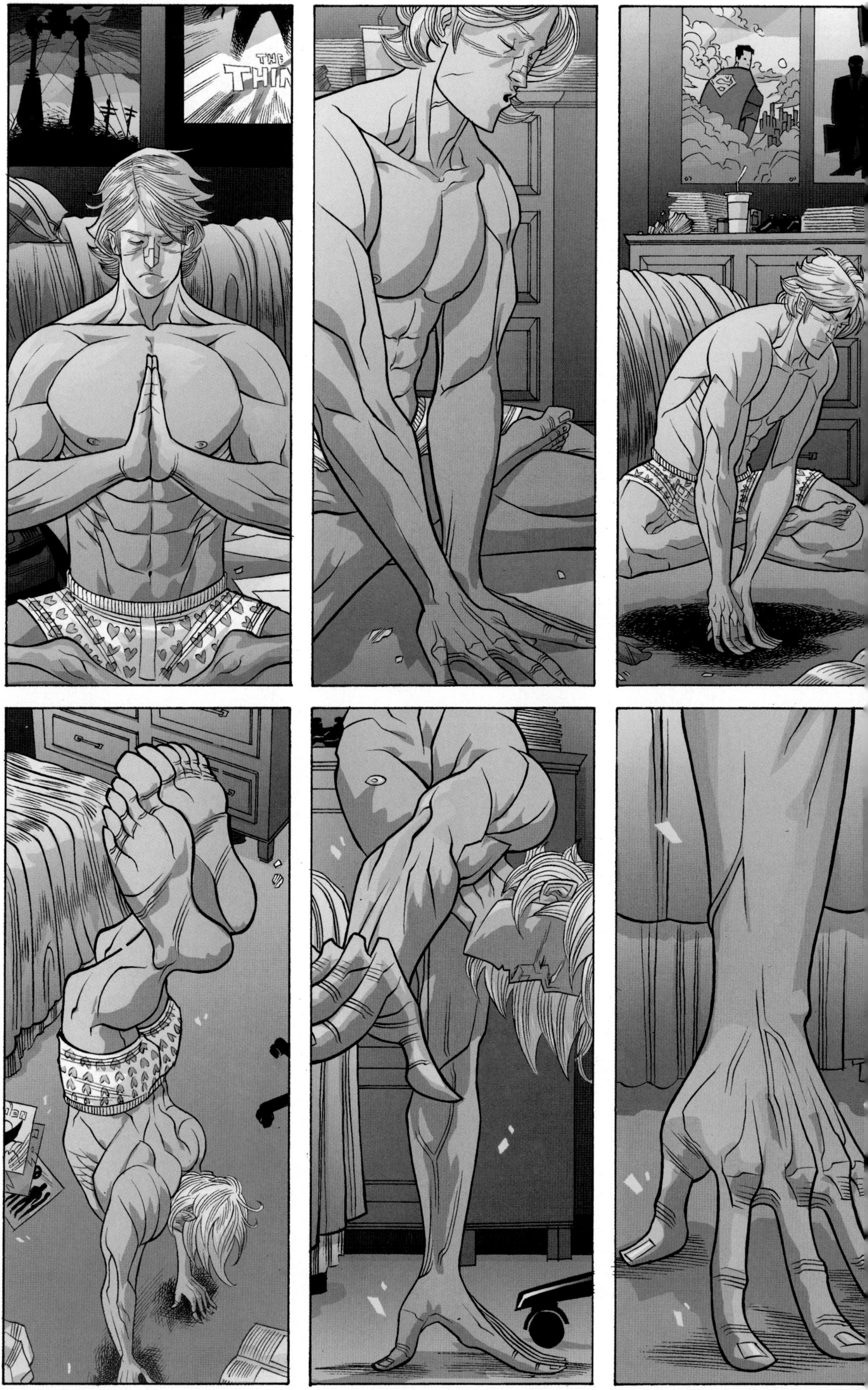
THE
THIN

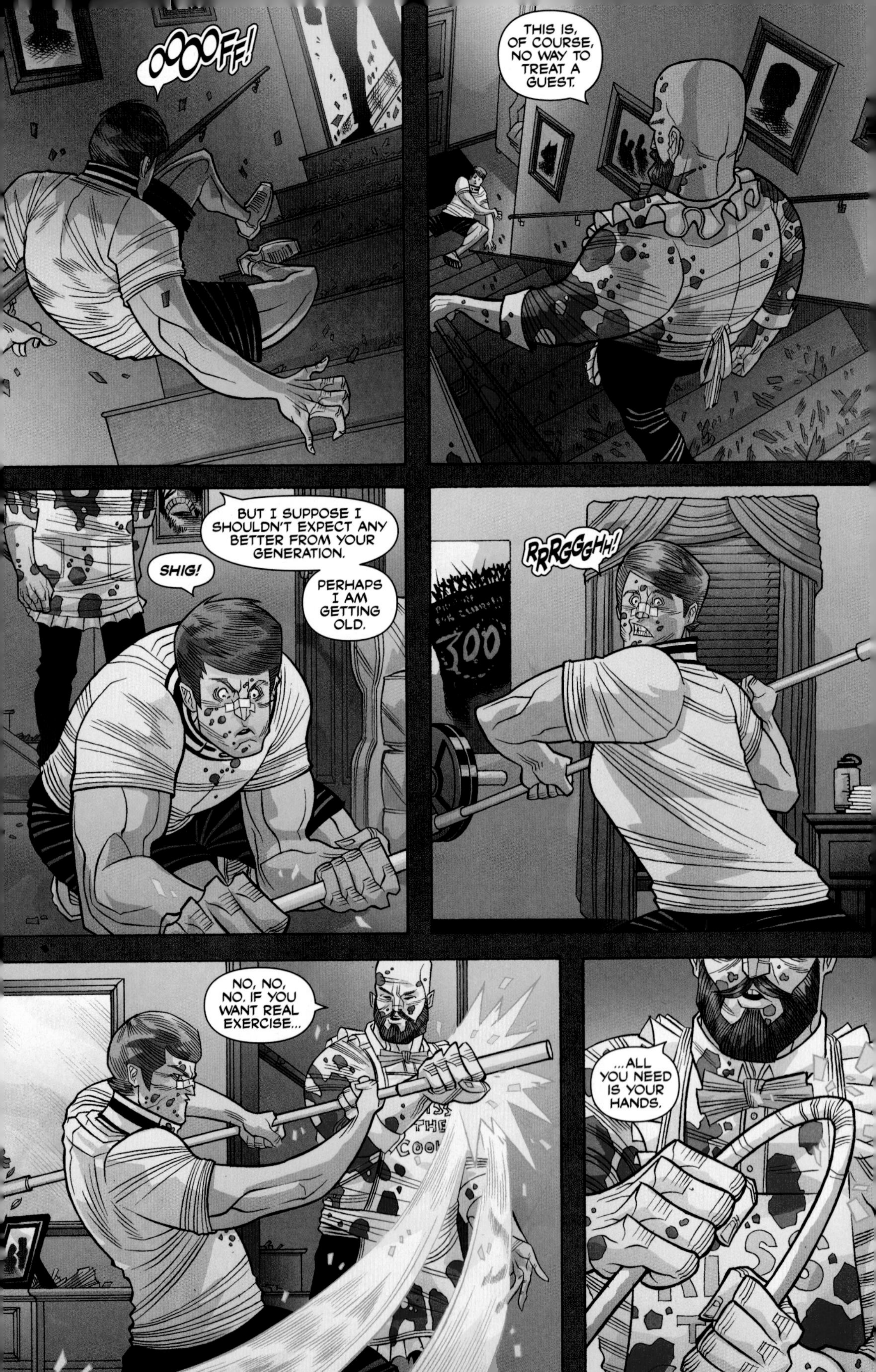
OOOOFF!
THIS IS, OF COURSE, NO WAY TO TREAT A GUEST.
BUT I SUPPOSE I SHOULDN'T EXPECT ANY BETTER FROM YOUR GENERATION.
SHIG!
PERHAPS I AM GETTING OLD.
RRRGGGHH!
300
NO, NO, NO, IF YOU WANT REAL EXERCISE...
...ALL YOU NEED IS YOUR HANDS.

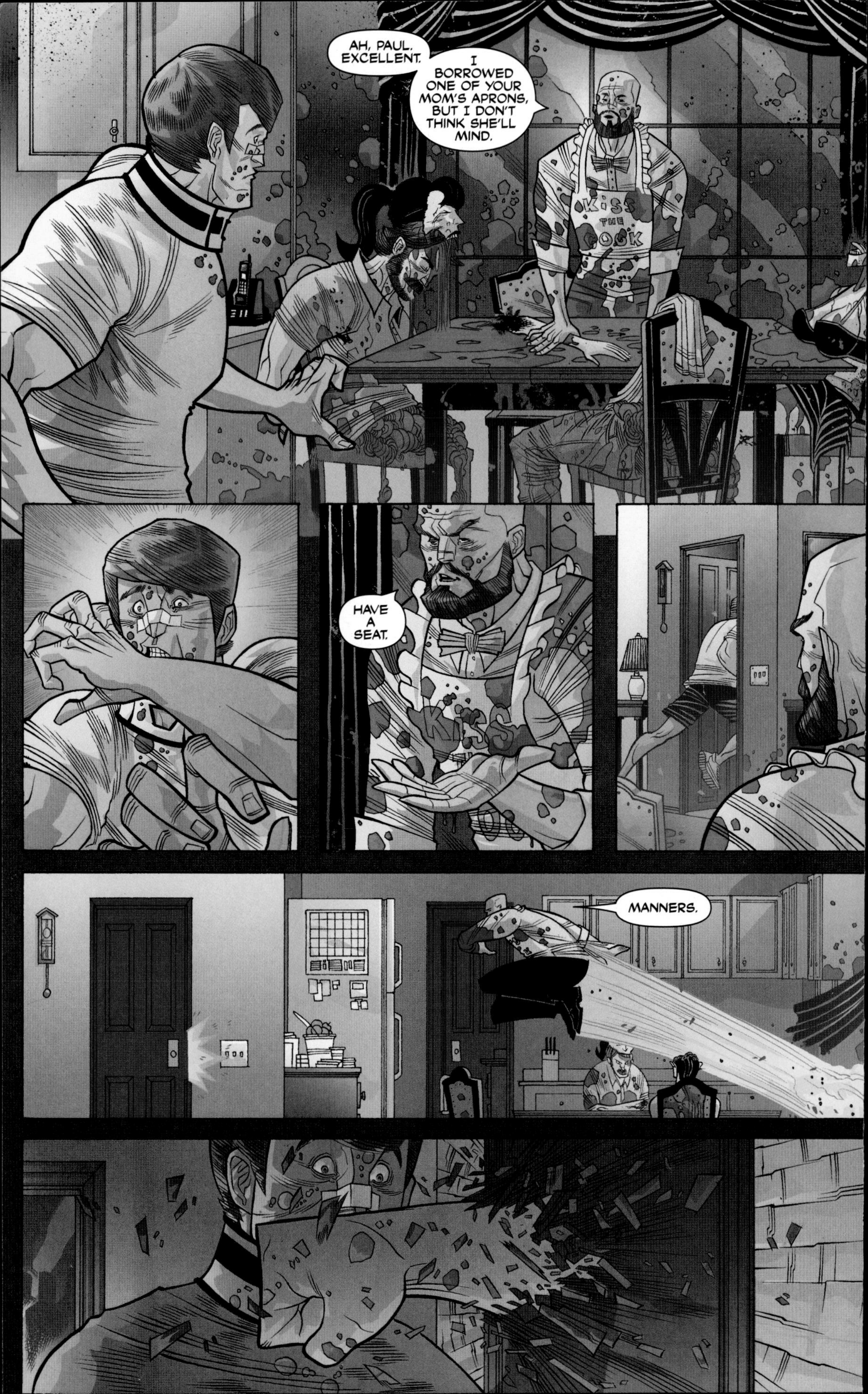
AH, PAUL, EXCELLENT.
I BORROWED ONE OF YOUR MOM'S APRONS, BUT I DON'T THINK SHE'LL MIND.
KISS THE COOK
HAVE A SEAT.
MANNERS.

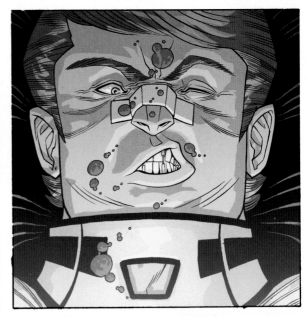

MUGGERFUGGER!

WUG?

MUG?! DUG?!

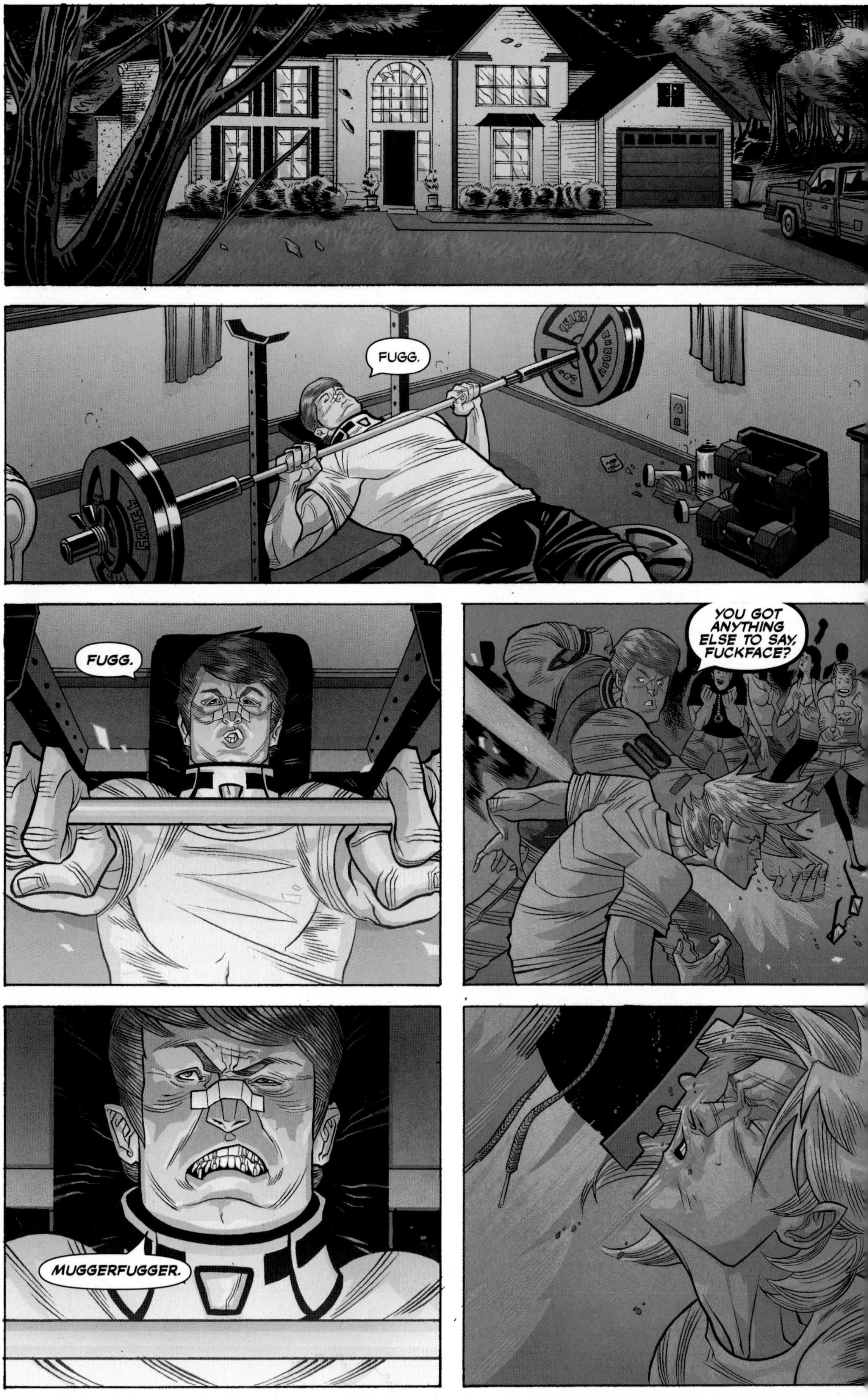
FUGG.
FUGG.
YOU GOT ANYTHING ELSE TO SAY, FUCKFACE?
MUGGERFUGGER.

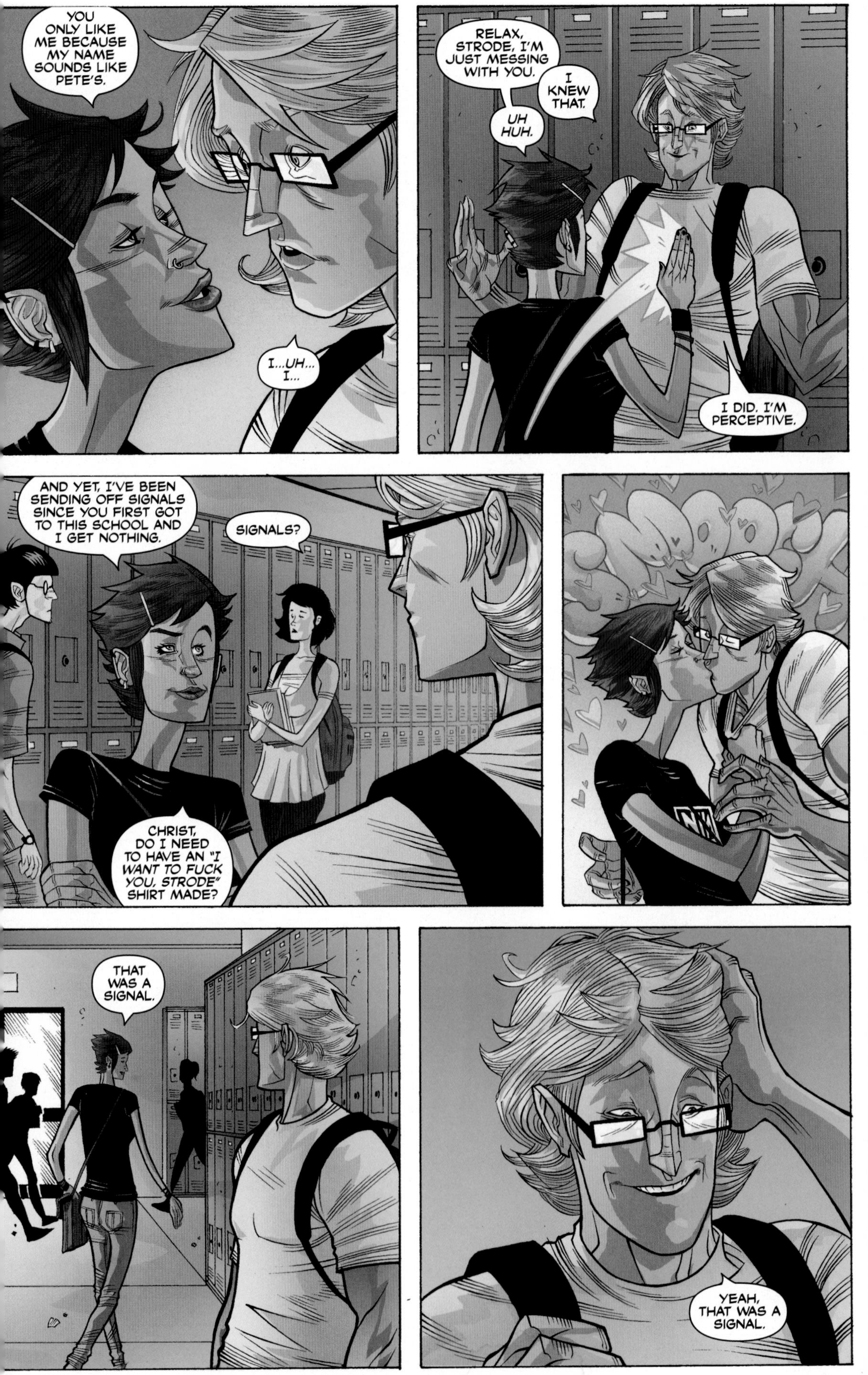
YOU ONLY LIKE ME BECAUSE MY NAME SOUNDS LIKE PETE'S.
I...UH... I...
RELAX, STRODE, I'M JUST MESSING WITH YOU.
I KNEW THAT.
UH HUH.
I DID. I'M PERCEPTIVE.
AND YET, I'VE BEEN SENDING OFF SIGNALS SINCE YOU FIRST GOT TO THIS SCHOOL AND I GET NOTHING.
SIGNALS?
CHRIST, DO I NEED TO HAVE AN "I WANT TO FUCK YOU, STRODE" SHIRT MADE?
THAT WAS A SIGNAL.
YEAH, THAT WAS A SIGNAL.

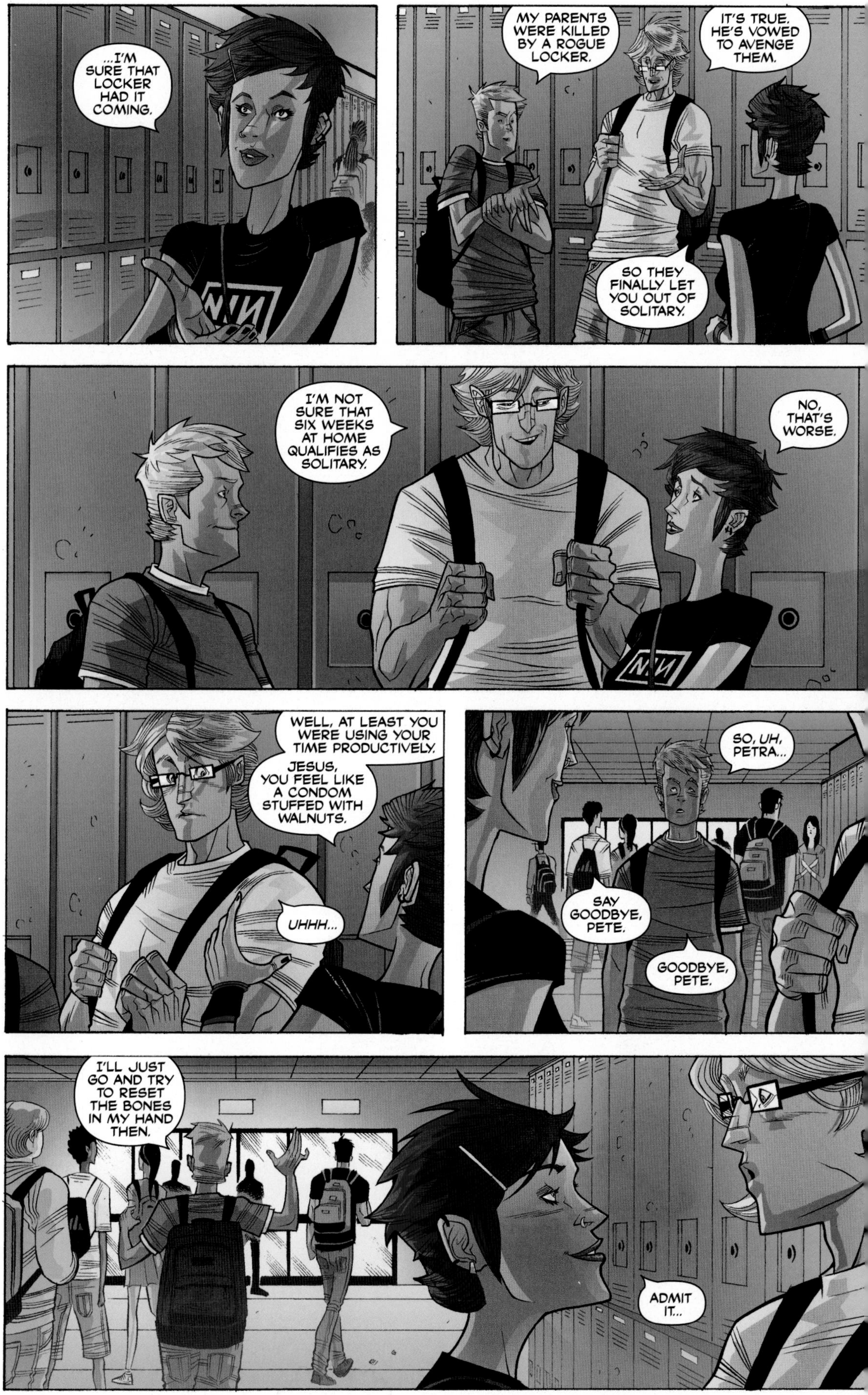
...I'M SURE THAT LOCKER HAD IT COMING.
MY PARENTS WERE KILLED BY A ROGUE LOCKER.
IT'S TRUE. HE'S VOWED TO AVENGE THEM.
SO THEY FINALLY LET YOU OUT OF SOLITARY.
I'M NOT SURE THAT SIX WEEKS AT HOME QUALIFIES AS SOLITARY.
NO, THAT'S WORSE.
WELL, AT LEAST YOU WERE USING YOUR TIME PRODUCTIVELY.
JESUS, YOU FEEL LIKE A CONDOM STUFFED WITH WALNUTS.
UHHH...
SO, UH, PETRA...
SAY GOODBYE, PETE.
GOODBYE, PETE.
I'LL JUST GO AND TRY TO RESET THE BONES IN MY HAND THEN.
ADMIT IT...

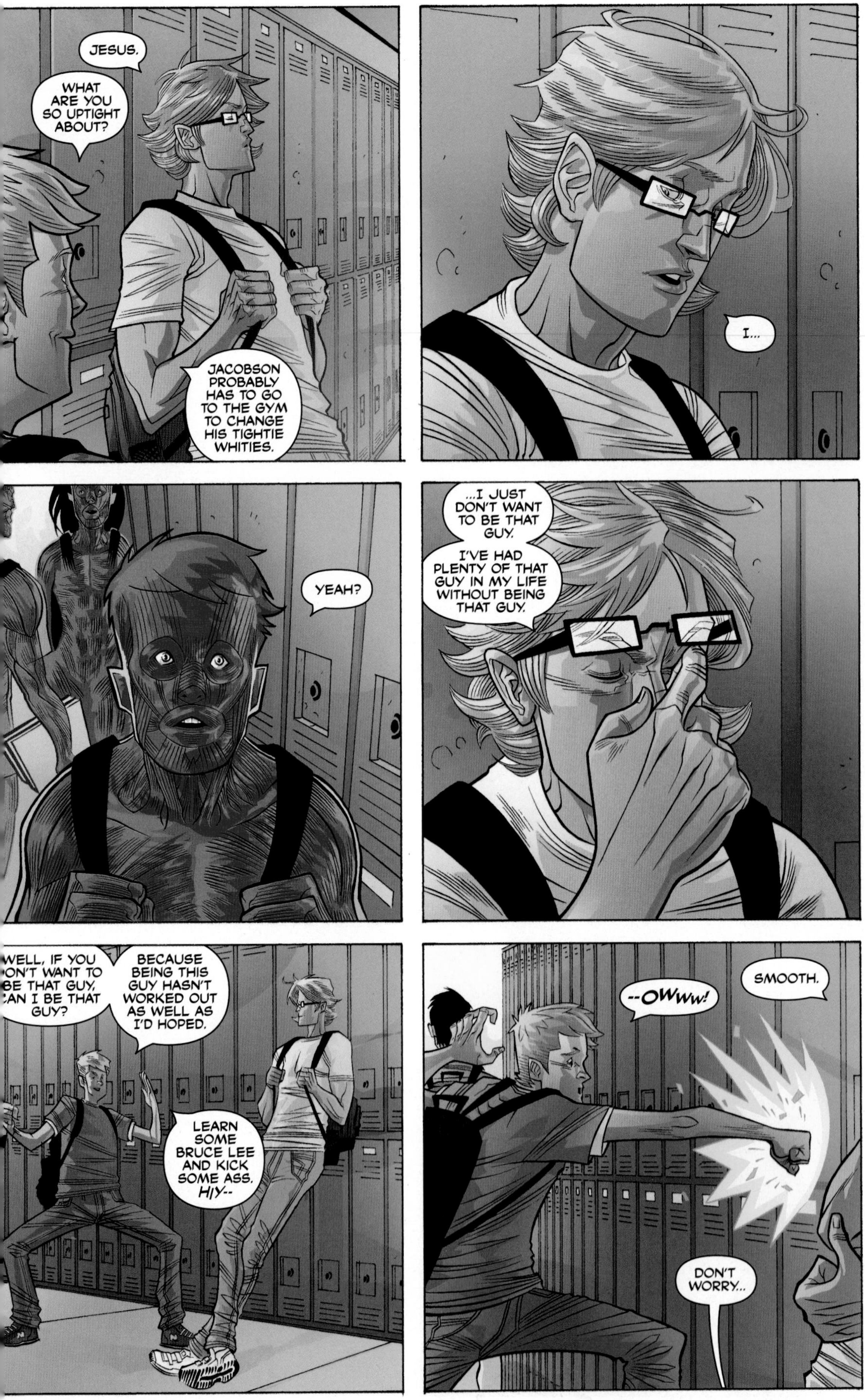
JESUS.
WHAT ARE YOU SO UPTIGHT ABOUT?
JACOBSON PROBABLY HAS TO GO TO THE GYM TO CHANGE HIS TIGHTIE WHITIES.
I...
YEAH?
...I JUST DON'T WANT TO BE THAT GUY.
I'VE HAD PLENTY OF THAT GUY IN MY LIFE WITHOUT BEING THAT GUY.
WELL, IF YOU DON'T WANT TO BE THAT GUY, CAN I BE THAT GUY?
BECAUSE BEING THIS GUY HASN'T WORKED OUT AS WELL AS I'D HOPED.
LEARN SOME BRUCE LEE AND KICK SOME ASS. HIY--
--OWWW!
SMOOTH.
DON'T WORRY...

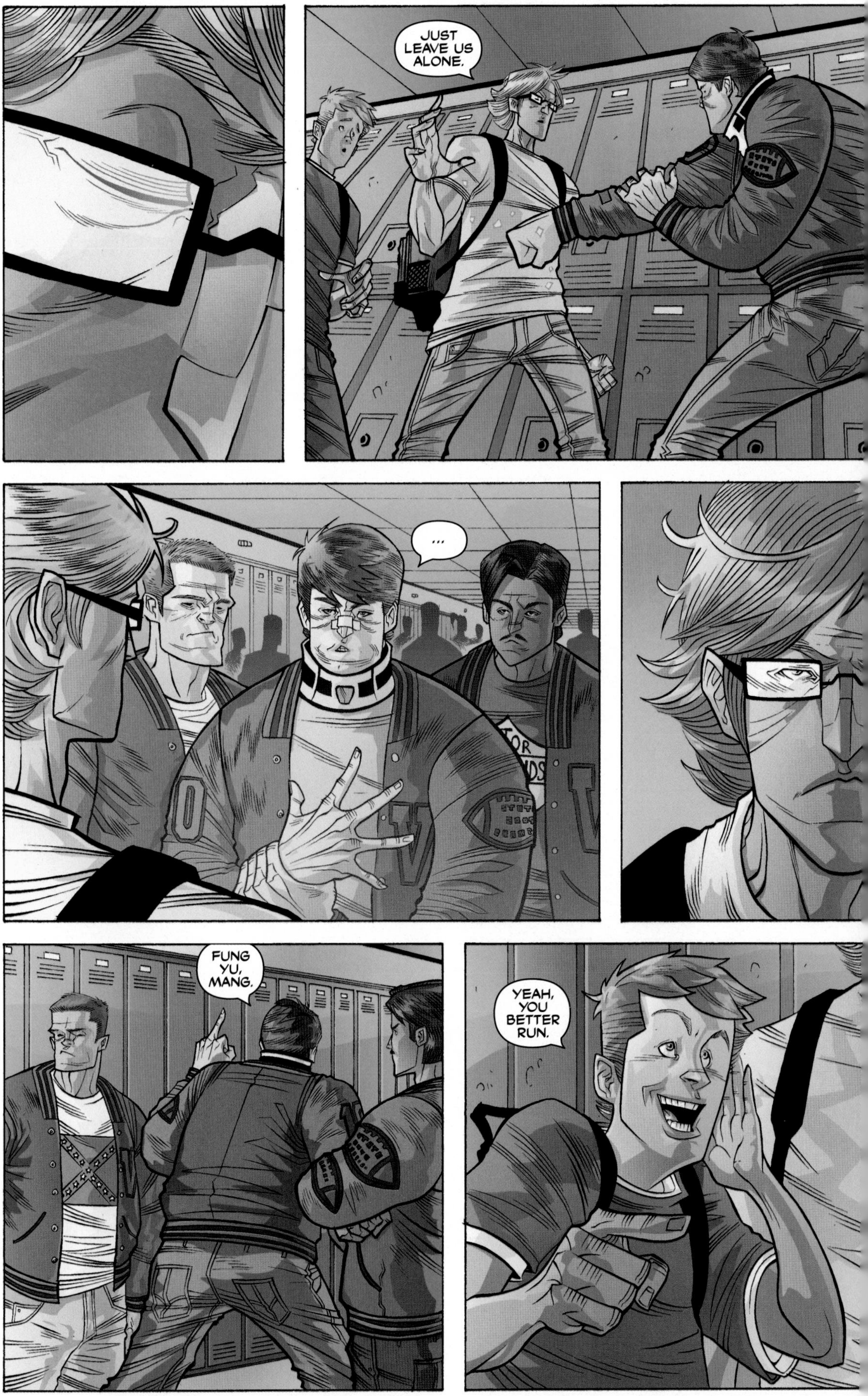
JUST LEAVE US ALONE.
...
FUNG YU, MANG.
YEAH, YOU BETTER RUN.

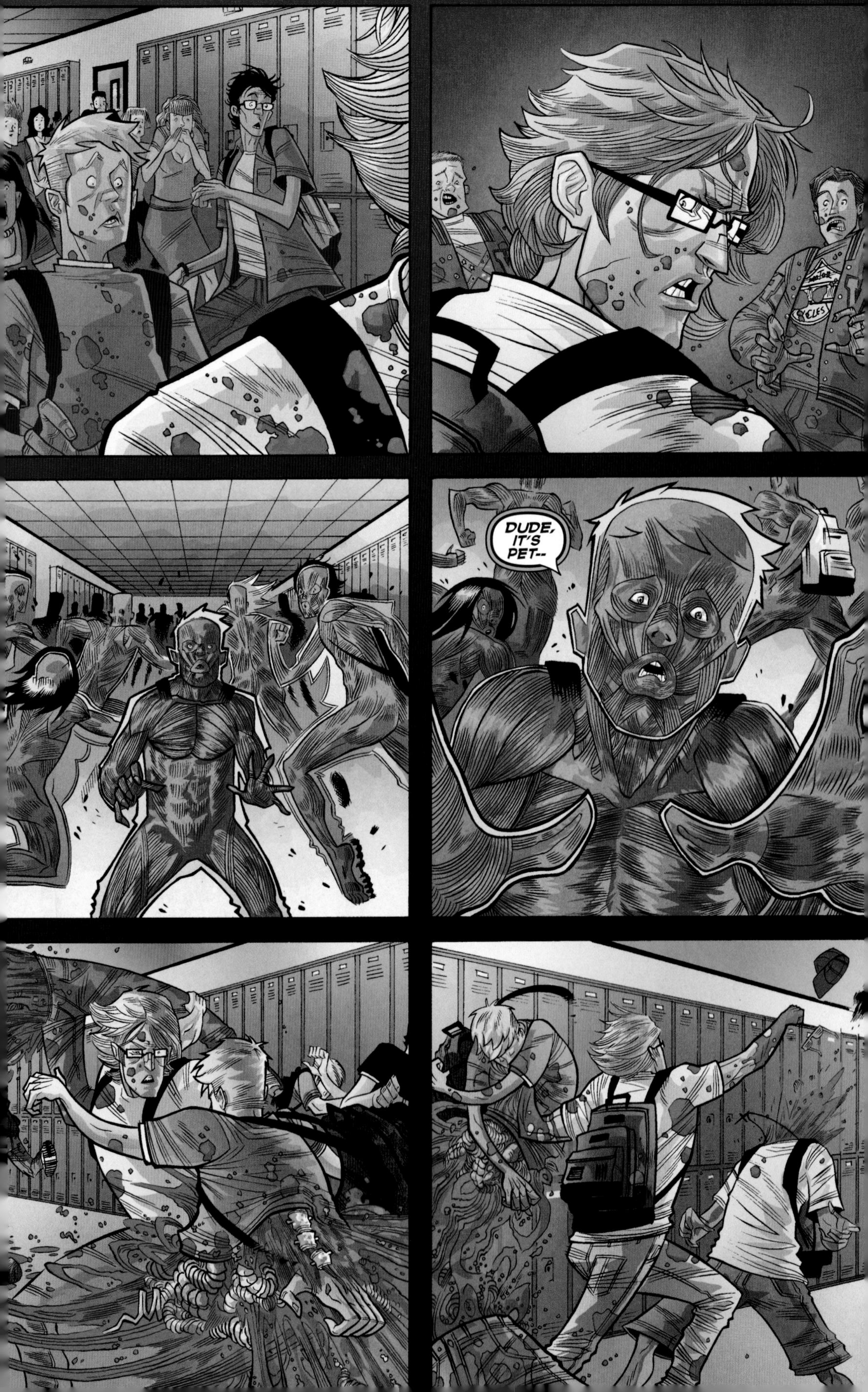
DUDE, IT'S PET--

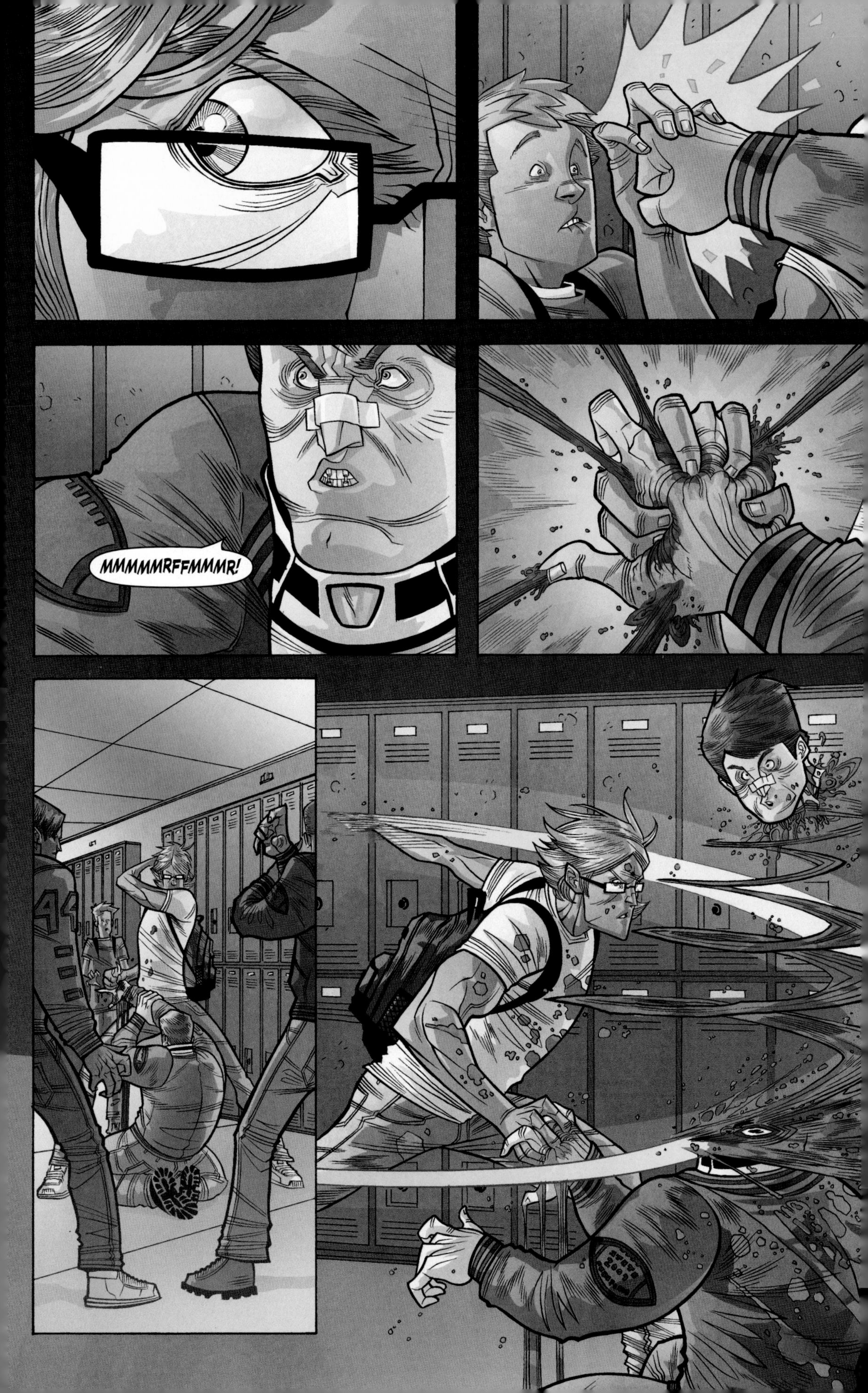
MMMMMRFFMMMR!

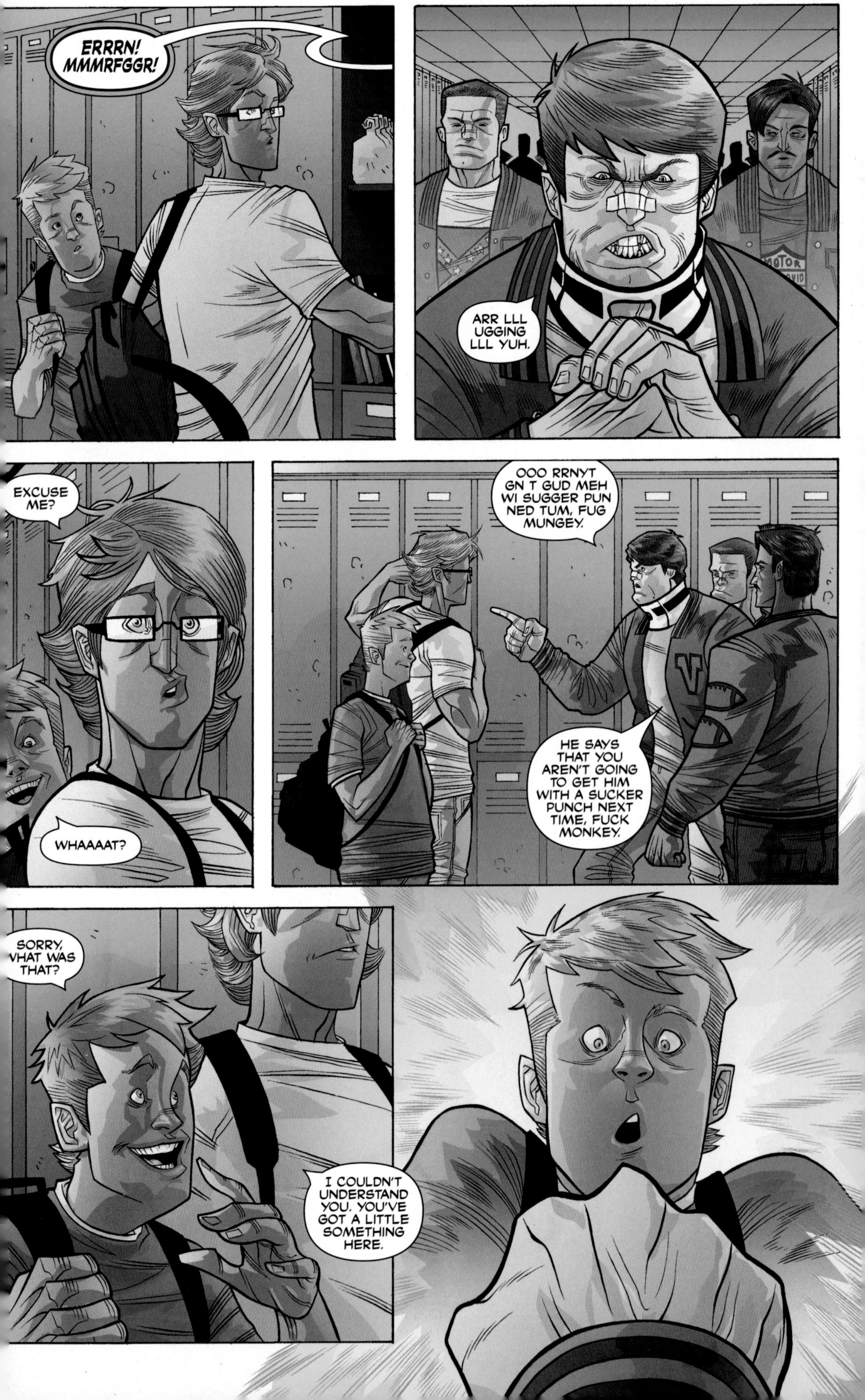
ERRRN! MMMRFGGR!
ARR LLL UGGING LLL YUH.
EXCUSE ME?
WHAAAAT?
OOO RRNYT GN T GUD MEH WI SUGGER PUN NED TUM, FUG MUNGEY.
HE SAYS THAT YOU AREN'T GOING TO GET HIM WITH A SUCKER PUNCH NEXT TIME, FUCK MONKEY.
SORRY, WHAT WAS THAT?
I COULDN'T UNDERSTAND YOU. YOU'VE GOT A LITTLE SOMETHING HERE.

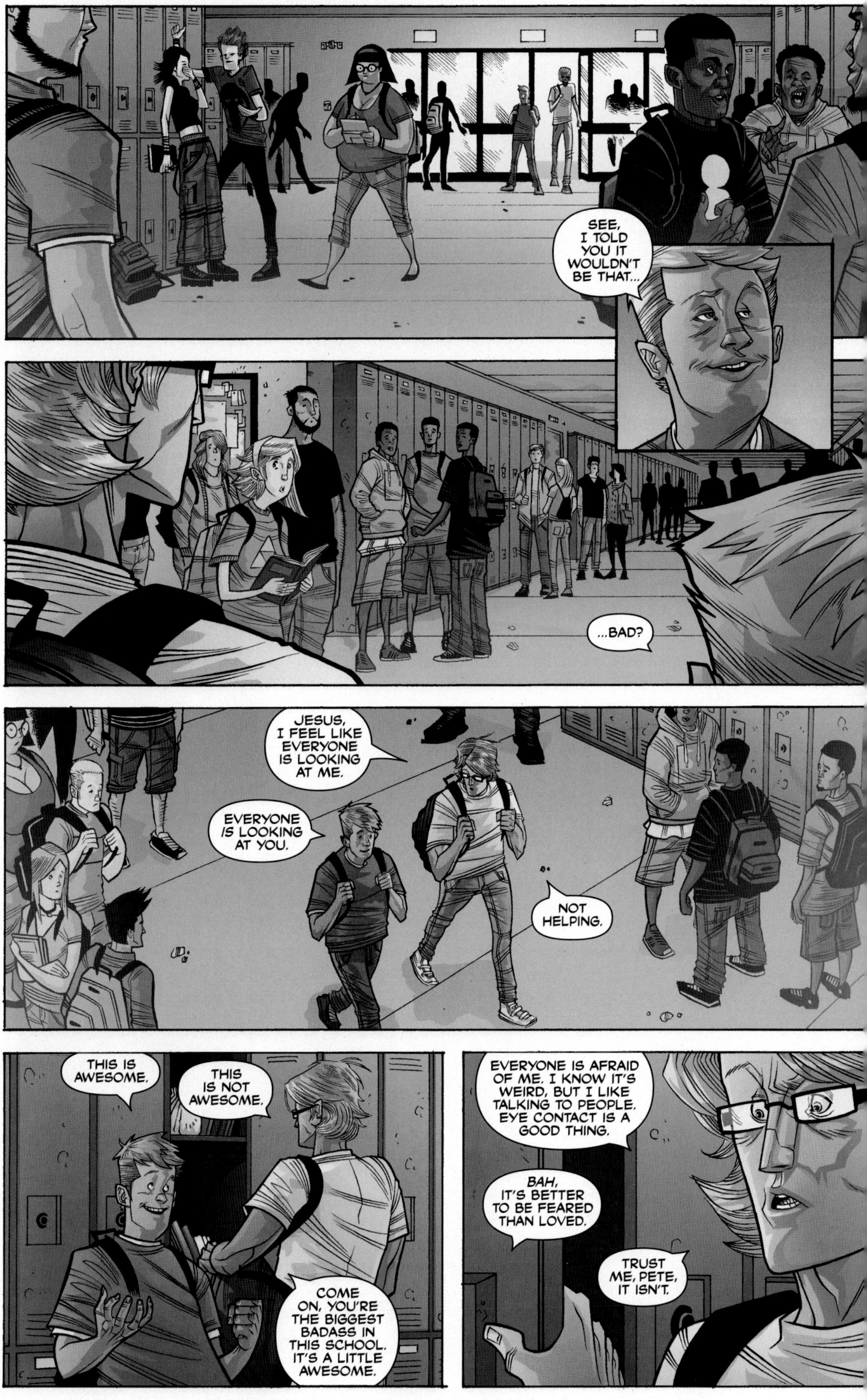
SEE, I TOLD YOU IT WOULDN'T BE THAT...
...BAD?
JESUS, I FEEL LIKE EVERYONE IS LOOKING AT ME.
EVERYONE IS LOOKING AT YOU.
NOT HELPING.
THIS IS AWESOME.
THIS IS NOT AWESOME.
COME ON, YOU'RE THE BIGGEST BADASS IN THIS SCHOOL. IT'S A LITTLE AWESOME.
EVERYONE IS AFRAID OF ME. I KNOW IT'S WEIRD, BUT I LIKE TALKING TO PEOPLE. EYE CONTACT IS A GOOD THING.
BAH, IT'S BETTER TO BE FEARED THAN LOVED.
TRUST ME, PETE, IT ISN'T.

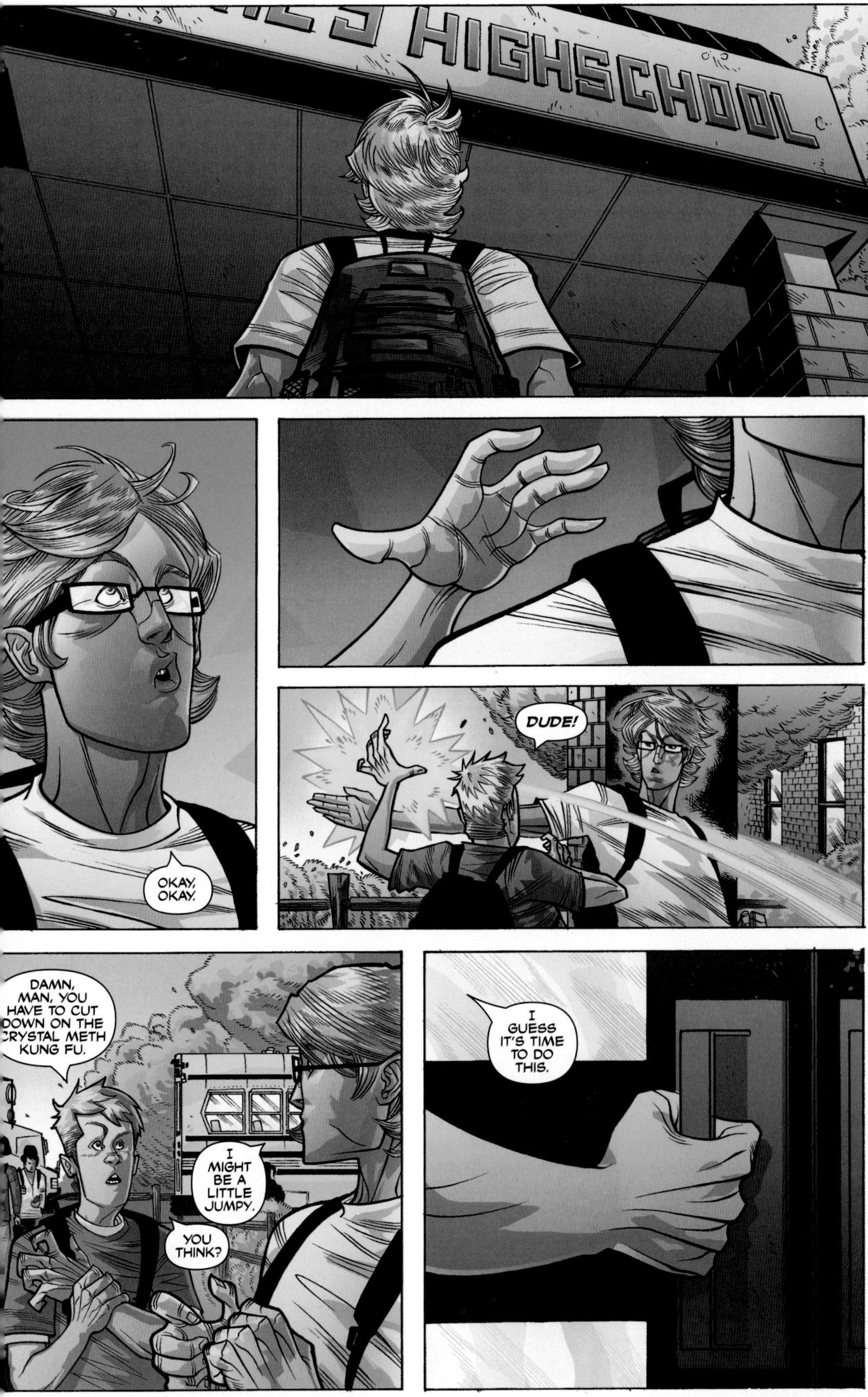

HIGHSCHOOL
OKAY, OKAY.
DUDE!
DAMN, MAN, YOU HAVE TO CUT DOWN ON THE CRYSTAL METH KUNG FU.
I MIGHT BE A LITTLE JUMPY.
YOU THINK?
I GUESS IT'S TIME TO DO THIS.

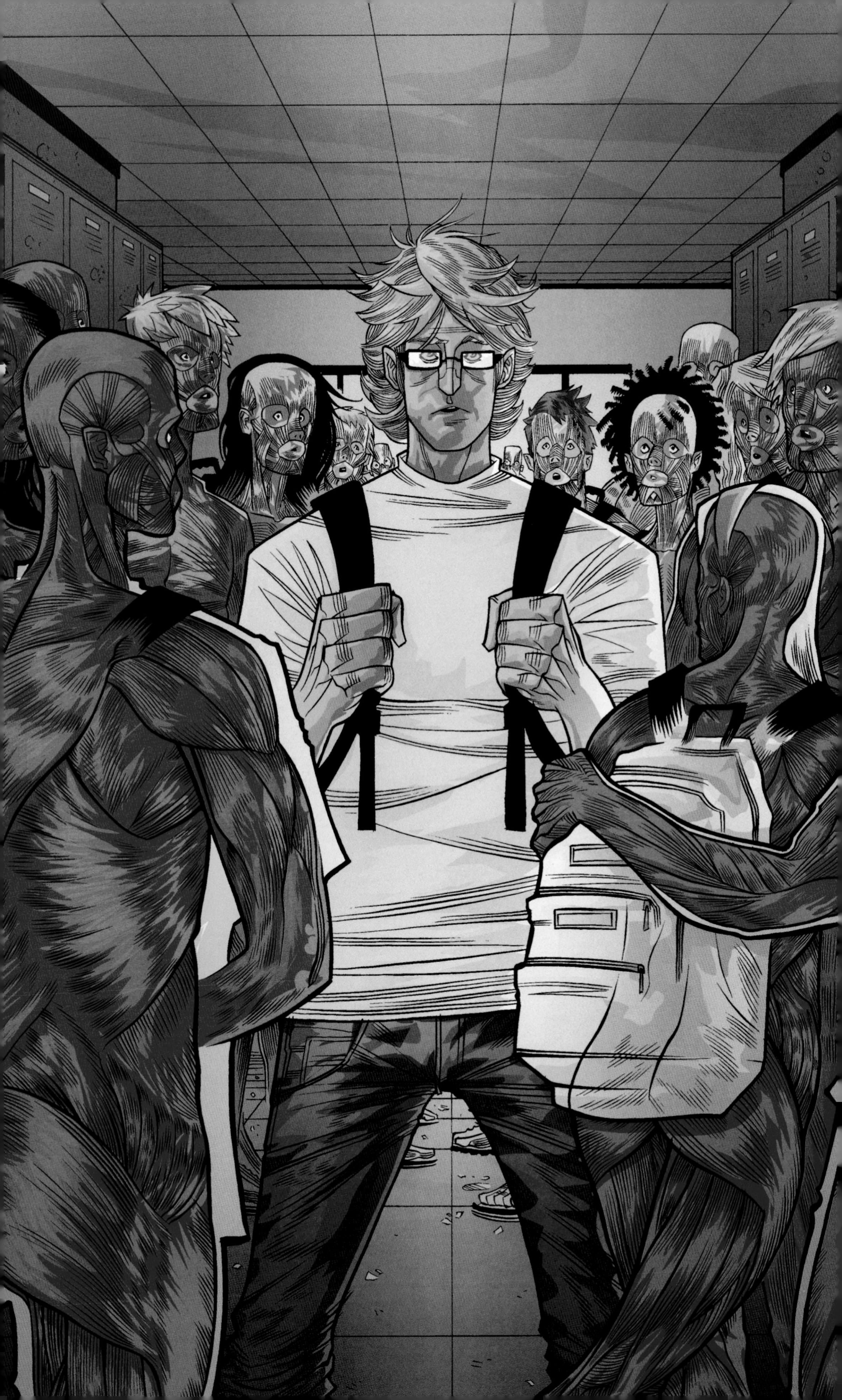

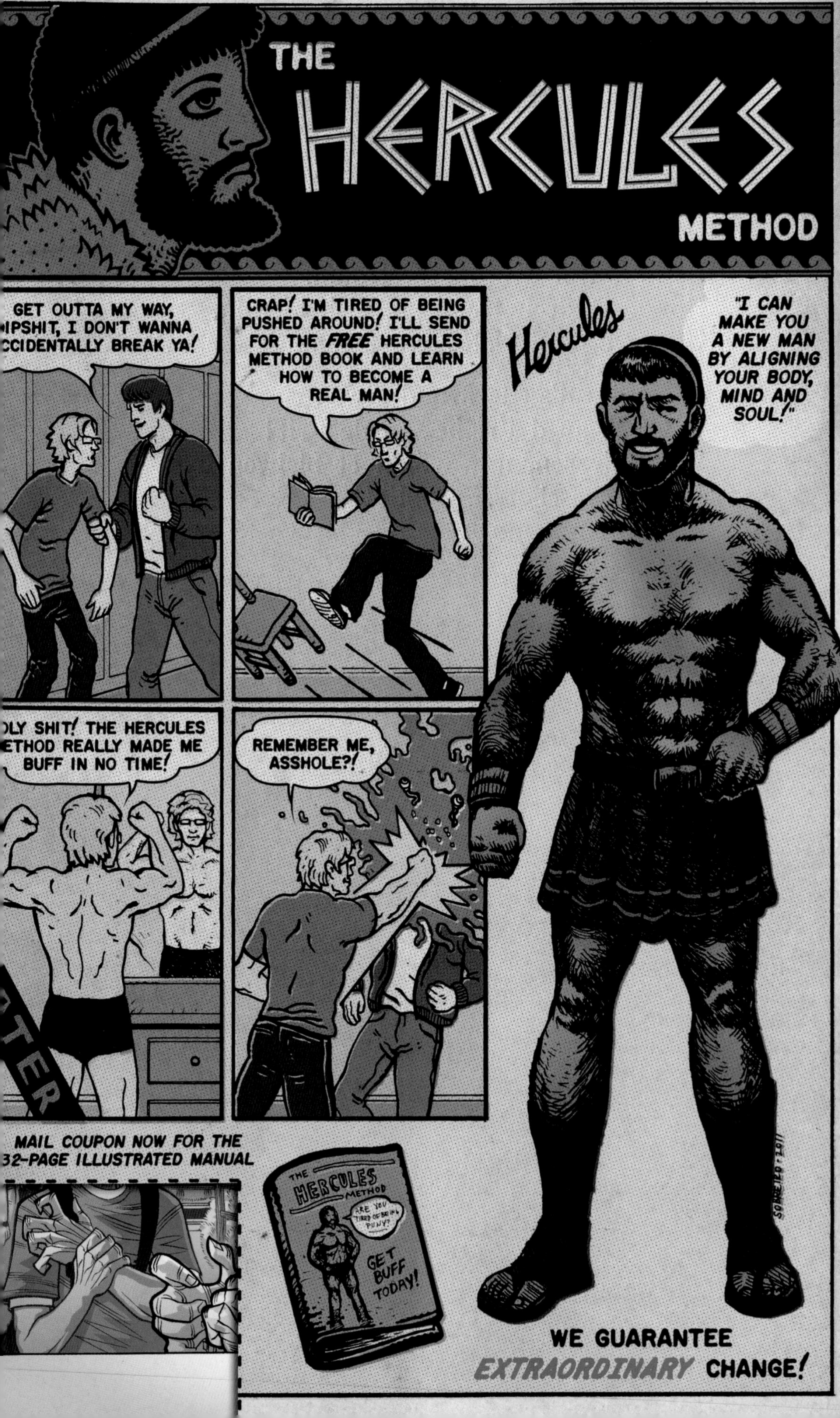
THE HERCULES METHOD
GET OUTTA MY WAY, IPSHIT, I DON'T WANNA CCIDENTALLY BREAK YA!
CRAP! I'M TIRED OF BEING PUSHED AROUND! I'LL SEND FOR THE FREE HERCULES METHOD BOOK AND LEARN HOW TO BECOME A REAL MAN!
Hercules
"I CAN MAKE YOU A NEW MAN BY ALIGNING YOUR BODY, MIND AND SOUL!"
OLY SHIT! THE HERCULES ETHOD REALLY MADE ME BUFF IN NO TIME!
TER
REMEMBER ME, ASSHOLE?!
MAIL COUPON NOW FOR THE 32-PAGE ILLUSTRATED MANUAL
THE HERCULES METHOD
ARE YOU TIRED OF BEING PUNY?
GET BUFF TODAY!
WE GUARANTEE EXTRAORDINARY CHANGE!

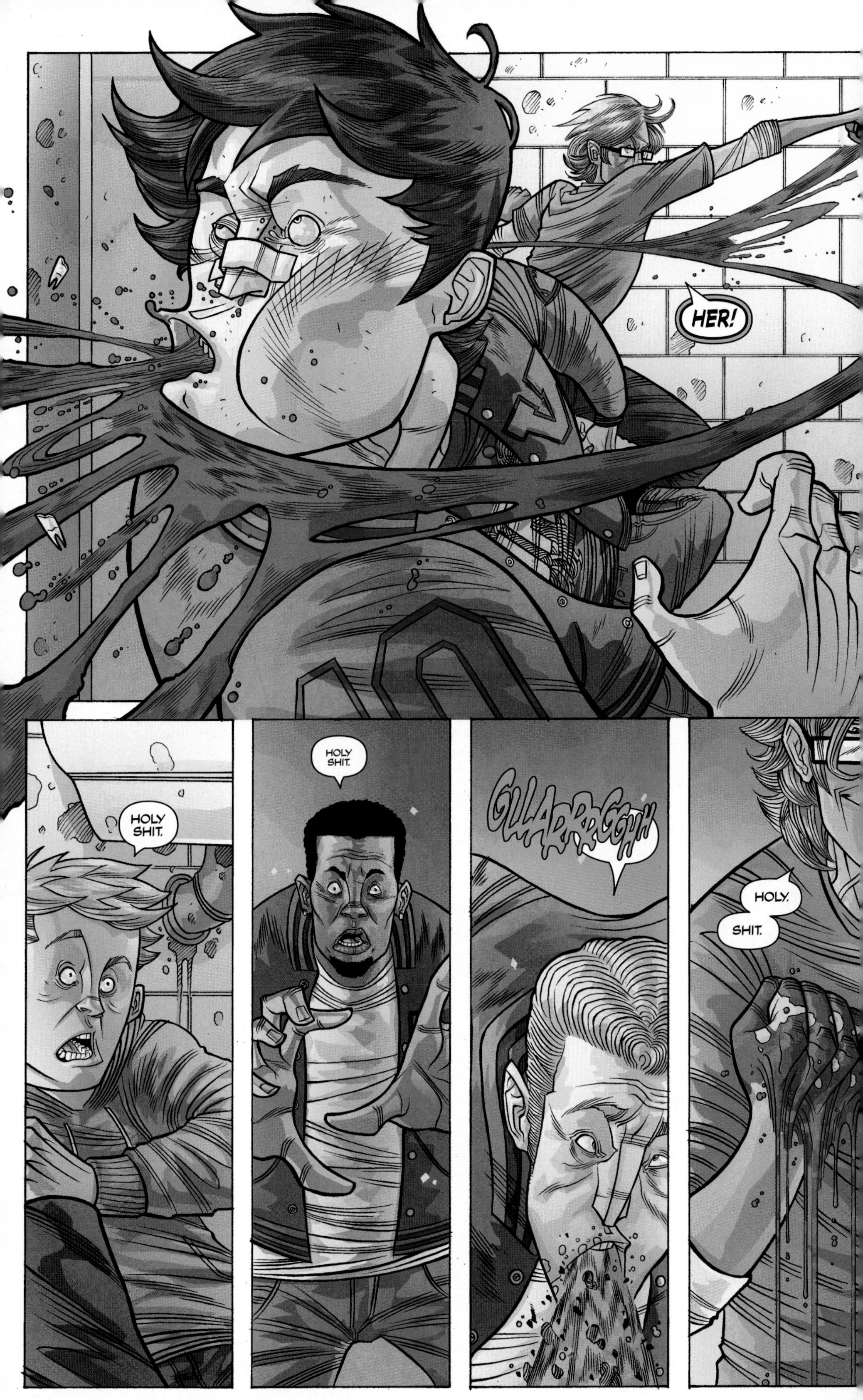
HER!
HOLY SHIT.
HOLY SHIT.
GULARRRGGHH
HOLY.
SHIT.

...THERE'S NOT GOING TO BE A FIGHT.

OOOFF!

YOU THINK THAT WAS FUCKING FUNNY? HITTING ME WITH THE BALL WHEN I WASN'T LOOKING?

HILARIOUS.

I'M GOING TO FUCK YOU UP SO BAD YOUR LITTLE BITCH WILL NEED A BARF BAG TO FUCK YOU.

DON'T.

YOU.

TALK.

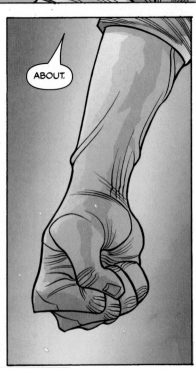

ABOUT.

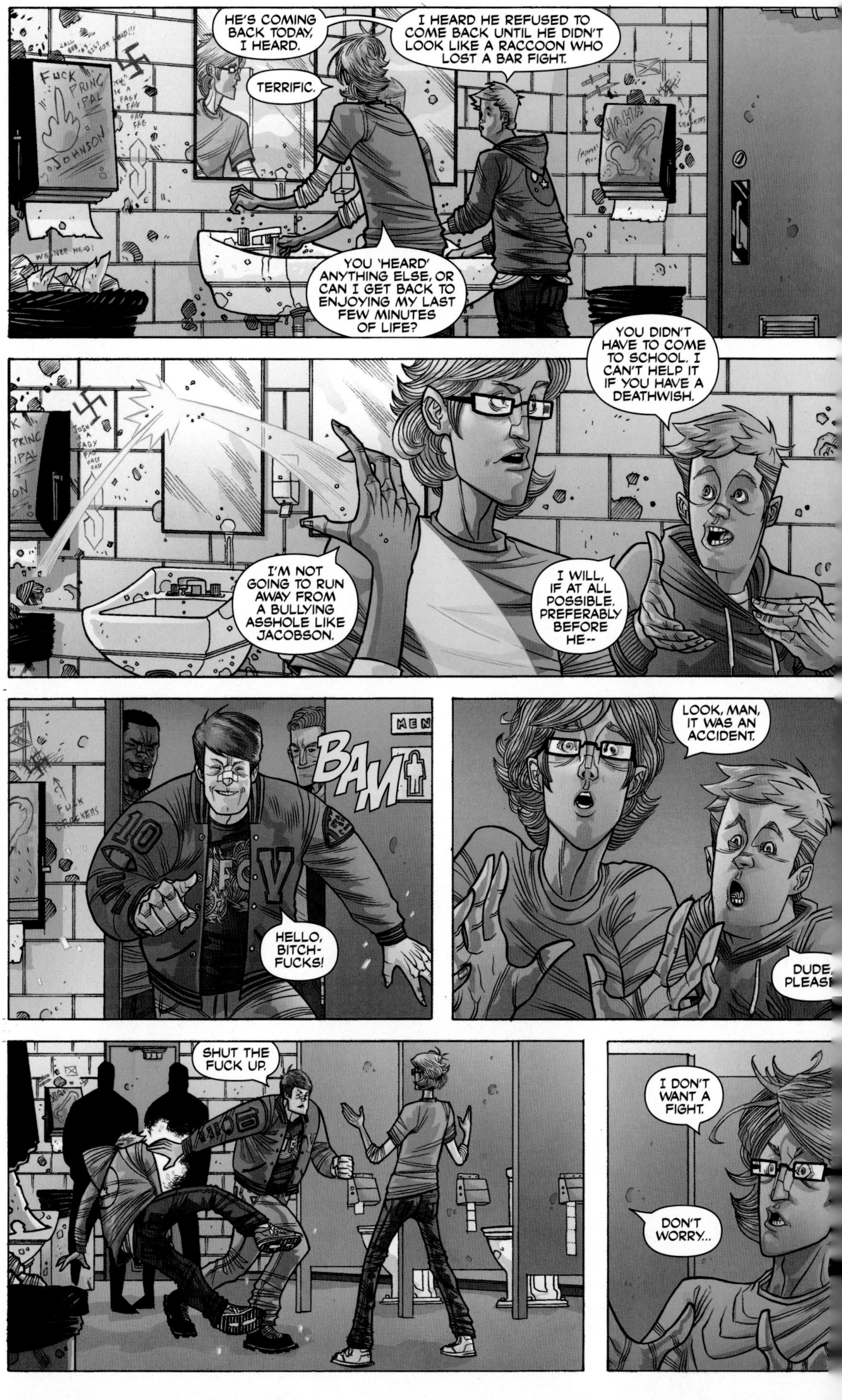
HE'S COMING BACK TODAY, I HEARD.
I HEARD HE REFUSED TO COME BACK UNTIL HE DIDN'T LOOK LIKE A RACCOON WHO LOST A BAR FIGHT.
TERRIFIC.
YOU 'HEARD' ANYTHING ELSE, OR CAN I GET BACK TO ENJOYING MY LAST FEW MINUTES OF LIFE?
FUCK PRINCIPAL
JOHNSON
YOU DIDN'T HAVE TO COME TO SCHOOL. I CAN'T HELP IT IF YOU HAVE A DEATHWISH.
I'M NOT GOING TO RUN AWAY FROM A BULLYING ASSHOLE LIKE JACOBSON.
I WILL, IF AT ALL POSSIBLE. PREFERABLY BEFORE HE--
MEN
BAM
HELLO, BITCH-FUCKS!
LOOK, MAN, IT WAS AN ACCIDENT.
DUDE, PLEAS
SHUT THE FUCK UP.
I DON'T WANT A FIGHT.
DON'T WORRY...

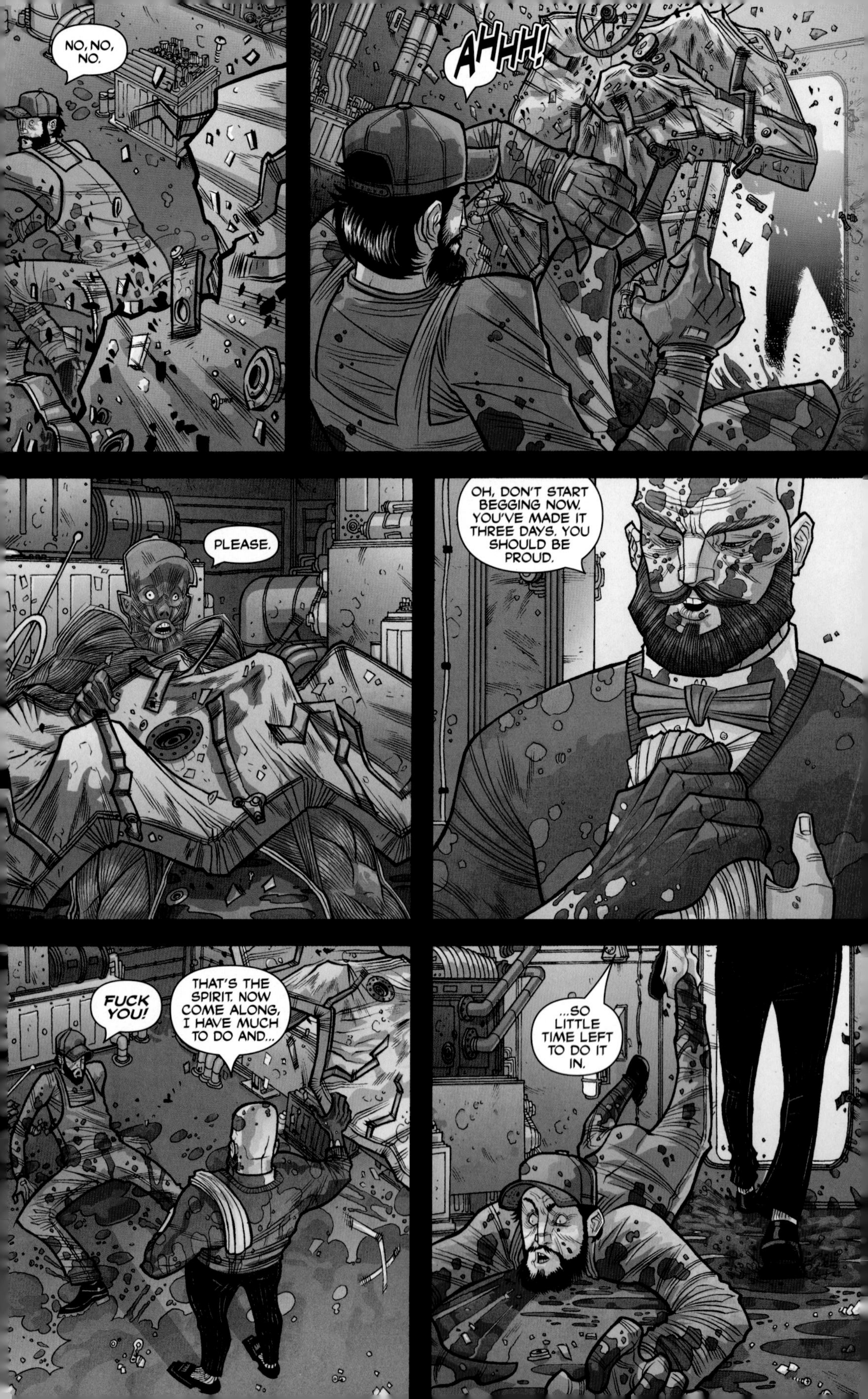
NO, NO, NO.
AHHH!
PLEASE.
OH, DON'T START BEGGING NOW. YOU'VE MADE IT THREE DAYS. YOU SHOULD BE PROUD.
FUCK YOU!
THAT'S THE SPIRIT. NOW COME ALONG, I HAVE MUCH TO DO AND...
...SO LITTLE TIME LEFT TO DO IT IN.

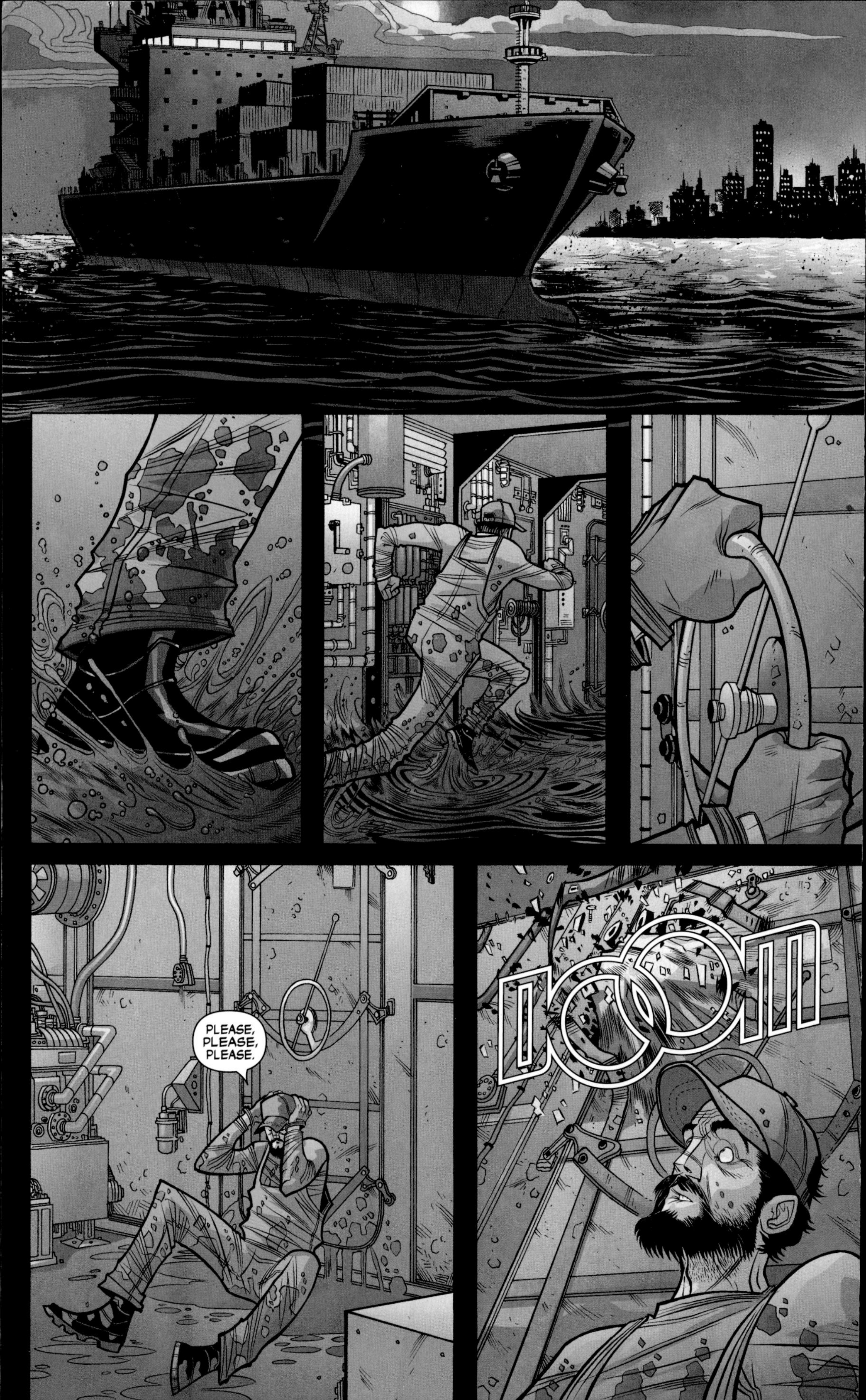
PLEASE, PLEASE, PLEASE.
boom

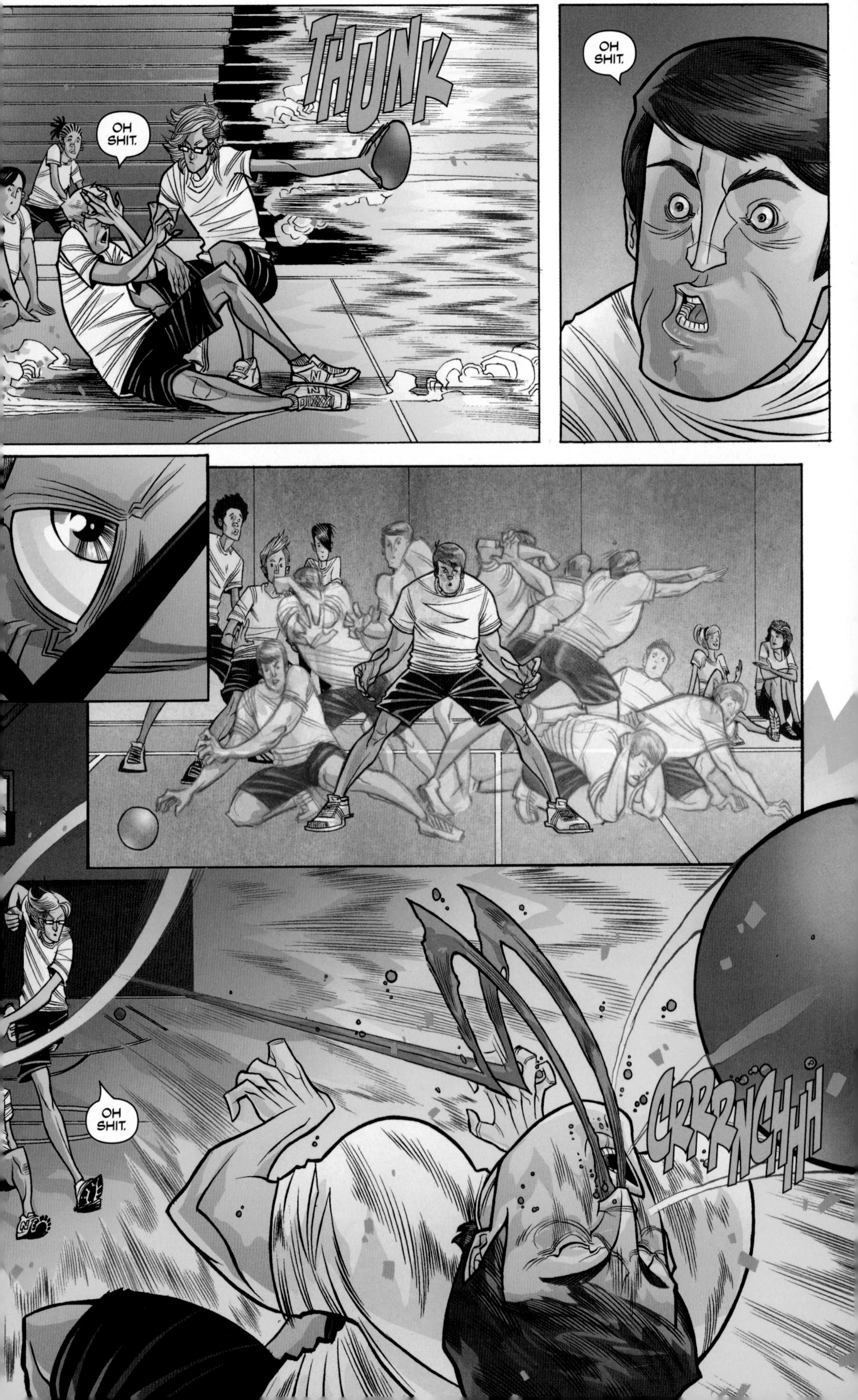
THUNK
OH SHIT.
OH SHIT.
OH SHIT.
CRRRNCHHH

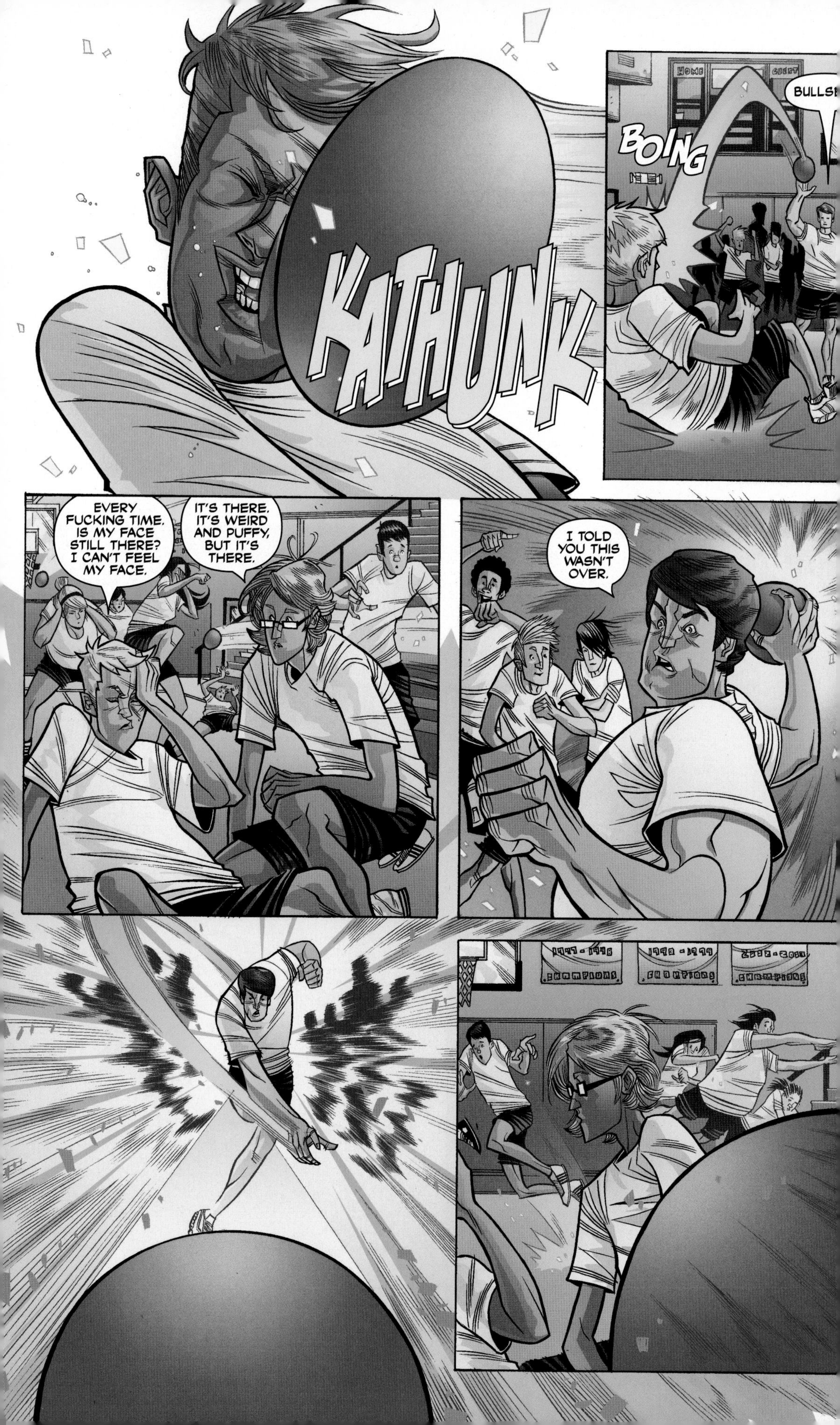
KATHUNK
HOME
GUEST
BULLS
BOING
EVERY FUCKING TIME. IS MY FACE STILL THERE? I CAN'T FEEL MY FACE.
IT'S THERE. IT'S WEIRD AND PUFFY, BUT IT'S THERE.
I TOLD YOU THIS WASN'T OVER.

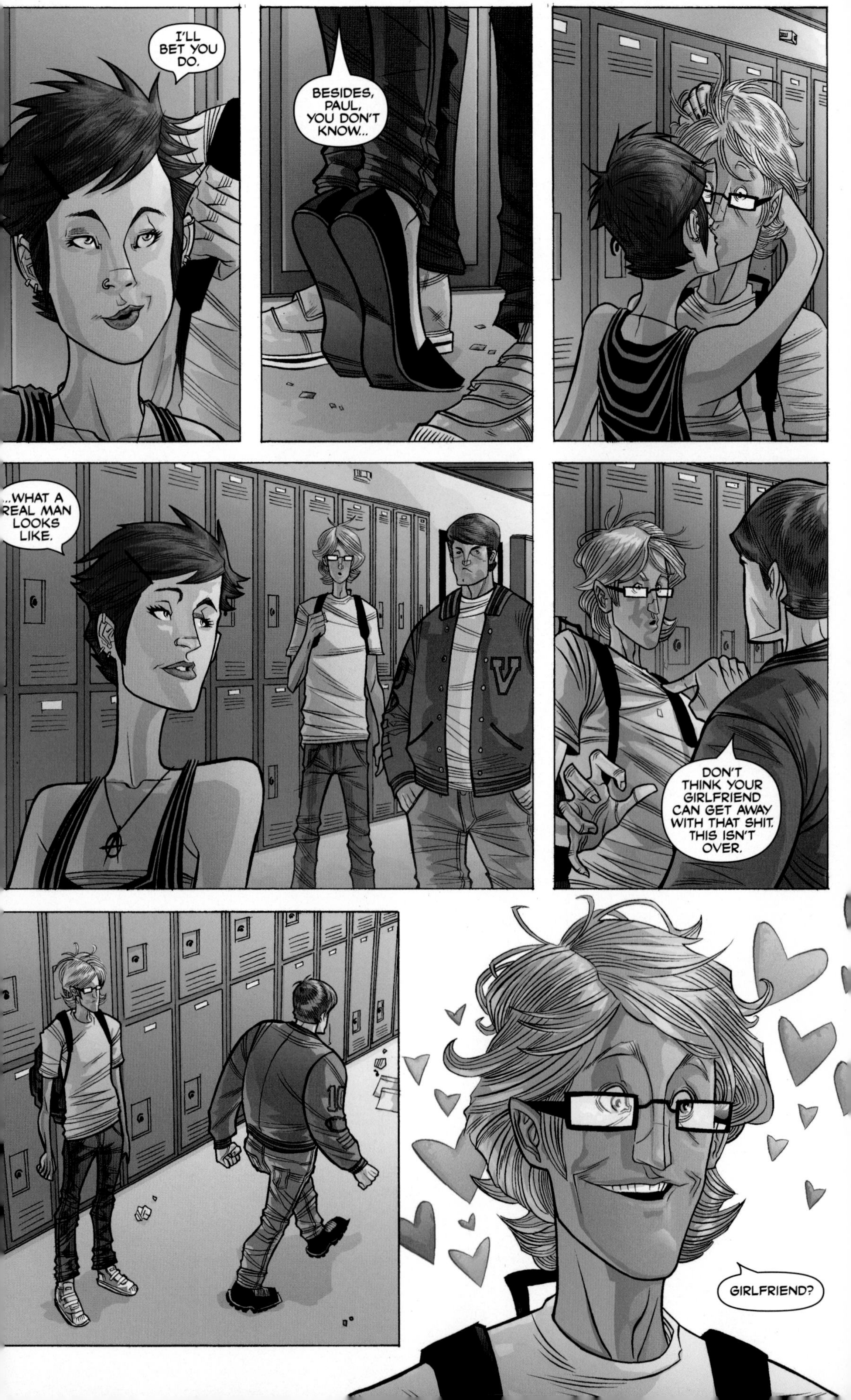
I'LL BET YOU DO.
BESIDES, PAUL, YOU DON'T KNOW...
...WHAT A REAL MAN LOOKS LIKE.
DON'T THINK YOUR GIRLFRIEND CAN GET AWAY WITH THAT SHIT. THIS ISN'T OVER.
GIRLFRIEND?

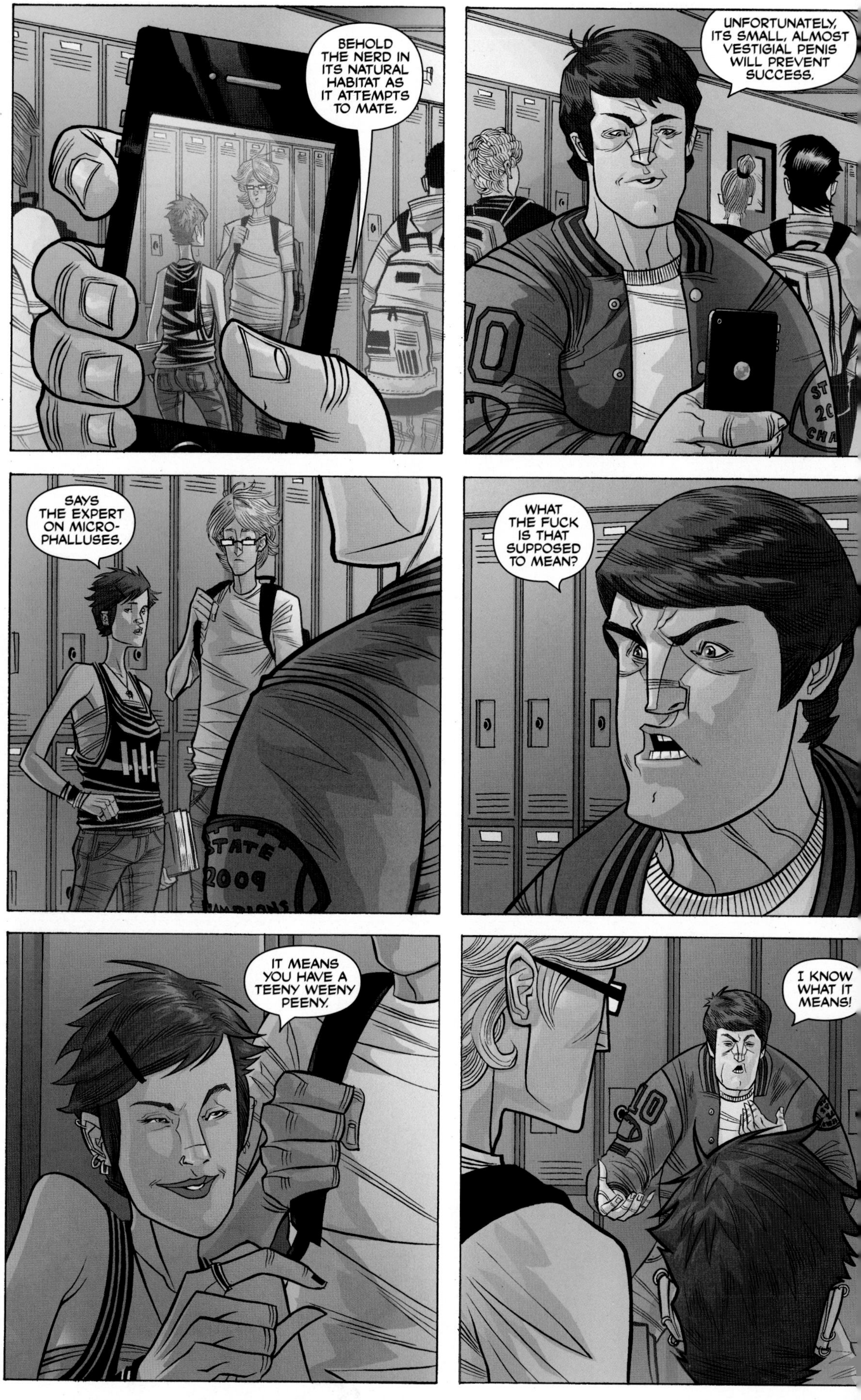
BEHOLD THE NERD IN ITS NATURAL HABITAT AS IT ATTEMPTS TO MATE.
UNFORTUNATELY, ITS SMALL, ALMOST VESTIGIAL PENIS WILL PREVENT SUCCESS.
SAYS THE EXPERT ON MICRO-PHALLUSES.
STATE 2009
WHAT THE FUCK IS THAT SUPPOSED TO MEAN?
IT MEANS YOU HAVE A TEENY WEENY PEENY.
I KNOW WHAT IT MEANS!

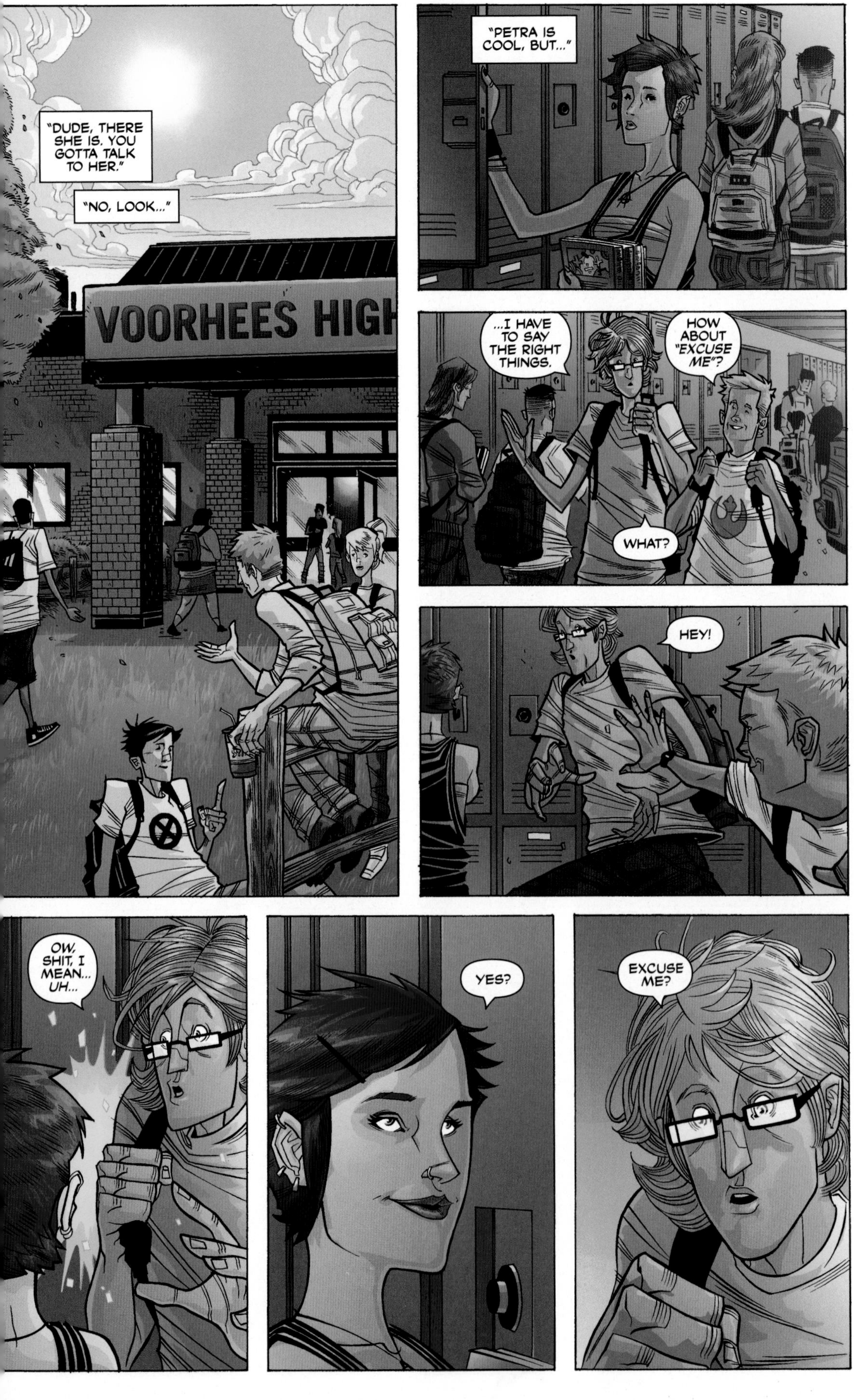
"DUDE, THERE SHE IS. YOU GOTTA TALK TO HER."
"NO, LOOK..."
VOORHEES HIGH
"PETRA IS COOL, BUT..."
...I HAVE TO SAY THE RIGHT THINGS.
HOW ABOUT "*EXCUSE ME*"?
WHAT?
HEY!
OW, SHIT, I MEAN... UH...
YES?
EXCUSE ME?

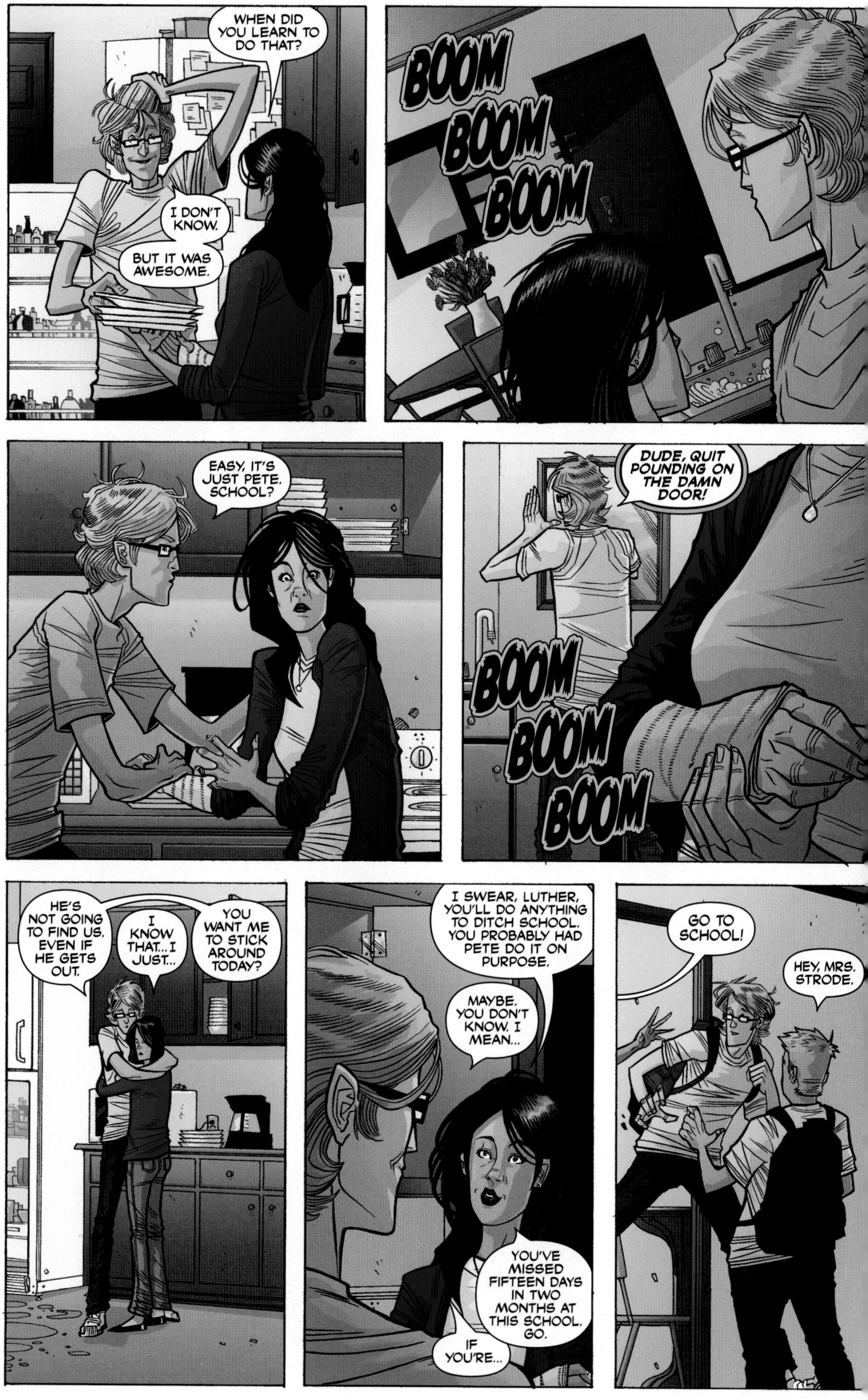
WHEN DID YOU LEARN TO DO THAT?
I DON'T KNOW.
BUT IT WAS AWESOME.
BOOM
BOOM
BOOM
EASY, IT'S JUST PETE. SCHOOL?
DUDE, QUIT POUNDING ON THE DAMN DOOR!
BOOM
BOOM
BOOM
HE'S NOT GOING TO FIND US, EVEN IF HE GETS OUT.
I KNOW THAT... I JUST...
YOU WANT ME TO STICK AROUND TODAY?
I SWEAR, LUTHER, YOU'LL DO ANYTHING TO DITCH SCHOOL. YOU PROBABLY HAD PETE DO IT ON PURPOSE.
MAYBE. YOU DON'T KNOW. I MEAN...
YOU'VE MISSED FIFTEEN DAYS IN TWO MONTHS AT THIS SCHOOL. GO.
IF YOU'RE...
GO TO SCHOOL!
HEY, MRS. STRODE.

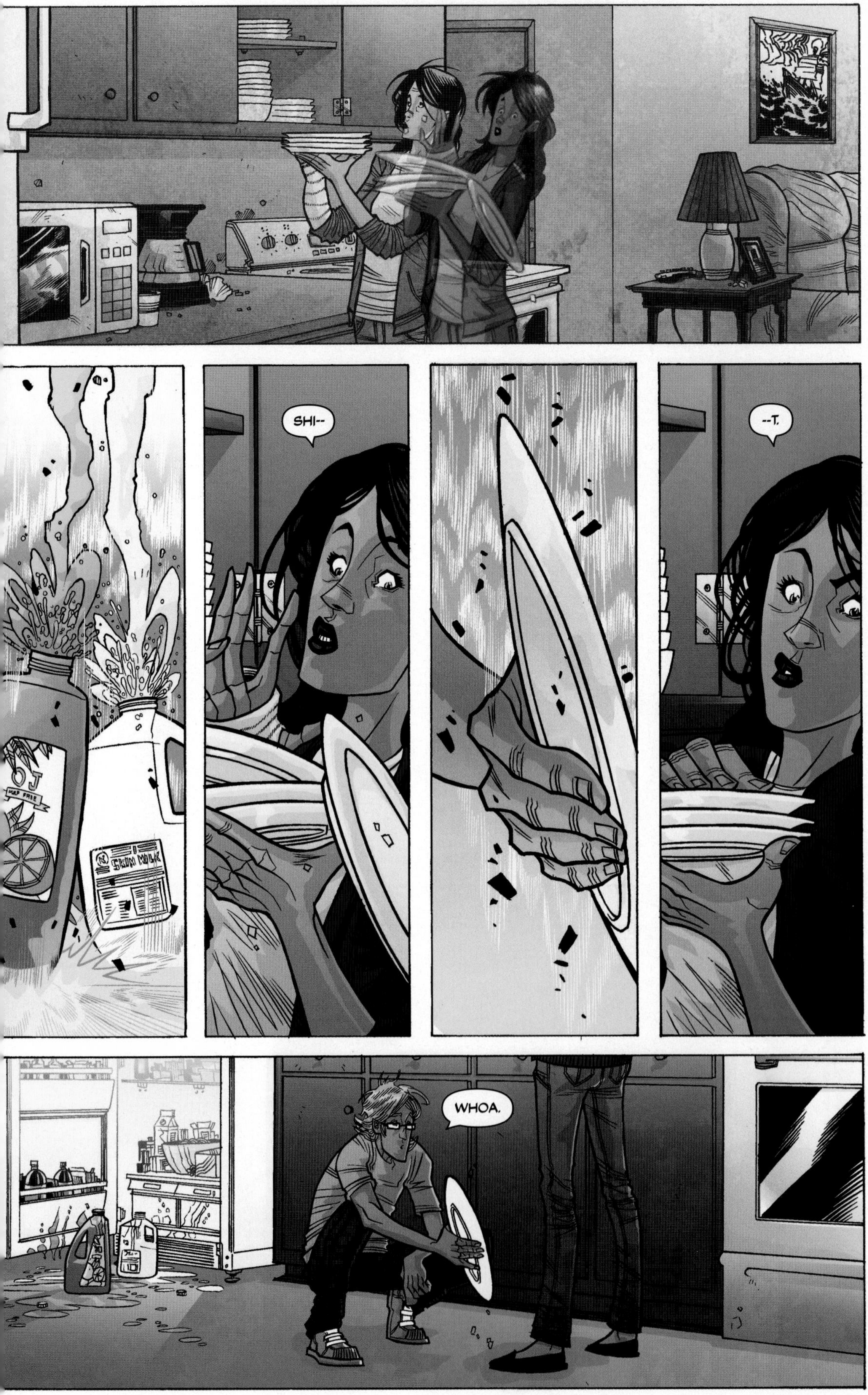

OJ
PULP FREE
SKIM MILK
SHI--
--T.
WHOA.

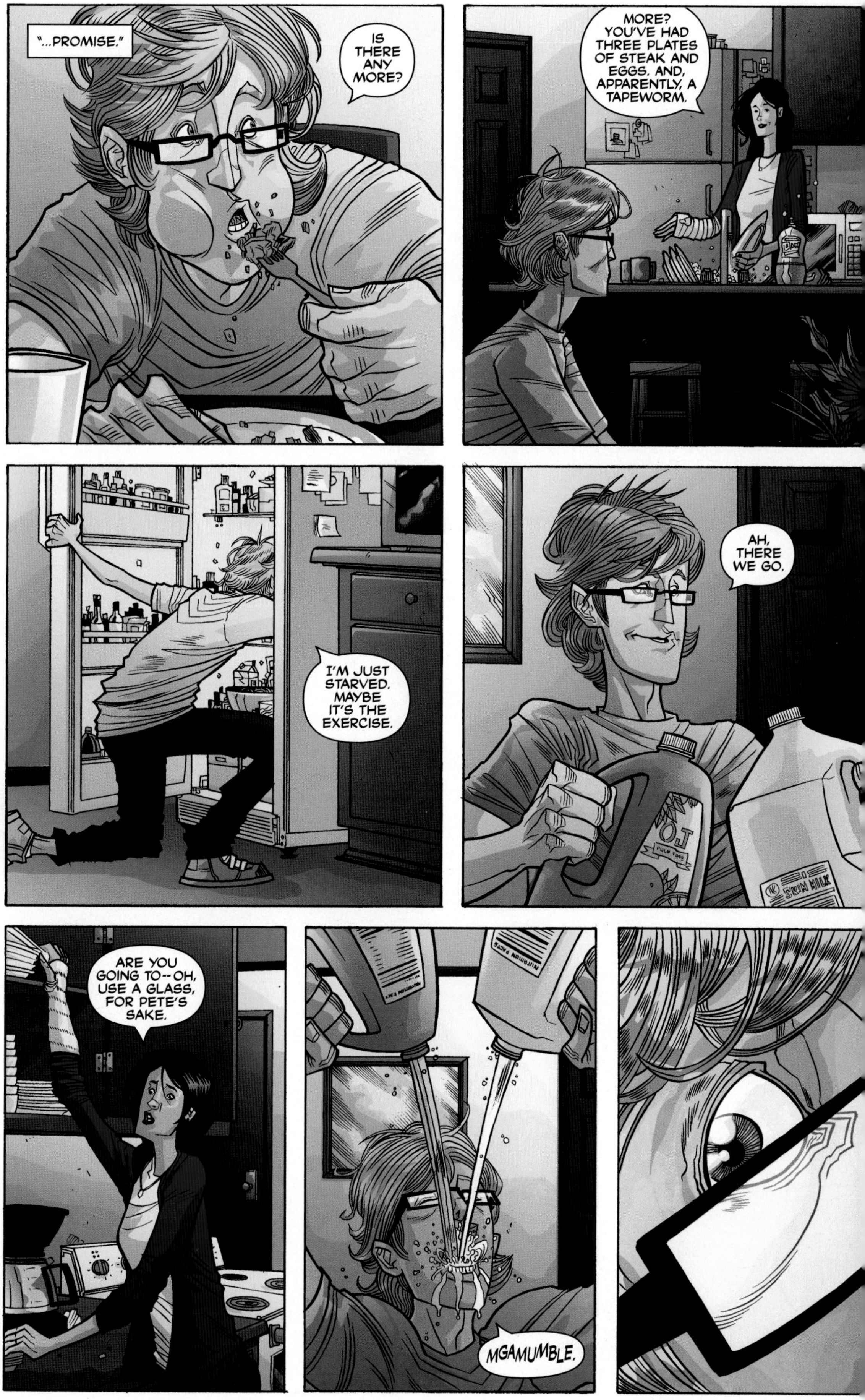
"...PROMISE."
IS THERE ANY MORE?
MORE? YOU'VE HAD THREE PLATES OF STEAK AND EGGS. AND, APPARENTLY, A TAPEWORM.
I'M JUST STARVED. MAYBE IT'S THE EXERCISE.
AH, THERE WE GO.
OJ
PULP FREE
SKIM MILK
ARE YOU GOING TO--OH, USE A GLASS, FOR PETE'S SAKE.
MGAMUMBLE.

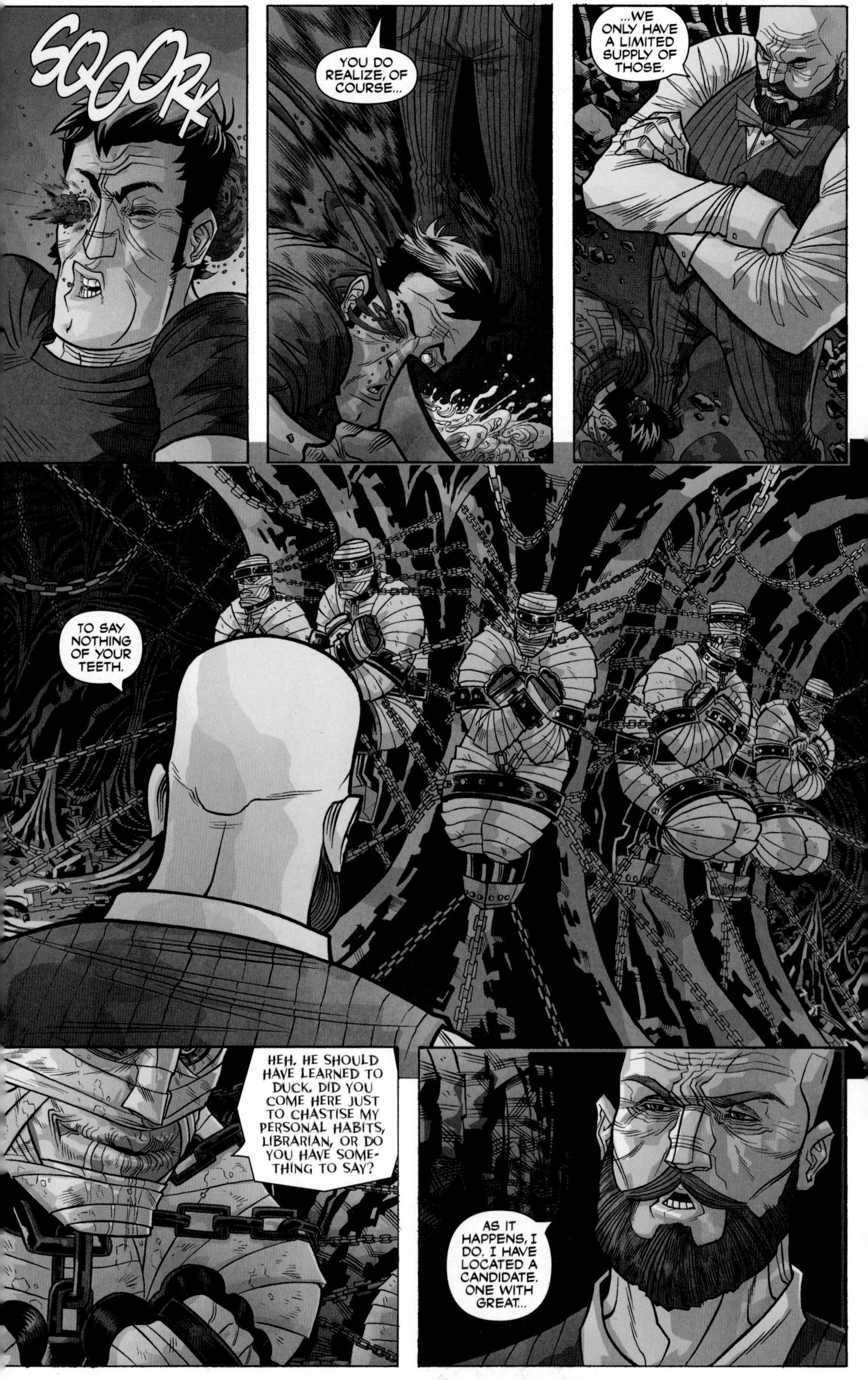
SQOORK
YOU DO REALIZE, OF COURSE...
...WE ONLY HAVE A LIMITED SUPPLY OF THOSE.
TO SAY NOTHING OF YOUR TEETH.
HEH. HE SHOULD HAVE LEARNED TO DUCK. DID YOU COME HERE JUST TO CHASTISE MY PERSONAL HABITS, LIBRARIAN, OR DO YOU HAVE SOME-THING TO SAY?
AS IT HAPPENS, I DO. I HAVE LOCATED A CANDIDATE. ONE WITH GREAT...

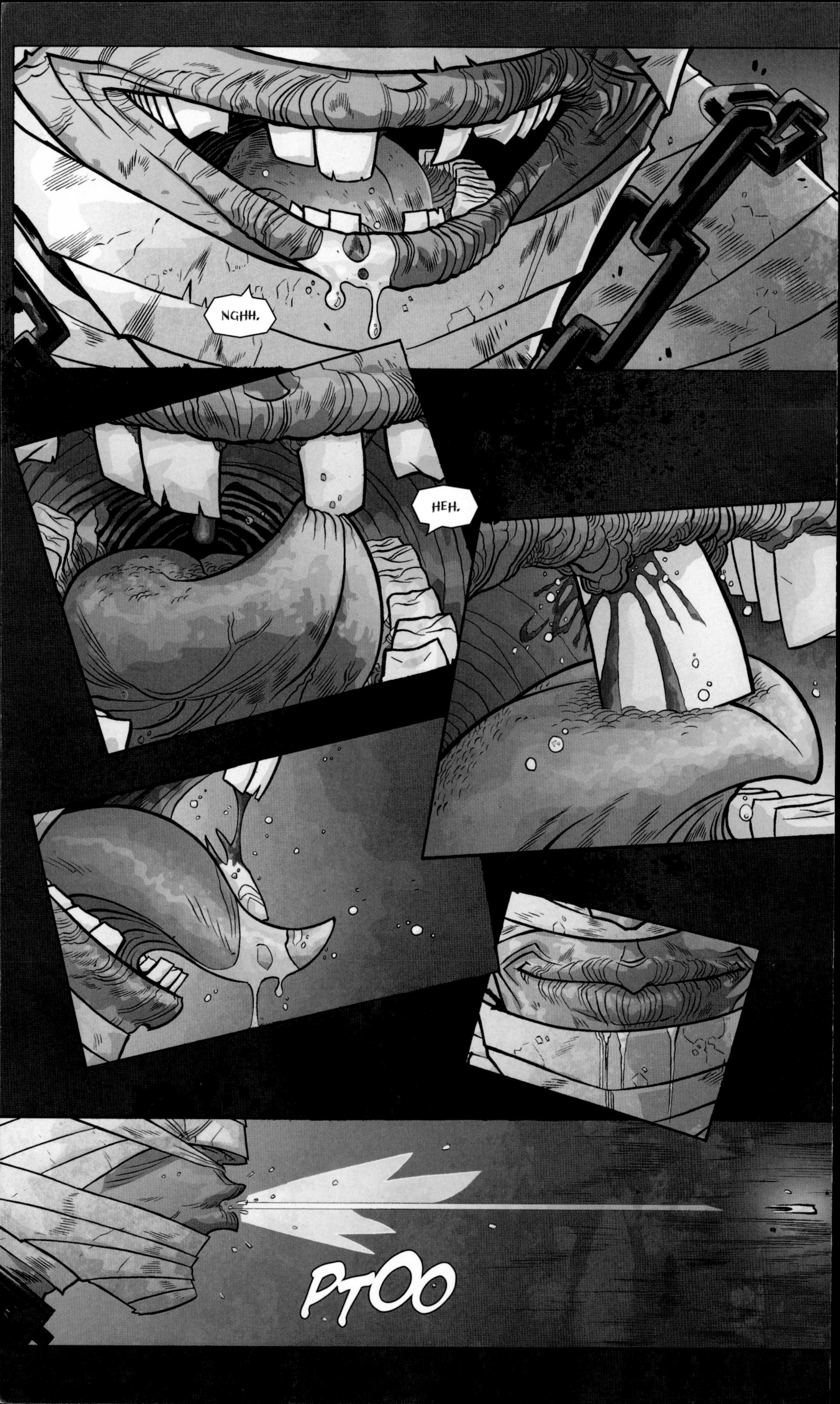
NGHH.
HEH.
PTOO

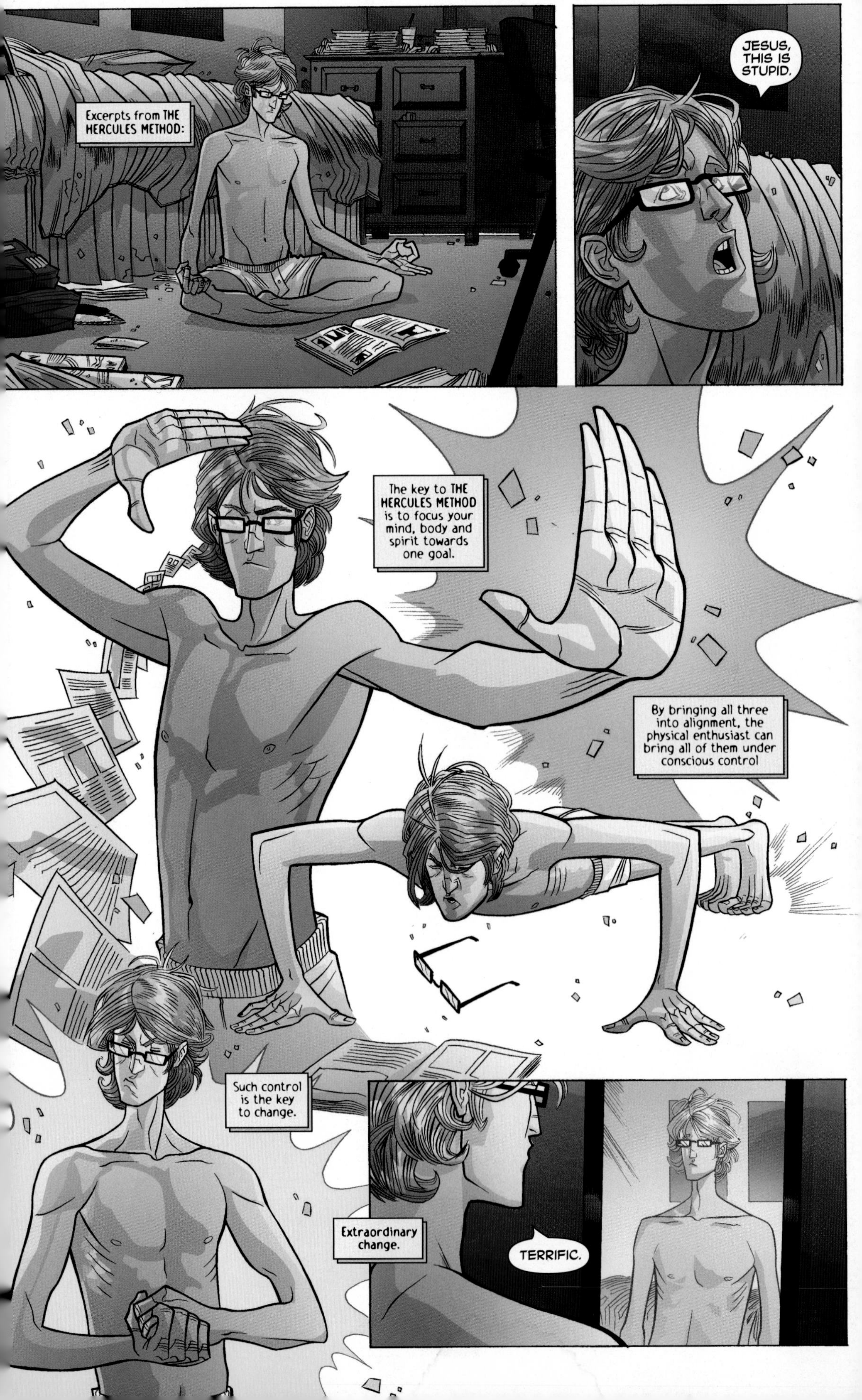

Excerpts from THE HERCULES METHOD:
JESUS, THIS IS STUPID.
The key to THE HERCULES METHOD is to focus your mind, body and spirit towards one goal.
By bringing all three into alignment, the physical enthusiast can bring all of them under conscious control
Such control is the key to change.
Extraordinary change.
TERRIFIC.

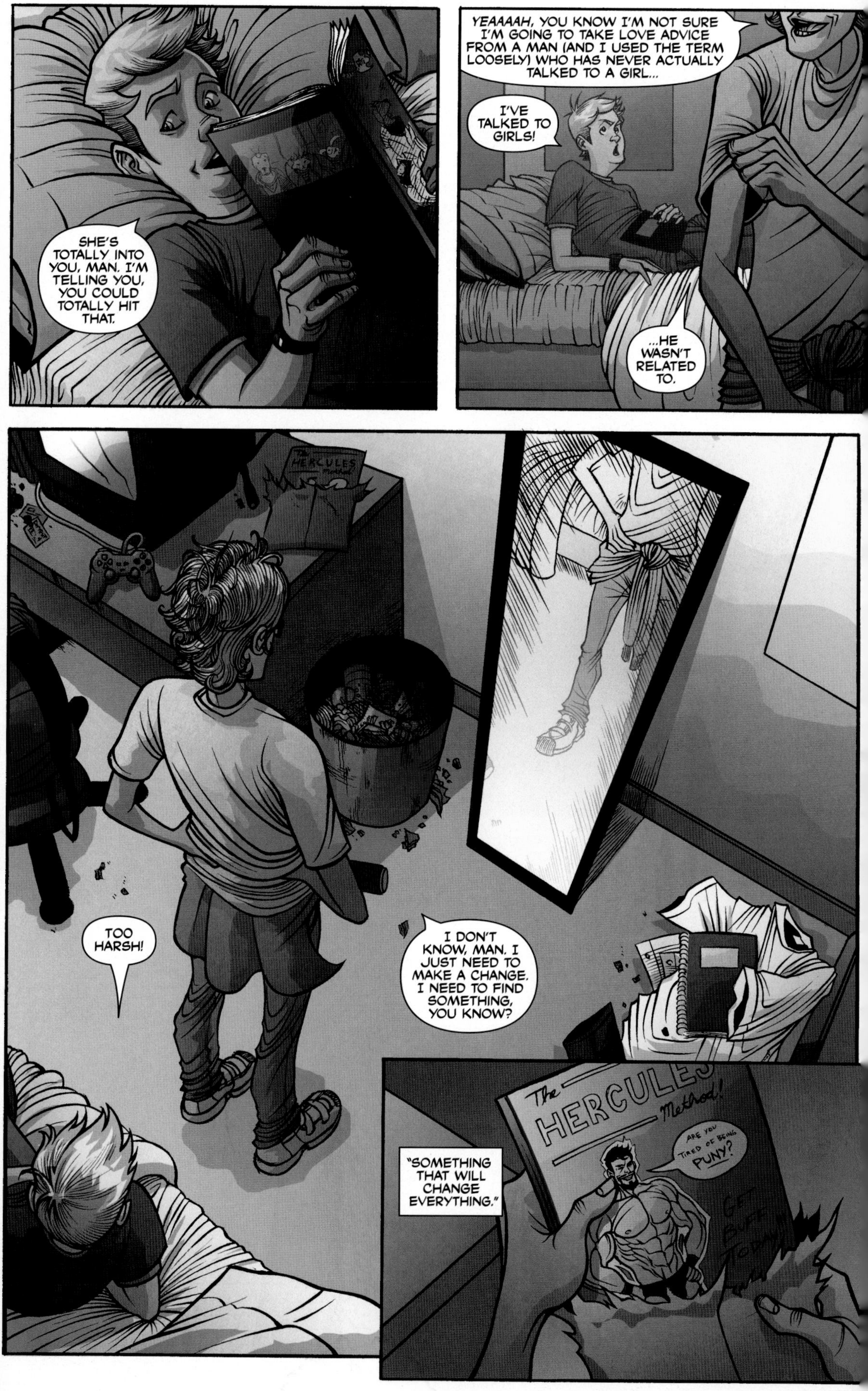
SHE'S TOTALLY INTO YOU, MAN. I'M TELLING YOU, YOU COULD TOTALLY HIT THAT.
YEAAAAH, YOU KNOW I'M NOT SURE I'M GOING TO TAKE LOVE ADVICE FROM A MAN (AND I USED THE TERM LOOSELY) WHO HAS NEVER ACTUALLY TALKED TO A GIRL...
I'VE TALKED TO GIRLS!
...HE WASN'T RELATED TO.
TOO HARSH!
I DON'T KNOW, MAN. I JUST NEED TO MAKE A CHANGE. I NEED TO FIND SOMETHING, YOU KNOW?
"SOMETHING THAT WILL CHANGE EVERYTHING."
The HERCULES Method!
ARE YOU TIRED OF BEING PUNY?
GET BUFF TODAY!

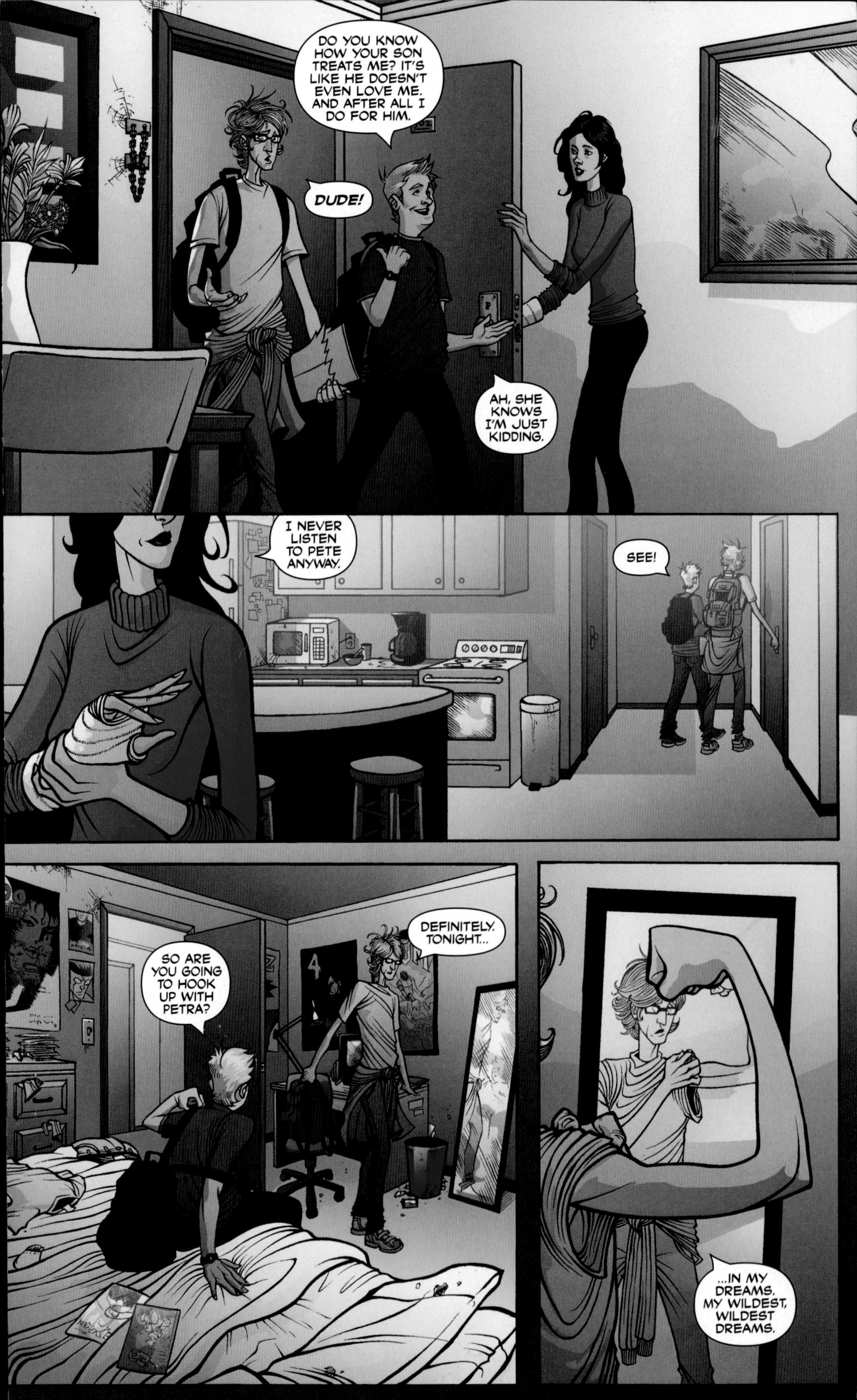
DO YOU KNOW HOW YOUR SON TREATS ME? IT'S LIKE HE DOESN'T EVEN LOVE ME. AND AFTER ALL I DO FOR HIM.
DUDE!
AH, SHE KNOWS I'M JUST KIDDING.
I NEVER LISTEN TO PETE ANYWAY.
SEE!
SO ARE YOU GOING TO HOOK UP WITH PETRA?
DEFINITELY. TONIGHT...
...IN MY DREAMS. MY WILDEST, WILDEST DREAMS.

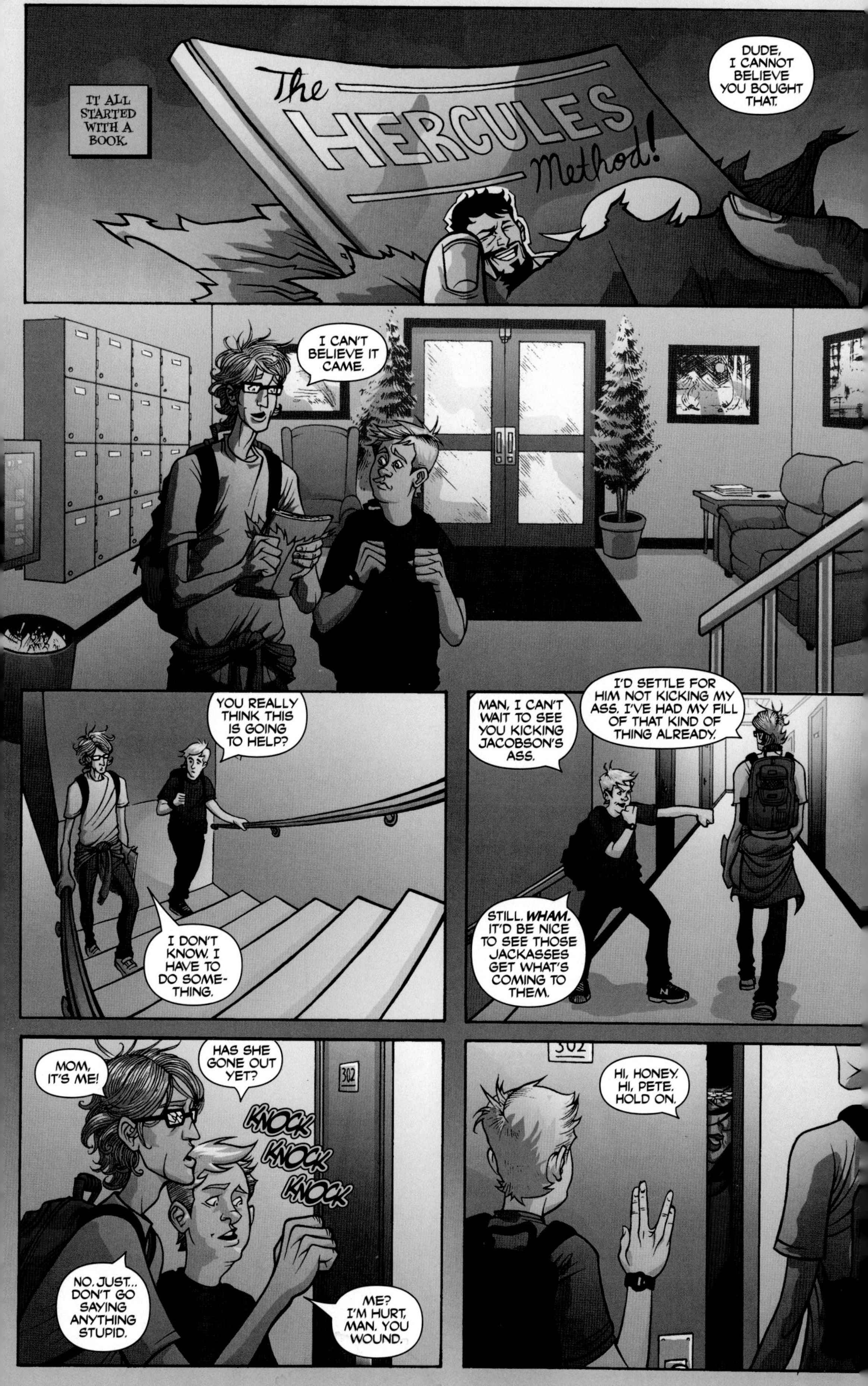

IT ALL STARTED WITH A BOOK.
The HERCULES Method!
DUDE, I CANNOT BELIEVE YOU BOUGHT THAT.
I CAN'T BELIEVE IT CAME.
YOU REALLY THINK THIS IS GOING TO HELP?
I DON'T KNOW. I HAVE TO DO SOME-THING.
MAN, I CAN'T WAIT TO SEE YOU KICKING JACOBSON'S ASS.
I'D SETTLE FOR HIM NOT KICKING MY ASS. I'VE HAD MY FILL OF THAT KIND OF THING ALREADY.
STILL. WHAM. IT'D BE NICE TO SEE THOSE JACKASSES GET WHAT'S COMING TO THEM.
MOM, IT'S ME!
HAS SHE GONE OUT YET?
302
KNOCK KNOCK KNOCK
NO. JUST... DON'T GO SAYING ANYTHING STUPID.
ME? I'M HURT, MAN. YOU WOUND.
302
HI, HONEY. HI, PETE. HOLD ON.

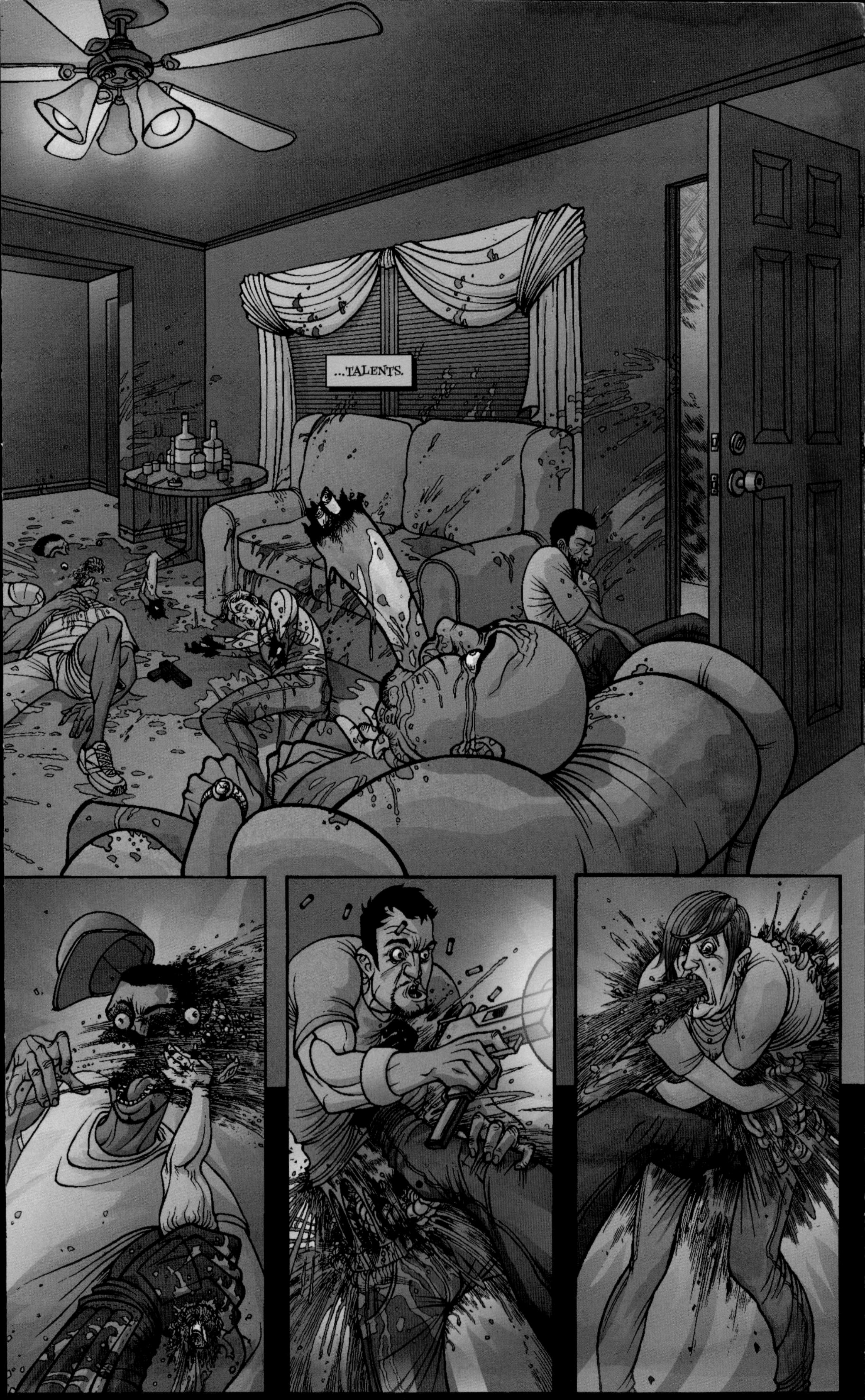
...TALENTS.

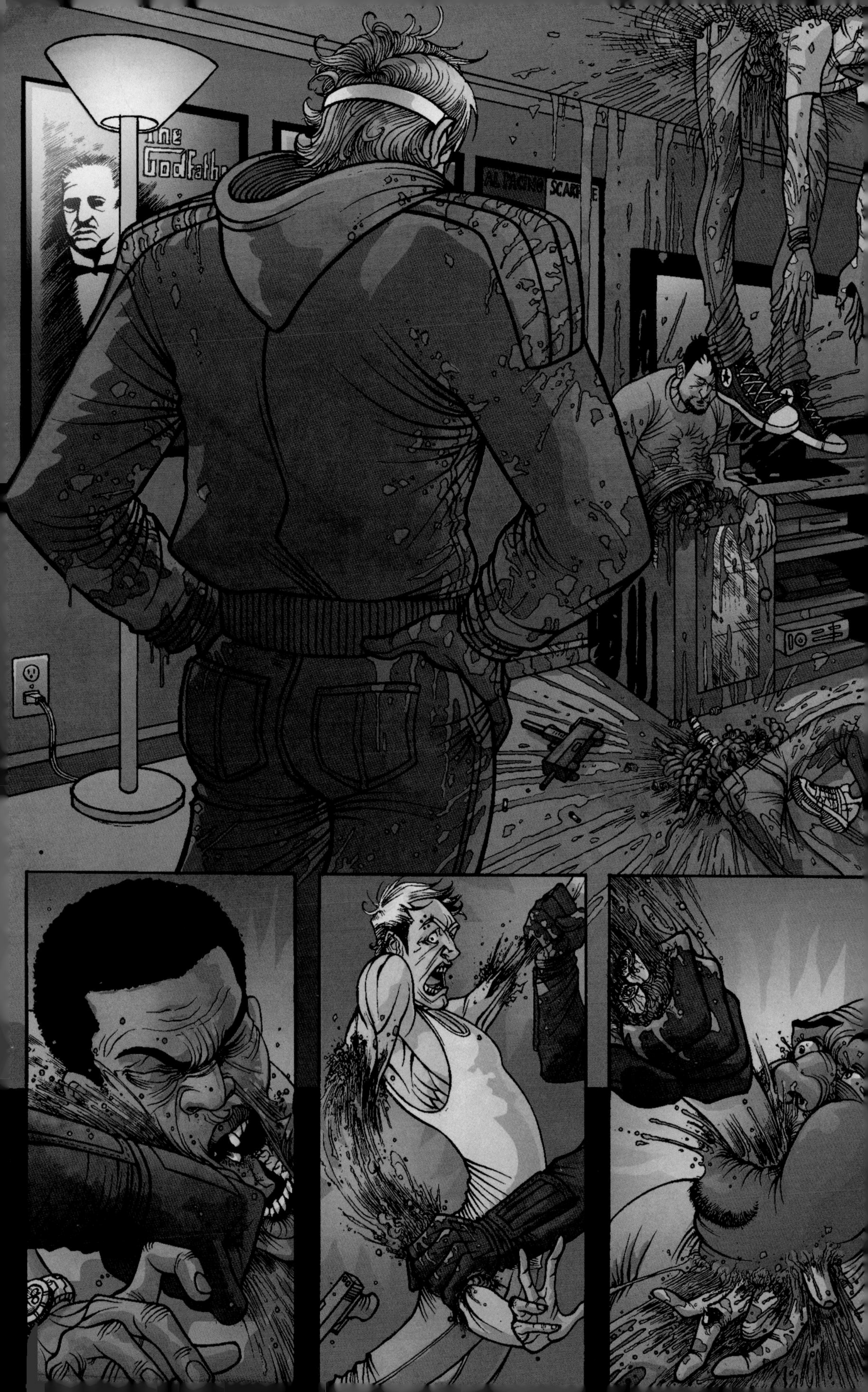
The
AL PACINO

MY NAME IS LUTHER STRODE, AND I WAS JUST SHOT SEVEN TIMES IN THE CHEST.

IT HURTS.

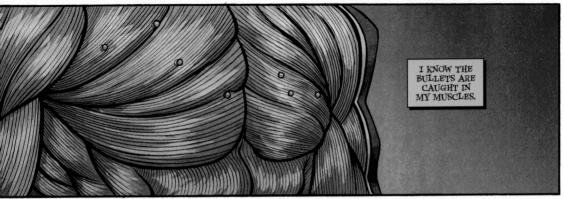

I KNOW THE BULLETS ARE CAUGHT IN MY MUSCLES.

I KNOW THAT'S IMPOSSIBLE. I ALSO KNOW THAT I CAN DO...

...THIS.

MY NAME IS LUTHER STRODE, AND I HAVE CERTAIN...

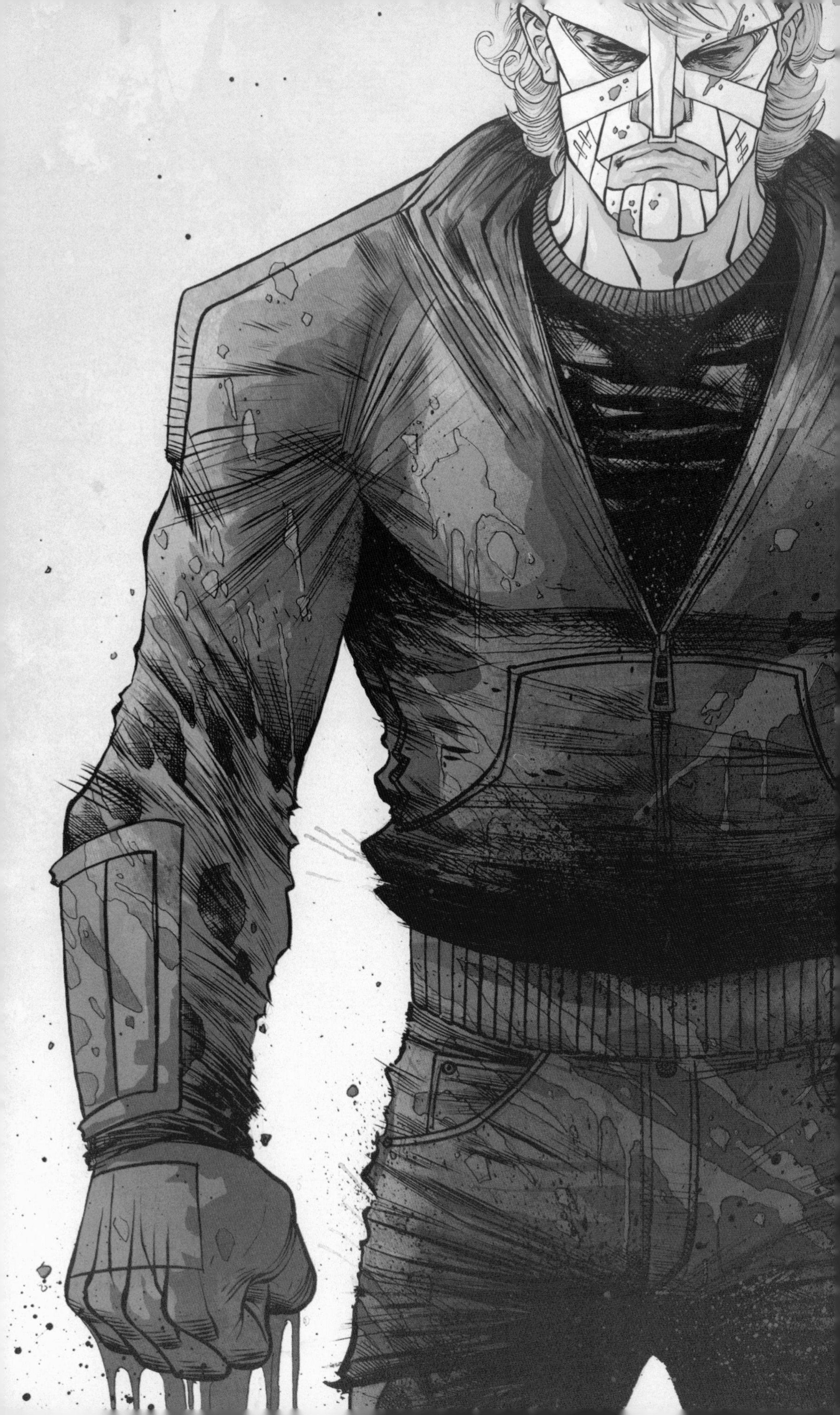

It's about power.

Well, okay, it's also about comic books, fathers and sons, slasher movies, and finding out that the girl of your dreams thinks you are the guy of her dreams, but mostly it's about power, and what happens when you've never had it and you suddenly get it.

It's all but a cliché that people that come into sudden wealth, be it from lotteries or record contracts or whatever tend to spend it poorly and end up back where they started from. I'm looking at you, MC Hammer. And, sadly, this is often the case. Because it's difficult to use money or power wisely when you've never had it before.

This is something that always interested me about superheroes, where the common narrative is that a normal person suddenly gets these incredible abilities and decides to use them to fight crime and help the world. Which, you hope, is exactly what a good person would do if they got powers.

But how do you actually do that? When you have power, how do you use it wisely? You can go out, as Luther does, and try to find crime and stop it as it happens, but then what? Have you really helped or have you made it worse? What are the long term consequences of using that power?

Luther is a fairly normal kid, all things considered. Maybe a little tougher than most, because he had to be, but fairly average. He's a good guy, because he's seen what a bad man is and doesn't want any part of it. He's got good intentions.

And now he has power. But what he doesn't necessarily have is wisdom. The problem with power isn't what you can do; it's what should you do with. How do you handle something like that?

So that is what the book is about. There were two specific ideas that glommed together in my brain and eventually became The Strange Talent of Luther Strode. The first was what would happen if those Charles Atlas type courses really did turn you into a perfect physical specimen?

The other was the notion that if you squinted, the line between a superhero like Rorschach or The Punisher and a horror movie slasher like Jason Voorhees or Michael Myers could get pretty blurry.

But mostly it's about power and the decisions that suddenly having it forces you to make. Well, that and sweet, sweet ultraviolence. But mostly the power thing.

- Justin